The Grace Awakening

BELIEVING IN GRACE IS ONE THING.
LIVING IT IS ANOTHER.

INCLUDES A THIRTY-DAY DEVOTIONAL

CHARLES R. SWINDOLL

THOMAS NELSON
Since 1798

NASHVILLE   DALLAS   MEXICO CITY   RIO DE JANEIRO

It is with great affection I dedicate this book to

Paul and Sue Sailhamer

and

Howie and Marilyn Stevenson,

whose lives and ministries radiate grace.

Because of our close friendship,

I know better what it means

to be free.

Dr. Charles R. Swindoll is senior pastor of Stonebriar Community Church, chancellor of Dallas Theological Seminary, and the Bible teacher on the internationally syndicated radio program *Insight for Living*. He has written more than thirty best-selling books, such as *Strengthening Your Grip*, *Laugh Again*, *The Grace Awakening*, and the million-selling *Great Lives from God's Word* series. Chuck and his wife, Cynthia, live in Frisco, Texas.

Contents

	Publisher's Preface	ix
	Acknowledgments	xiii
	Introduction	xvii
1	Grace: It's *Really* Amazing!	1
2	The Free Gift	13
3	Isn't Grace Risky?	31
4	Undeserving, Yet Unconditionally Loved	49
5	Squaring Off against Legalism	67
6	Emancipated? Then Live Like It!	93
7	Guiding Others to Freedom	115
8	The Grace to Let Others Be	139
9	Graciously Disagreeing and Pressing On	159
10	Grace: Up Close and Personal	179
11	Are You *Really* a Minister of Grace?	195
12	A Marriage Oiled by Grace	217
13	The Charming Joy of Grace Giving	239
14	Grace: It's *Really* Accepting!	255
	Conclusion	277
	Notes	281
	The Grace Awakening Devotional	287

Publisher's Preface

WE LIVE IN A CHANGING WORLD. Perhaps no era in history has seen so many dramatic changes in such a short time as our own. We are witnessing a tremendous explosion of interest in spiritual matters throughout all segments of society. Today, the Christian faith is going through one of the greatest periods of growth in modern times.

When *The Grace Awakening* first appeared in 1990, Chuck Swindoll wanted to address what he perceived as "grace killers" . . . people who restrain and limit the dynamic potential of the Christian life. Among the most visible and vicious are those who criticize, condemn, and crush our hopes of joyful living. Chuck warned that legalism in the church—hiding behind the mask of orthodoxy or piety—was stealing the happiness of believers and holding faith hostage. What we needed at that hour was awakening.

Within days of the book's release, the responses began flooding in. Letters, cards, and reviews came from grateful pastors, teachers, and other Christians all over the country. Some said they had often felt imprisoned in their faith until they recognized their own need for a "grace awakening." Suddenly they understood the reality of the regeneration that Christ had meant for us to enjoy. If we are "new creatures in Christ," they asked, why aren't we rejoicing more and worrying less? Tragically, some Christian leaders became weary of the assaults, lost the battle, and resigned from positions they had once occupied.

Chuck Swindoll points out that Paul gave us the right perspective in his letter to the church at Ephesus when he writes, "For by grace you have been saved through faith; and that not of yourselves, it is the gift of God; not as a result of works, so that no one may boast" (Eph. 2:8–9). Most are quick to adopt a grace-based salvation, but how often, Swindoll asks, have we fallen into the trap of a works-related Christian life? And how often have we traded the freedom and spontaneity of our walk of faith for a man-made code of dos and don'ts? Nothing so stifles our faith, he insists, as the cold scowl of legalism, which brings with it a critical and judgmental spirit.

On numerous occasions since this book was released, Chuck Swindoll has been stopped by total strangers to listen to stories of an individual's transforming awakening of grace. One such occasion occurred at an airport when a woman walked up and asked if he happened to be the author of "the best book I ever read on grace" (her exact words). After the two introduced themselves, she told how it had not only changed her life but the lives of everyone in her entire family.

Her husband had been a pastor of an extremely legalistic church in a denomination known for its rigidity and judgmental spirit. In fact, he had been reared and schooled in that kind of stifling, demanding, religious atmosphere. It was all he knew. Performance lists were common as those in charge spelled out what was expected of all who wished to please God. The pressure mounted, especially in that pastor's home.

Not only did the teenage children begin to rebel, the pastor's wife became disenchanted with the whole system of "works theology." Instead of graciously and carefully teaching the Word of God, her husband—and all who filled his pulpit—harassed and threatened the flock. She became depressed, seeing no hope of change and no way of escape. It was then she came upon *The Grace Awakening*, which she "devoured in a few days," even though it was not among the books her denomination approved.

Seeing his wife's enthusiasm and joy returning led her husband to read the book as well. Before he finished it, he began to see how twisted and misguided he had been. He had the courage to go public and admit from the pulpit that an awakening of grace had so changed him, he could no longer promote the legalism, hypocrisy, and joyless religion that was so much a part of their church and denomination. He refused to continue filling the role of a grace killer.

His resignation was met with cold stares; the family was virtually ostracized by those who had been long-time "church friends." But this man, his wife, and even their teenagers now know a joy and relief in their relationship with each other (and with the Lord) they never dreamed existed. Their Christian walk, now based on grace, has been literally revolutionized. As Chuck put it, "She is radiant with a joy that is contagious. I've rarely seen a person who exudes the love and grace of Christ so naturally, so enthusiastically. Grace has truly awakened within her!"

Since the release of the book, the world has continued its dramatic changes. In addition to the political changes around the world, there have been startling moral and ethical revolutions as well—an awakening of conscience and character of amazing proportions. Christianity has been breaking out around the world.

We have witnessed prayer movements ushered in by open confession of sin and repentance on college campuses. Outpourings of the Spirit have called congregations and even denominations back to their first love for Christ. We have witnessed the birth of Christ-centered men's and women's movements that have already touched hundreds of thousands of lives with strong admonitions and biblical teaching on the importance of character, integrity, fidelity, facing their pressures, and keeping their promises. Chuck Swindoll and his sister, Luci Swindoll, have been a part of these movements, not only by speaking at Promise Keepers and Women of Faith events around the nation, but through the ongoing ministry of this important book.

It is clear now that *The Grace Awakening* was prophetic in many ways. So many of the signs of liberation that the author described in these pages have come to fulfillment. And that is the reason for this new edition, repackaged and re-presented for another generation of believers. It is our hope that the timeless message of *The Grace Awakening* may now begin to touch the lives of an entirely new group of Christians and to encourage men and women everywhere in their walk of faith.

Even though the message of this book has already had a dramatic impact on our thinking about the Christian life, the wisdom and counsel contained in these pages is needed today more than ever. Since 9/11, the challenges in the world around us are greater than ever, but the need for Christians who will live out their witness in freedom and compassion is even greater.

Paul writes in Romans 12:6 that "since we have gifts that differ according to the grace given to us, let each exercise them accordingly." Indeed, each one of us has gifts, but it is the hope of the publisher that this book can help us become a generation of believers, molded into the image of Christ, walking boldly in the freedom of faith that our Lord intended. For when that occurs, *The Grace Awakening* is not simply a book worth reading but a life worth living.

Acknowledgments

I AM A GRATEFUL MAN. I have every reason to be. It is my joy to have numerous people surrounding me with encouragement, affirmation, honest feedback, and an abundant supply of fresh hope to stay at tough tasks. I consider them more than friends; they are partners with me, true to the end. To say that they have been helpful in seeing this book to completion is a gross understatement of the fact.

Contrary to a recurring rumor, I have no writing staff or team of researchers who provide me with historical and illustrative material or serve as my ghost writers. Every word comes from my own pen through the age-old process most authors still use: blood, sweat, tears, sleepless nights, lengthy stares at blank sheets of paper, unproductive days when everything gets dumped into the trash, and periodic moments when inspiration and insight flow. My method is so obsolete I don't even use a word processor in the writing of my books, and I have a thick, pen-worn callous on my finger to prove it.

But what I do have are faithful partners who believe in me enough to pray for me while I'm in the midst of giving birth to a book. They do more than pray, however. Some make suggestions. Others offer ideas and toss out warnings as well as goad me with questions. One types, another edits, several read, and many patiently listen. Because I am a pastor, having started a brand-new church far north of Dallas, in Frisco, Texas, I also have a lot of ears who hear the things I later put into a book. They help me hone my words by responding to what I have said with comments that are often poignant. And then there are those who serve with me on the same pastoral staff—my closest colleagues—with whom I have an enviable and rare relationship. As I acknowledge their value in my life and their contribution to my writing, I could not be more sincere or grateful. These are all my unnamed yet eminently appreciated "partners."

Specifically, I am indebted to David Moberg of Thomas Nelson for his enthusiasm over the revision of this book. His support has been relentless since its inception. In addition, the late Kip Jordon and Ernie Owen, both longtime friends of mine at Thomas Nelson, gave me great encouragement, being convinced that my perspective and convictions on grace deserved to be published so all could read what we have discussed and agreed on for years. While acknowledging my appreciation for those in the Thomas Nelson family, I dare not forget to mention my editor, Beverly Phillips, with whom I have worked for over a decade. She continues to model the qualities an author needs most in an editor—a discerning eye, a sensitive spirit, wise counsel, accuracy mixed with flexibility, penetrating questions that make me think, and a kind of convincing criticism that forces me to reevaluate and (ugh!) rewrite.

My list would be incomplete if I failed to mention Sealy Yates, who supplied invaluable assistance behind the scenes. Being the man of integrity that he is, his advice and suggestions rang true and proved to be best. I am grateful that he cared more about *The Grace Awakening* project than his own schedule, and when my patience wore thin, he demonstrated the kind of grace I write about. And, of course, I must again express my profound thanks to Helen Peters, whose diligence knew no bounds. With tireless determination she proofread the manuscript numerous times, corrected my spelling, typed every word, secured approval for my quotations and illustrations, adapted her personal calendar to meet the demands of my deadlines, put the final copy into perfect form ahead of schedule—in itself, a minor miracle—and all without one word of exasperation or complaint. Helen could sit for a portrait of amazing grace.

Finally, I acknowledge the support of my entire family, whose attitudes and expressions of grace were nothing short of incredible. In spite of the storms we have weathered and the pain we have endured together, not once have I felt anything but their unconditional love and absolute support. Rather than being pulled apart, we have bonded closer than ever. So thank you, Cynthia, and all in our family along with Luci, my dear sister, for your unfailing loyalty and love.

> 'Tis grace hath brought us safe thus far
> And grace will lead us home.[1]

Introduction

THE HUMAN HEART CRIES OUT TO BE FREE. Everything within us fights against the bondage of tyranny and oppression. Our souls were not made to live in cages of fear that restrict us from the joys of liberty. Once we get a taste of such relief, our appetite for more becomes consuming. This is true for those who lived behind the Iron Curtain in Eastern Europe or under the fanatical rules and regulations of the Taliban in Afghanistan or beneath the brutal dictatorship of Saddam Hussein's torturous regime in Iraq. And it is every bit as true for God's people who have existed too long in the suffocating grip of legalistic demands and expectations. Long enough have those who wish to control and intimidate others in the body of Christ been allowed to do so.

I am pleased to announce that their grip is loosening as grace is awakening.

Two decades have passed since I wrote and released the first printing of this book. Back then, I mentioned that a new movement was on the horizon—a movement of freedom from the things that had bound us much too long. With the passing of these recent years, it has been wonderful to witness the growth of that movement. We who have always stood firmly on the grace of God for our salvation from sin's domination are finally learning to take our stand on that same grace for deliverance from others' tight restrictions and shame-based manipulations. Having tasted the sweet delights of liberty in Christ, more and more in the Christian family are satisfied with nothing less. Nor should we be.

Based on the response of so many who have spoken to me personally or written letters of gratitude for their liberation from legalism, I have decided to provide this newly revised edition of *The Grace Awakening*. The time seems right.

My hope is that this volume will make a fresh impact on an entirely new generation of believers who are longing to be free from bondage to others but have not known how to make that happen. It is gratifying to think that these pages will provide the keys you have been looking for that will unlock those iron bars and release you from the shackles of slavery to others, awakening you to what it means to be truly free.

Free in Christ. Free indeed. Free at last.

—CHARLES R. SWINDOLL
Dallas, Texas

1
Grace: It's Really *Amazing!*

[The] moralizing and legalizing of the Gospel of God's grace
is a dull heresy peddled to disappointed people who are angry
because they have not received what they had no good reason to expect.

—RICHARD J. NEUHAUS

THERE ARE KILLERS ON THE LOOSE TODAY. The prob-
lem is that you can't tell by looking. They don't wear little buttons that
give away their identity, nor do they carry signs warning everybody to stay
away. On the contrary, a lot of them carry Bibles and appear to be clean-
living, nice-looking, law-abiding citizens. Most of them spend a lot of time
in churches, some in places of religious leadership. Many are so respected
in the community, their neighbors would never guess they are living next-
door to killers.

They kill freedom, spontaneity, and creativity; they kill joy as well as
productivity. They kill with their words and their pens and their looks.
They kill with their attitudes far more often than with their behavior. There
is hardly a church or Christian organization or Christian school or missionary group or media ministry where such danger does not lurk. The
amazing thing is that they get away with it, day in and day out, without
being confronted or exposed. Strangely, the same ministries that would not
tolerate heresy for ten minutes will step aside and allow these killers all the

1

space they need to maneuver and manipulate others in the most insidious manner imaginable. Their intolerance is tolerated. Their judgmental spirits remain unjudged. Their bullying tactics continue unchecked. And their narrow-mindedness is either explained away or quickly defended. The bondage that results would be criminal were it not so subtle and wrapped in such spiritual-sounding garb.

This day—this very moment—millions who should be free, productive individuals are living in shame, fear, and intimidation. The tragedy is they think it is the way they should be. They have never known the truth that could set them free. They are victimized, existing as if they were living on death row instead of enjoying the beauty and fresh air of the abundant life Christ modeled and made possible for all of His followers to claim. Unfortunately, most don't have a clue about what they are missing.

That whole package, in a word, is *grace*. That's what is being assaulted so continually, so violently. Those who aren't comfortable denying it have decided to debate it. Similar to the days of the Protestant Reformation, grace has again become a theological football kicked from one end of the field to the other as theologians and preachers, scholars and students argue over terms like frustrated coaches on opposite sides trying to gain advantage over each other. It is a classic no-win debate that trivializes the issue and leaves the masses who watch the fight from the stands confused, polarized, or, worst of all, bored. Grace was meant to be received and lived out to the fullest, not dissected and analyzed by those who would rather argue than eat. Enough of this! Grace must be awakened and released, not denied . . . enjoyed and freely given, not debated.

Grace received but unexpressed is dead grace. To spend one's time debating how grace is received or how much commitment is necessary for salvation, without getting into what it means to live by grace and enjoy the magnificent freedom it provides, quickly leads to a counterproductive argument. It becomes little more than another tedious trivial pursuit where the majority of God's people spend days looking back and asking, "How did we receive it?" instead of looking ahead and announcing, "Grace is ours . . . Let's live it!" Deny it or debate it, and we kill it. My plea is that we claim it and allow it to set us free. When we do, grace will become what it was meant to be—*really* amazing! When that happens, our whole countenance changes.

"NO" FACES . . . "YES" FACES

Dr. Karl Menninger, in a book entitled *The Vital Balance*, at one point discusses the negativistic personality. That's the type of person who says no to just about everything. Calling these sad folks "troubled patients," Menninger (no doubt with tongue in cheek) mentions several of the things that characterize their lives: they have never made an unsound loan, voted for a liberal cause, or sponsored any extravagances. Why? He suggests it is because they cannot permit themselves the pleasure of giving. He describes them in vivid terms: "rigid, chronically unhappy individuals, bitter, insecure, and often suicidal."[1]

I would add one further description—they have never given themselves permission to be free. Still imprisoned behind the bars of petty concerns and critical suspicions, they have learned to exist in a bondage that has hindered their ability to see beyond life's demands. Lacking grace, they have reduced life to the rules and regulations essential for survival. Their God is too small, their world is too rigid, and therefore their faces shout "No!"

Candidly, I know of nothing that has the power to change us from within like the freedom that comes through grace. It's so amazing that it will change not only our hearts but also our faces. And goodness knows, some of us are overdue for a face change! Were you reared by parents whose faces said "No"? Or are you married to someone with a "No" face? If that is true, you may envy those who had "Yes"-face parents or are married to

"Yes"-face mates. All of us are drawn to those whose faces invite us in and urge us on.

During his days as president, Thomas Jefferson and a group of companions were traveling across the country on horseback. They came to a river that had left its banks because of a recent downpour. The swollen river had washed the bridge away. Each rider was forced to ford the river on horseback, fighting for his life against the rapid currents. Each rider was threatened with the very real possibility of death, which caused a traveler who was not part of their group to step aside and watch. After several had plunged in and made it to the other side, the stranger asked President Jefferson if he would carry him across the river. The president agreed without hesitation. The man climbed on, and shortly thereafter the two of them made it safely to the other side. As the stranger slid off the back of the horse onto dry ground, one in the group asked him, "Tell me, why did you select the president to ask this favor of?" The man was shocked, admitting he had no idea it was the president who had helped him. "All I know," he said, "is that on some of your faces was written the answer 'No,' and on some of them was the answer 'Yes.' His was a 'Yes' face."[2]

Freedom gives people a "Yes" face. I am confident Jesus had a "Yes" face. I have never seen Him, but I've determined from what I've read about Him that this was true. What a contrast He must have been! He was surrounded by lettered men, religious, robed, *righteous*, law-quoting, professional men whose very demeanor announced "No!" Pious without, killers within . . . yet none of their poison seeped into His life. On the contrary, He revolutionized the entire direction of religion because He announced "Yes" while all His professional peers were frowning "No." That has intrigued me for years. How could it be? What was it that kept Him from getting caught in their grip? In one word, it was grace. He was so full of truth and grace, He left no inner space for their legalistic poison.

While thinking back on his days with Jesus, John (one of the Twelve) remembers there was something about Him that was like no one else, during which time His disciples "beheld His glory." His uniqueness was that incredible "glory," a glory that represented the very presence of God. In addition, this glorious One was "full of grace and truth." Pause and let that sink in. It was His glory mixed with grace and truth that made Him different. In a world of darkness and demands, rules and regulations, requirements and expectations demanded by the hypocritical religious leaders, Jesus came and ministered in a new and different way—He alone, full of grace and full of truth, introduced a revolutionary, different way of life.

Remembering that uniqueness, John adds, "For of His fullness we have all received, and grace upon grace" (John 1:16).

Don't miss the tie-in with John 1:14. Initially, John wrote, "We beheld His glory," and then he added, in effect, "We received His fullness." John and the other disciples became marked men as a result. Grace heaped upon grace rubbed off, leaving them different. His style became theirs. His tolerance, theirs. His acceptance, love, warmth, and compassion were absorbed by those men, so much so it ultimately transformed their lives. By the end of the first century, the ministry of those same men had sent shock waves throughout the Roman world.

John puts the capstone on his introductory remarks by summing up the difference between contrastive styles of ministry: "For the Law was given through Moses; grace and truth were realized through Jesus Christ" (John 1:17).

With the Mosaic Law came requirements, rules, regulations. With those exacting demands came galling expectations, which fueled the Pharisees' fire. By adding to the laws, the Pharisees not only lengthened the list, they intensified everyone's guilt and shame. Obsessed with duty, external conduct, and a constant focusing only on right and wrong (especially in others' lives), they promoted a system so demanding there was no room left for joy.

This led to harsh, judgmental, even prejudicial pronouncements as the religious system they promoted degenerated into external performance rather than internal authenticity. Obedience became a matter of grim compulsion instead of a joyous overflow prompted by love.

But when "grace and truth were realized through Jesus Christ," a long-awaited revolution of the heart began to set religious captives free. Fearful bondage motivated by guilt was replaced with a fresh motivation to follow Him in truth simply out of deep devotion and delight. Rather than focusing on the accomplishments of the flesh, He spoke of the heart. Instead of demanding that the sinner fulfill a long list of requirements, He emphasized faith, if only the size of a mustard seed.

The change spelled freedom, as the Lord Himself taught: "You shall know the truth, and the truth shall make you free" (John 8:32). Rigid, barren religion was, at last, replaced by a grace-oriented relationship—liberating grace. His followers loved it. His enemies hated it . . . and Him. Without a doubt, the earliest grace killers were the Pharisees.

GRACE: LET'S UNDERSTAND THE TERM

What exactly is grace? And is it limited to Jesus' life and ministry? You may be surprised to know that Jesus never used the word. He just taught it, and, equally important, He lived it. Furthermore, the Bible never gives us a one-statement definition, though grace appears throughout its pages . . . not only the word itself but numerous demonstrations of it. Understanding what grace means requires our going back to an old Hebrew term that meant "to bend, to stoop." By and by, it came to include the idea of "condescending favor."

If you have traveled to London, you have perhaps seen royalty. If so, you may have noticed sophistication, aloofness, distance. On occasion, royalty in England will make the news because someone in the ranks of nobility will stop, kneel down, and touch or bless a commoner. That is grace. There is nothing in the commoner that deserves being noticed or touched or blessed by the royal family. But because of grace in the heart of the royal person, there is the desire at that moment to pause, to stoop, to touch, even to bless.

The late pastor and Bible scholar Donald Barnhouse perhaps said it best: "Love that goes upward is worship; love that goes outward is affection; love that stoops is grace."[3]

To show grace is to extend favor or kindness to one who doesn't deserve it and can never earn it. Receiving God's acceptance by grace always stands in sharp contrast to earning it on the basis of works. Every time the thought of grace appears, there is the idea of its being undeserved. In no way is the recipient getting what he or she deserves. Favor is being extended simply out of the goodness of the heart of the giver.

I vividly remember the last spanking I ever received. It was on my thirteenth birthday, as a matter of fact. Having just broken into the sophisticated ranks of the teen world, I thought I was something on a stick. My father wasn't nearly as impressed as I was with my great importance and newfound independence. I was lying on my bed. He was outside the window on a muggy October afternoon in Houston, weeding the garden. He said, "Charles, come out and help me weed the garden." I said something like: "No . . . it's my birthday, remember?" My tone was sassy, and my deliberate lack of respect was eloquent. I knew better than to disobey my dad, but, after all, I was the ripe old age of thirteen. He set a new 100-meter record that autumn afternoon. He was in the house and all over me like white on rice, spanking me all the way out to the garden. As I recall, I weeded until the moonlight was shining on the pansies.

That same night he took me out to a surprise dinner. Earlier he had given me what I deserved. Later he gave me what I did not deserve. The birthday dinner was grace. He condescended in favor upon this rebellious young man. That evening I enjoyed what a proper theologian named Benjamin Warfield called "free sovereign favor to the ill-deserving."[4] I enjoyed grace.

One more thing should be emphasized about grace: It is absolutely and totally free. You will never be asked to pay it back. You couldn't even if you tried. Most of us have trouble with that thought because we work for everything we get. As the old saying goes, "There ain't no free lunch." But in this case, grace comes to us free and clear, no strings attached. We should not even try to repay it; to do so is insulting.

Imagine going to the house of a friend who has invited you over to enjoy a meal. You finish the delicious meal and then listen to some fine music and visit for a while. Finally, you stand up and get your coat as you prepare to leave. But before you leave, you reach into your pocket and say, "Now, how much do I owe you?" What an insult! You don't do that with someone who has graciously given you a meal. Isn't it strange, though, how this world is running over with people who think there's something they must do to pay God back? Somehow they are hoping God will smile on them if they work really hard and earn His acceptance, but that's an acceptance on the basis of works. That's not the way it is with grace.

And now that Christ has come and died and thereby satisfied the Father's demands on sin, all we need to do is claim His grace by accepting the free gift of eternal life. Period. He smiles on us because of His Son's death and resurrection. It's grace, my friend, amazing grace. That is enough to give anybody a "Yes" face!

GRACE: A MANY-SPLENDORED THING

We use *grace* to describe many things in life:

- a well-coordinated athlete or dancer
- good manners and being considerate of others

- beautiful, well-chosen words
- consideration and care for other people
- various expressions of kindness and mercy

Those statements remind me of Christ. What a perfect illustration of grace! Think of several examples with me. He stood alongside a woman caught in adultery. The Law clearly stated, "Stone her." The grace killers who set her up demanded the same. Yet Christ said to those self-righteous Pharisees, "He who is without sin, let him cast the first stone." What grace! Under the Law they had every legal right to bury her beneath the rocks in their hands . . . and they were ready. There they stood with self-righteous fire in their eyes, but He intervened in grace.

When His friend Lazarus died, Martha met Him on the road and Mary later faced Him in the house. Both blamed Him for not coming earlier: "If You had been here, my brother would not have died!" (John 11:21). There is strong accusation in those words. He took them in grace. With the turn of His hand, He could have sent them to eternity, but He refused to answer them in argument. That is grace.

When He told stories, grace was a favorite theme. He employed a gracious style in handling children. He spoke of the prodigal son in grace. As He told stories of people who were caught in helpless situations, grace abounded . . . as with the good Samaritan. And instead of extolling the religious official who spoke of how proud God must be to have him in His family, Christ smiled with favor on the unnamed sinner who said, "God, be merciful to me, a sinner." Even from the cross, He refused to be angry with His enemies. Remember His prayer? "Father, forgive them . . ." No resentment, no bitterness. Amazing, this grace! Remarkable, the freedom and release it brought. And it came in full force from the only One on earth who had unlimited power, the Son of God.

My plea is that we not limit it to Him. We, too, can learn to be just as gracious as He. And since we can, we must . . . not only in our words and in great acts of compassion and understanding but in small ways as well.

Sir Edward C. Burne-Jones, the prominent nineteenth-century English artist, went to tea at the home of his daughter. As a special treat, his young granddaughter was allowed to come to the table; she misbehaved, and her mother made her stand in the corner with her face to the wall. Sir Edward, a well-trained grandfather, did not interfere with his grandchild's training, but the next morning he arrived at his daughter's home with paints and palette. He went to the wall where the little girl had been forced to stand, and there he painted pictures—a kitten chasing its tail, lambs in a field, goldfish swimming. He decorated the wall on both sides of that corner with paintings for his granddaughter's delight. If she had to stand in the corner again, at least she would have something to look at.[5]

And so it is with our Lord. When we do the things we should not, He may administer discipline, sometimes quite severely, but He never turns His back . . . He doesn't send His child to hell! Neither do we fall from grace and get slammed behind the iron bars of the Law. He deals with His own in grace . . . beautiful, charming, unmerited favor. It is really amazing!

There will always be some—as those who glared at the woman taken in adultery—who will urge us to be stern, rigid, and cold-hearted. Yes, there are always a few who prefer stoning to forgiving, who will vote for judgment rather than tolerance. But my hope is that we might join the swelling ranks of those who decide that Christlike grace (with all its risks) is so much more effective, we opt for it every time. God honors such an attitude.

SOME PRACTICAL EXPECTATIONS

Most of you are familiar with the story of Rip Van Winkle, the man in the children's fairy tale who went to sleep for twenty years and awoke to a very different world from the one he had known before his two-decade slumber. All the while he was asleep, wonderful changes were taking place around him about which he was totally ignorant. Like Rip Van Winkle, many of us are slumbering under the oppressive opiate of those who would keep us from experiencing the marvelous grace-filled life available to those of us who would be made fully alive to its liberating potential. Wake up! Sleep no longer! The grace awakening is upon us. And what can you expect upon rising from your uninformed stupor? Let me close this first chapter by mentioning four practical expectations you can anticipate as you get a firm grasp on grace.

First, *you can expect to gain a greater appreciation for God's gifts to you and others.* What gifts? Several come to mind. The free gift of salvation (which we shall consider in depth in the next chapter). The gift of life. The gifts of laughter, of music, of beauty, of friendship, of forgiveness. Those who claim the freedom God offers gain an appreciation for the gifts that come with life.

Second, *you can expect to spend less time and energy critical of and concerned about others' choices.* Wouldn't that be a refreshing relief? When you get a grasp on grace—when you begin to operate in a context of freedom—you become increasingly less petty. You will allow others room to make their own decisions in life, even though you may choose otherwise.

Third, *you can expect to become more tolerant and less judgmental.* Externals will not mean as much to you by the time you've finished the book. You'll begin to cultivate a desire for authentic faith rather than endure a religion based on superficial performance. You will find yourself so involved in your own pursuit of grace, you'll no longer lay guilt trips on those with whom you disagree.

Fourth, *you can expect to take a giant step toward maturity.* As your world expands, thanks to an awakening of your understanding of grace, your maturity will enlarge. Before your very eyes, new vistas will open. It will be so transforming, you will never be the same.

That reminds me of something that happened to me when I was about ten or eleven years old. If you can believe it, I had never seen a football game . . . I mean an official high school, college, or professional football game played in a stadium. My world was incredibly small because my knowledge of life outside our little home in East Houston was so limited. We did not own a television set as I grew up, which also restricted my awareness. One weekend, while visiting friends in Austin, the father of that family asked all of us kids if we would like to go to a University of Texas football game. I wasn't sure what he meant, but if it had to do with football, I was interested since I played sandlot ball almost every afternoon.

Was I in for a surprise! As we walked up the ramp at the stadium, my eyes must have been the size of saucers. And when we stepped into the bleachers, I literally could not believe the scene that stretched before me. Warming up down on the field stood Bobby Layne, who later that day went on to lead the Longhorns to a victory. The immediate outcome was great—winning is always fun—but the ultimate change in my life was enormous. In one brief afternoon my world exploded! I had had a taste of the excitement, the color, the competition of grown-up football, and I would never be the same. I would not have returned even if I could. The exposure resulted in my taking a giant step toward growing up.

Trust me, once you have tasted the grown-up freedom that grace provides, you will never again be satisfied with sandlot living . . . and I really mean *never*.

2

The Free Gift

FOR THE NEXT FEW MINUTES LET'S THINK ABOUT HERESY. To begin with, answer this question: What would you consider the most dangerous heresy on earth? Stop and think before you answer. The one I have in mind is not so bold and ugly that it would make angels blush. This one is subtle, rather attractive. For a long, long time it's been a favorite of many. Actually, it has been around since the Garden of Eden. Let me give you a few hints:

- It is a philosophy found in numerous self-help books, many poems, and most rags-to-riches biographies.
- It is a recurring theme in political speeches and commencement addresses. It flourishes in academia.
- It feeds our pride, it fuels our self-centered bent, it pleases our flesh.

In a word, it's humanism.

William Ernest Henley, born in Gloucester, England, in 1849—crippled since childhood—was among the early humanists. He wrote a piece that is commonly quoted by valedictorians at high school graduations all across America.

INVICTUS

> Out of the night that covers me,
>   Black as the Pit from pole to pole,
> I thank whatever gods may be
>   For my unconquerable soul.
>
> In the fell clutch of circumstance
>   I have not winced nor cried aloud.
> Under the bludgeonings of chance
>   My head is bloody, but unbowed.
>
> Beyond this place of wrath and tears
>   Looms but the Horror of the shade,
> And yet the menace of the years
>   Finds and shall find me unafraid.
>
> It matters not how strait the gate,
>   How charged with punishments the scroll,
> I am the master of my fate;
>   I am the captain of my soul.[1]

Pretty heady stuff, isn't it? Makes you want to get at it, to dig in deeper and try harder, right? After all, if you and I have souls that are unconquerable, the sky's the limit. If we really are our own master and captain, watch out, world!

The Free Gift

You've heard words like that, haven't you? If you're like me, you've heard them since you were just a child. They sound so right, so inspiring. "Just reach down real deep and pull up hard on your own bootstraps, and you can make it all on your own. You can endure whatever. Nothing is out of reach, so press on . . . climb higher! You can make anything of yourself. You can even attain heaven!" (Or, as in Luther's day, at least buy a quicker way to heaven for someone else.)

What seems so right is, in fact, heresy—the one I consider the most dangerous heresy on earth. What is it? *The emphasis on what we do for God, instead of what God does for us.* Some are so convinced of the opposite, they would argue nose to nose. They are often the ones who claim that their favorite verse of Scripture is "God helps those who help themselves" (which doesn't appear in the Bible). Talk about killing grace! The fact is, God helps the helpless, the undeserving, those who don't measure up, those who fail to achieve His standard. Nevertheless, the heresy continues louder now than ever in history. Most people see themselves as "masters" of their own fate, "captains" of their own souls. It's an age-old philosophy deeply ingrained in the human heart. And why not? It supports humanity's all-time favorite subject: self.

Let me show you one of the first times it reared its head back in the earliest days of the Scriptures. Many, many centuries before Christ, even before there were multiple languages and dialects, tribes and nations, the people of the earth lived in an area called Shinar and spoke the same universal language. By unanimous vote they agreed to build an enormous structure—a tower whose top would reach into heaven itself. The biblical account puts it this way:

Now the whole earth used the same language and the same words. And it came about as they journeyed east, that they found a plain in the land of

15

Shinar and settled there. And they said to one another, "Come, let us make bricks and burn them thoroughly." And they used brick for stone, and they used tar for mortar. And they said, "Come, let us build for ourselves a city, and a tower whose top will reach into heaven, and let us make for ourselves a name." (Gen. 11:1–4)

The Living Bible calls this construction project "a proud eternal monument to themselves." Doesn't that sound appealing? Doesn't that sound like a project that would attract everyone's attention? I mean, nobody could resist! This was the choice opportunity of a lifetime. I can just imagine the Shinar Chamber of Commerce promoting the new slogan, "Glory to man in the highest," as they recruited workers. Everybody pitched in.

This tower has intrigued me for years, especially its top that would "reach into heaven." As a little boy in Sunday school, I remember seeing pictures of the Tower of Babel. Each picture of the tower portrayed its top far up in the clouds. I assumed in my little mind that the top literally went right up to the heavens into the very throne room of God. But there was no way such an immense, towering structure could have been erected. Sizable construction projects were possible but certainly nothing that tall.

Several years ago I went back and did a little extra digging in the Genesis text and discovered some helpful information. I found that a crucial part of verse 4 reads literally, "whose upper part is with the heavens." The little preposition "with" is a preposition of accompaniment or representation. Somehow the topmost part of the tower was designed and constructed so that it would "represent" the heavens.

In my study I also learned that an extensive excavation took place in the land of Shinar numerous decades ago. Not just one tower, but many of these ziggurats (cone-shaped structures built with a spiral road around them for journeying up and down) were constructed. And among all the cone-shaped dwellings in this particular area, one tower stood above all the rest. Chances are good that the tallest was the tower referred to in Genesis 11. What is most interesting is that they discovered in that particular tower the signs of the zodiac etched into the stonework up toward its peak. Signs and symbols that represented the stellar spaces, which are commonly called "the heavens," appeared at the top. It was like an ancient religious shrine up there . . . almost as if they were saying, "Good old God. He's looking down on our city and is pleased with our efforts. Just think of the fame that will come our way as we make a name for ourselves. God can't help but bless us for all we have achieved." It was humanism's finest hour.

The question is, What *did* God think of this original building constructed for and dedicated to the glory of man? To begin with, He immediately saw through their thinking:

> And the Lord came down to see the city and the tower which the sons of men had built. And the Lord said, "Behold, they are one people, and they all have the same language. And this is what they began to do, and now nothing which they purpose to do will be impossible for them." (Gen. 11:5–6)

Make no mistake about it. Human effort can accomplish incredible feats. No one should underestimate the ability of human beings. God himself acknowledges such when He says, in effect, "This is just the beginning of a lifetime of such thinking. There's no limit. Whatever they purpose to do, they will do." Realizing that, He quickly put a stop to the project:

> Come, let Us go down and there confuse their language, that they may not understand one another's speech. (Gen. 11:7)

(Read the next two verses carefully. Notice that God never destroyed the Tower of Babel; the workers deliberately left it unfinished.)

So the Lord scattered them abroad from there over the face of the whole earth; and they stopped building the city. Therefore its name was called Babel, because there the Lord confused the language of the whole earth; and from there the Lord scattered them abroad over the face of the whole earth. (Gen. 11:8–9)

One wonders how many generations traveled through Shinar and stared at that city as time slowly deteriorated those towers. Candidly, the answer is *not enough*. Humanity failed to learn the lesson Babel was designed to teach. Instead, we seem to have restored and enshrined what God attempted to erase. Too many of us continue to believe that doing what we want to do will result in being what we ought to be. "I want to build a tower," one announces. Why? "Because I want to be famous. I want to have a name. I ought to be great. And I need that sense of accomplishment, the feeling of pride that comes from making a name for myself. I'll do it my way!" God steps in and says, in effect, "There's no way." But still the self-made towers continue to be erected. After all, "God helps those who help themselves," the workers confidently proclaim. But their self-centered efforts represent heresy . . . a gospel of works, a grace killer in its worst form.

James Russell Lowell was a contemporary of William Ernest Henley. They were separated by the Atlantic Ocean geographically and by an even larger distance theologically. Lowell, an American, wrote in his work "The Present Crisis" of a philosophy that was much different from the one in Henley's "Invictus":

> Truth forever on the scaffold,
> Wrong forever on the throne—
> Yet that scaffold sways the future, and,
> behind the dim unknown,

Standeth God within the shadow,

keeping watch above his own.[2]

DEFENDING: TRUTH ON THE SCAFFOLD

While most people in the world are busy building towers with highest hopes of making a name and gaining fame, God's truth sets the record straight. On the basis of God's Book, His Holy Word, it is my plea that we simply admit our need and claim God's grace. Instead of striving for a man-made ticket to heaven based on high achievement and hard work (for which we get all the credit), I suggest we openly declare our own spiritual bankruptcy and accept God's free gift of grace. "Why?" you ask. "Why not emphasize how much I do for God instead of what He does for me?" Because that is heresy, plain and simple. How? By exalting our own effort and striving for our own accomplishments, we insult His grace and steal the credit that belongs to Him alone.

Let's leave the land of Shinar with its city of towers and turn to a man who lived shortly thereafter. His name was Abraham . . . a man who, in himself, had quite a name, not to mention an impressive reputation. Yet, when it came to his being righteous before God, he had nothing in himself that earned God's acceptance. All this is clearly stated in Romans 4:1–2:

> What then shall we say that Abraham, our forefather according to the flesh, has found? For if Abraham was justified by works, he has something to boast about; but not before God.

That closing statement is worth pursuing. Anyone who has a lot of accomplishments to his credit has something to boast about before the public. People are impressed with human achievement. They will applaud you. They will give you credit. They will honor your name. They may even build a statue out of bronze or name schools and streets after you. You have something to boast about before others on earth, no question. But according to the statement in Romans 4, there is no room for boasting before God. Not even a great man like Abraham could earn God's favor and blessing.

In the final analysis, it was not the result of Abraham's hard work that caused him to find favor with God; it was the result of God's great grace. Apart from anything Abraham owned or earned, bought or achieved, God declared the man righteous. He "justified" Abraham:

> The day came when, in the accounting of God, ungodly Abraham was suddenly declared righteous. There was nothing in Abraham that caused the action; it began in God and went out to the man in sovereign grace. Upon a sinner the righteousness of God was placed. In the accounting the very righteousness of God was reckoned, credited, imputed. The Lord God Himself, by an act of grace moved by His sovereign love, stooped to the record and blotted out everything that was against Abraham, and then wrote down on the record that He, God, . . . credited . . . this man Abraham to be perfect even at a moment when Abraham was ungodly in himself. That is justification.[3]

How could anyone say a great man like Abraham was "ungodly"? Well, when you look behind the scenes of his life (or any life), you find out. Deep within Abraham was an emptiness. Spiritual death. Behind all of the possessions and human greatness there was a background of idolatry (according to the Old Testament book of Joshua, chapter 24). He had been reared by an idolater. He had married a woman who had come from the same region of idolatry. He was by birth, by nature, and by choice a sinner. However, God in sovereign grace penetrated through all of that. And when He heard Abraham say, "I believe," God, in grace, credited perfect righteousness to the man's account. The Scriptures call this "justification."

May I suggest a definition? Justification is the sovereign act of God whereby He declares righteous the believing sinner—while he is still in a sinning state. Even though Abraham (after believing and being justified) would continue to sin from time to time, God heard Abraham when he said, "I believe . . . I believe in You." And God credited divine righteousness to his account. This occurred even though Abraham was still in a sinning state. But never again would the man have to worry about where he stood before his God. He was, once and for all, declared righteous. He received what he did not deserve and could never earn. Once again I remind you, that's grace. But is Abraham unique? The answer is in the next two verses:

> Now to the one who works, his wage is not reckoned as a favor but as what is due. But to the one who does not work, but believes in Him who justifies the ungodly, his faith is reckoned as righteousness. (Rom. 4:4–5)

Most people I know look forward to payday. You do too, right? For a week, or perhaps a two-week period, you give time and effort to your job. When payday arrives, you receive a hard-earned, well-deserved paycheck. I have never met anyone who bows and scrapes before his boss, saying, "Thank you. Oh, thank you for this wonderful, undeserved gift. How can I possibly thank you enough for my paycheck?" If we did, he would probably faint. Certainly, he would think, *What is wrong with this guy?* Why? Because your paycheck is not a gift. You've earned it. You deserve it. Cash it! Spend it! Save it! Invest it! Give it! After all, you had it coming. In the workplace, where wages are negotiated and agreed upon, there is no such thing as grace. We earn what we receive; we work for it. The wage "is not reckoned as a favor but as what is due."

But with God the economy is altogether different. There is no wage relationship with God. Spiritually speaking, you and I haven't earned any-thing but death. Like it or not, we are absolutely bankrupt, without eter-nal hope, without spiritual merit; we have nothing in ourselves that gives us favor in the eyes of our holy and righteous heavenly Father. So there's nothing we can earn that would cause Him to raise His eyebrows and say, "Um, now maybe you deserve eternal life with Me." No way. In fact, the individual whose track record is morally pure has no better chance at earning God's favor than the individual who has made a wreck and waste of his life and is currently living in unrestrained disobedience. Everyone who hopes to be eternally justified must come to God the same way: on the basis of grace; it is a gift. And that gift comes to us absolutely free. Any other view of salvation is heresy, plain and simple.

So much for Abraham. Our next stop-off is Romans 5. It will help me explain how this free gift flows over into our lives and the lives of all who will believe:

> Therefore having been justified by faith, we have peace with God through
> our Lord Jesus Christ. (Rom. 5:1)

Study those words carefully. We, being justified by faith, not works, get the one thing we've longed for—peace with God. Is it through our merits? Not at all. The verse states we've been justified by faith. It is through Jesus Christ our Lord who paid the absolute, final payment for sin when He died in our place at the Cross. Sin against God required the payment of death. And Jesus Christ, the perfect Substitute, made the ultimate, once-and-for-all payment on our behalf. It cost Him His life. As a result, God gives the free gift of salvation to all who believe in His Son.

Because this is foundational to an understanding of grace, I have set aside this second chapter as a declaration and explanation of God's free gift. Once we grasp its vertical significance as a free gift from God, much of horizontal grace—our extending it to others—automatically falls into place. Once we accept the seldom-announced fact that we have nothing to give God or impress God with that will prompt Him to credit righteousness to our account, we will be ready to take His free gift.

This sounds so simple. And it is—except for one troublesome barrier. It is the problem of sin. No amount of education, no amount of reading, no amount of churchgoing will take away our problem. We are contaminated with sin:

> Therefore, just as through one man sin entered into the world, and death through sin, and so death spread to all men, because all sinned. (Rom. 5:12)

Learn a little theology. It is vital to understanding and appreciating grace. We were born wrong with God. The same sin that Adam introduced has polluted the entire human race. No one is immune to the sin disease. And no human accomplishment can erase the internal stain that separates us from God. Because Adam sinned, all have sinned. This leads to one conclusion: We all need help. We need forgiveness. We need a Savior.

So . . . how do we get out of this mess? Read the next two verses slowly and carefully:

> So then as through one transgression there resulted condemnation to all men, even so through one act of righteousness there resulted justification of life to all men. For as through the one man's disobedience the many were made sinners, even so through the obedience of the One the many will be made righteous. (Rom. 5:18–19)

Wonderful! Marvelous reassurance!

"You're telling me, Chuck, that by simply believing in Jesus Christ I can have eternal life with God, my sins forgiven, a destiny secure in heaven, all of this and much more without my working for that?" Yes, that is precisely what Scripture teaches. I remind you, it is called *grace*. It's what the Protestant Reformation was all about. Salvation is offered by divine grace, not by human works. Do you want a classic scriptural example? How about a man who was breathing his last? The man I have in mind is one who was dying on a cross, hanging next to Jesus at our Lord's crucifixion. Remember the scene?

He was saying, "Jesus, remember me when You come in Your kingdom!" (Luke 23:42). Those are words of faith, the simple statement of a man who has been an unbeliever all of his life. Suddenly, with his last sigh (unable to do one religious deed . . . he couldn't even be baptized!), he turns to Christ, hanging helplessly on a cross, and he believes. He states his faith in Christ: "Lord . . . remember me." And Jesus answers with this promise: "Truly . . . today you shall be with Me in Paradise" (23:43). The man's faith without works, without conditions, was rewarded with Jesus' grace.

Once again, back to Romans 5, verse 20, where we read, "And the Law came in that the transgression might increase." Did it ever! Some misread that and assume there's something wrong with the Law if it brings an increase in transgression—an inaccurate assumption. Let me put it this way. When the Law came in, our transgression was identified and our guilt was intensified. By reading for the first time "Thou shalt not . . . thou shalt not . . . thou shalt not . . . ," we realized what sin was. God's demands are right; His commands are pure and clean. They are God's expectation of a holy people. The Law came, declaring what it took to measure up to God's standard of righteousness—but we couldn't do it. The Law kept hammering away, "Don't . . . don't . . . don't!" But mankind still failed. The Law gave us the demands of perfection, but no assistance, no encouragement. The best thing the Law did was identify sin and intensify our guilt. As a matter of fact, it still does so. To this day, the Law makes us painfully aware of our wrongs.

I remember when I was in my early teens, one of my first jobs was throwing a paper route. I threw the *Houston Press* for a couple of years during junior high school. It was a good job and kept me out of mischief, but it got tiring.

After a long afternoon of folding about two hundred papers, throwing my route, and turning toward home on my bike, I remember coming to the backyard of a large lawn at the corner across the street from our house. I thought to myself, *I'm tired . . . no need to go all the way down to the end of the street and around this big yard. I'll just cut across and be home in a jiffy.* It was a quick-and-easy shortcut. The first time I did that I entertained a little twinge of guilt as I rode my bike across that nice, plush grass. You need to understand, this was a beautiful yard. To make matters worse, our neighbor was very particular about it. I had watched him manicure it week after week. Still, I figured it wouldn't hurt just this once. Late the next afternoon I came tooling down the same street, thinking, *I wonder if I ought to use that same shortcut?* I did . . . with less guilt than the first time. Theoretically, something told me I shouldn't; but practically, I rationalized around the wrong.

In less than two weeks my bicycle tires had begun to wear a narrow path across the yard. By then, I knew in my heart I really should be going down and around the corner, but I didn't. I just shoved all those guilt feelings down out of sight.

By the end of the third week, a small but very obvious sign appeared near the sidewalk, blocking the path I had made. It read: "Keep Off the Grass—No Bikes." Everything but my name was on the sign! I confess, I ignored it; I went around the sign and rode right on over my path, glancing at the sign as I rode by. Admittedly, I felt worse! Why? The sign identified my sin which, in turn, intensified my guilt. But what is most interesting, the sign didn't stop me from going across the yard. As a matter of fact, it held a strange fascination. It somehow prodded me into further wrong.

It's like a Wet Paint sign. I have touched more wet paint just because somebody put a sign there, haven't you? I've thought that if they just wouldn't identify it as wet, I wouldn't touch it. But when it says Do Not Touch, I have to touch it. Something inside me forces my fingers onto wet paint. It's called sinful depravity. Signs don't help a bit.

One of my close friends told me about a trip he took to San Francisco, during which time he saw a most unusual sign. It read "*Try* to Keep off the Grass." My point? When you see a sign, the sign has no power whatsoever to make you obey. It certainly identifies the sin in us, and it intensifies the guilt when we ignore it, but it offers no power to restrain us.

And so it is with the Law. The Law came and in bold letters etched by the finger of God it read, "This is holiness! Honor My name by keeping My Law!" But the fact is, nobody could keep it, which explains the statement in Romans 5:20 that says "sin increased." The Law arouses sin but never arrests it. So how can the tailspin stop? What hope is there? The answer is found in the same verse: "where sin increased, grace abounded all the more." Isn't that great! Grace overshadowed sin; it outranked it and thereby brought hope.

Let me amplify the scriptural statement even more. Where sin overflowed, grace flooded in. Where sin measurably increased, grace immeasurably increased. Where sin was finite, grace was infinite. Where sin was colossal, grace was supercolossal. Where sin abounds, grace superabounds. The sin identified by the Law in no way stopped the flow of the grace of God. Jesus' death on the cross was the sufficient payment for sin, putting grace into action that was not simply adequate but *abundant*.

Augustus Toplady wrote it this way:

> The terrors of Law and of God
> with me can have nothing to do;
> My Savior's obedience in blood
> hide all my transgressions from view.[4]

The Free Gift

For the next few moments, graze slowly over this paragraph of truth recorded by Paul in the letter to the Ephesians. Take your time. Don't hurry.

And you were dead in your trespasses and sins, in which you formerly walked according to the course of this world, according to the prince of the power of the air, of the spirit that is now working in the sons of disobedience. Among them we too all formerly lived in the lusts of our flesh, indulging the desires of the flesh and of the mind, and were by nature children of wrath, even as the rest. But God, being rich in mercy, because of His great love with which He loved us, even when we were dead in our transgressions, made us alive together with Christ (by grace you have been saved), and raised us up with Him, and seated us with Him in the heavenly places, in Christ Jesus, in order that in the ages to come He might show the surpassing riches of His grace in kindness toward us in Christ Jesus. For by grace you have been saved through faith; and that not of yourselves, it is the gift of God; not as a result of works, that no one should boast. (Eph. 2:1–9)

Pay close attention to ten single-syllable words, "by grace . . . through faith . . . it is the gift of God."

One of my greatest anticipations is some glorious day being in a place where there will be no boasting, no namedropping, no selfishness. Guess where it will be? Heaven. There will be no spiritual-sounding testimonies that call attention to somebody's supercolossal achievements. None of that! Everybody will have written across his or her life the word *grace*.

"How did you get up here?"

"Grace!"

"What made it possible?"

"Grace."

"What's your name?"

"Grace."

There will be more Graces up there than any other name. Everywhere, grace, grace, grace!

When I was in seminary, one fellow who struggled with academics—I mean really struggled—was grateful just to get through school. I can still remember going to the mailroom where everybody got their tests back. Invariably, there would be a handful of guys in the corner, asking, "What did you get on Number 4?"

"Well, I got so and so."

"Really? I wrote the same thing, and he counted me wrong on 4."

But one dear guy never did any of that nonsensical comparison stuff. He would quietly open his box, pull out his test booklet, and before he ever looked at his grade, he wrote in big bold letters across the front of the test "Grace." If he did poorly: "Grace." If he did well: "Grace!" If he passed, that was sufficient: "Grace!" I learned a valuable lesson from my friend. That's all any of us have to claim.

> Nothing in my hands I bring,
> Simply to Thy Cross I cling.[5]

And when grace is our only claim, who gets the glory? The One who went to the Cross.

Now for the big question: Can you understand why the grace killers would attack this great truth? Of course! It cuts the heart out of do-it-yourself-and-get-the-glory religion. As they did in Luther's day, they appear in every generation with convincing arguments, saying, "You know, you have to try really hard." Or, "You need to give up such and such." Or, "You need to start doing so and so." Or, "You must prove the sincerity of your faith." Or, "Before God can do this in your life, you must earn it by doing such and such." Forget it! God, in grace, offers you the free gift of forgiveness. All you can do is take it. Once you take it, you will be given the power to give up, to put on, to take off, to quit, to start— whatever. But don't confuse the issue of salvation. It is yours strictly on the basis of God's free gift. In spite of all the stuff you may hear to the contrary, the emphasis is not on what we do for God; instead, it is on what God has done for us.

Some time ago, while digging deeply into this subject of God's amazing grace, I happened upon a piece by Dorothea Day, in which she answers Henley's "Invictus" with words that cut to the heart of his humanistic philosophy.

MY CAPTAIN

Out of the light that dazzles me,
   Bright as the sun from pole to pole,
I thank the God I know to be
   For Christ the conqueror of my soul.

Since His the sway of circumstance,
   I would not wince nor cry aloud.
Under that rule which men call chance
   My head with joy is humbly bowed.

Beyond this place of sin and tears
   That life with Him! And His the aid,
Despite the menace of the years,
   Keeps, and shall keep me, unafraid.
I have no fear, though strait the gate,
   He cleared from punishment the scroll.

Christ is the Master of my fate,

Christ is the Captain of my soul.[6]

Can you honestly say that Christ is the Master of your fate, the Captain of your soul? Trust me, His name is the only name that will take you from earth to heaven when you die. And it won't be your achievements or your fame or your fortune that will get you there. You will be granted entrance because you accepted the free gift of eternal life — nothing more, nothing less, nothing else.

There is one and only one password for entering heaven: grace.

3

Isn't Grace Risky?

BY NOW SOME OF YOU MAY BE THINKING, *The reason you are emphasizing grace is that you spent so much time in California.*

That kind of comment always makes me smile inside. Spending years of one's life in California means you have to tolerate the looks and comments from those who think all Californians are like the stereotype image—suntanned surfers who sport a casual, carefree look, think shallow thoughts, and operate on a rather relaxed mentality. When interpreted, that means Californians live near the edge of extremes and conduct themselves in a questionable lifestyle. As my sister, Luci, has said, "Just living in California means we live on the fault line in more ways than one." Too bad, but I suppose it comes with the territory (pun intended).

When I was in California, I received a strongly critical letter from one of my radio listeners. Among several things the lady unloaded on me, she had a bone to pick about my family's picture that appears on the back of the jacket of one of my books. We are all there—kids, grandkids, and our dog, Sah Sha—the whole tribe. She said that she didn't like it, that we all looked "so *Californian.*" And then she added, "Even your *dog* looks Californian!" What are we supposed to look like, *Latvian?* I mean, can Sah Sha help it if her thick coat of fur is snow white? It's pretty difficult to find a Samoyed puppy with black or red fur these days.

At the risk of sounding a lot like former President Richard Nixon, *I want to make something perfectly clear.* I believed in the grace of God before I ever stepped foot into the state of California. I was, in fact, reared in a family that believed in grace. I studied at a seminary that upheld grace. I have loved and taught the importance of living by grace in every place I have lived—Texas, the Far East, New England, the West Coast, and now back in the Lone Star State again. It is a message that is welcomed because it fits any geographical location: the Midwest, the Deep South, the great Northwest, the sun-drenched Southwest, the islands, the Third World, *anywhere.* Everywhere I have even visited I have observed one common denominator: Most people yearn to be free. They hate living under bondage. They want liberty, yet many have no idea where or how to find it. There is nothing like an accurate understanding of God's matchless grace to help make that happen. One of my joys in life is helping people gain an understanding of God's grace.

But isn't it risky? Won't some people take it to an extreme? In California—or anywhere—doesn't a minister run the risk that some in his flock may take unfair liberties if he presents the message of grace with the same gusto that I'm emphasizing in this book? Couldn't an awakening of grace lead to an abusing of grace?

Before I answer those questions, I invite you to travel with me across the Atlantic Ocean. Of all the countries in the world, England has to be considered among the most understated. In my travels, I have observed that very little is flaunted in the British Isles. When it comes to Christianity, *evangelical* Christianity that is, perhaps it is as conservative there as it is anywhere around the globe. And to go one step further, few evangelical British ministers would qualify as being more conservative than the late Martyn Lloyd-Jones, pastor of Westminster Chapel for decades. As a staunch Calvinist of the Puritan school of thought, Dr. Lloyd-Jones was a biblicist of the first order. His expositions represent a conservative position to the ultimate degree. I mention all that so you will understand that this man I am about to quote was one who would be the furthest removed from the popular (albeit erroneous) stereotype of a Californian mentality.

Twelve years before his retirement and until the day he completed his ministry, the man taught the book of Romans from the historic Westminster Chapel pulpit. His expositions would be considered tedious by some, but no one could ever say they were casual or loose. And yet in no uncertain terms, Martyn Lloyd-Jones (of all people!) states that preaching grace is not only risky, but the fact that some take it to an unwise extreme is proof that a minister is indeed preaching the true grace of God. Hold on to your surfboards as you read his remarks concerning Paul's question at the beginning of Romans 6: "Are we to continue in sin that grace may increase?"

If it is true that where sin abounded grace has much more abounded, well then, 'shall we continue in sin, that grace may abound yet further?'

First of all let me make a comment, to me a very important and vital comment. The true preaching of the gospel of salvation by grace alone always leads to the possibility of this charge being brought against it. There is no better test as to whether a man is really preaching the New Testament gospel of salvation than this, that some people might misunderstand it and misinterpret it to mean that it really amounts to this, that because you are saved by grace alone it does not matter at all what you do; you can go on sinning as much as you like because it will redound all the more to the glory of grace. That is a very good test of gospel preaching. If my preaching and presentation of the gospel of salvation does not expose it to that misunderstanding, then it is not the gospel. Let me show you what I mean.

If a man preaches justification by works, no one would ever raise this question. If a man's preaching is, 'If you want to be Christians, and if you want to go to heaven, you must stop committing sins, you must take up good works, and if you do so regularly and constantly, and do not fail to keep on at it, you will make yourselves Christians, you will reconcile yourselves to God, and you will go to heaven'. Obviously a man who preaches in that strain would never be liable to this misunderstanding. Nobody would say to such a man, 'Shall we continue in sin, that grace may abound?', because the man's whole emphasis is just this, that if you go on sinning you are certain to be damned, and only if you stop sinning can you save yourselves. So that misunderstanding could never arise. . . .

. . . Nobody has ever brought this charge against the Church of Rome, but it was brought frequently against Martin Luther; indeed that was precisely what the Church of Rome said about the preaching of Martin Luther. They said, 'This man who was a priest has changed the doctrine in order to justify his own marriage and his own lust', and so on. 'This man', they said, 'is an antinomian; and that is heresy.' That is the very charge they brought against him. It was also brought against George Whitefield two hundred years ago. It is the charge that formal dead Christianity—if there is such a thing—has always brought against this startling, staggering message, that God 'justifies the ungodly'. . . .

That is my comment; and it is a very important comment for preachers. I would say to all preachers: If your preaching of salvation has not been misunderstood in that way, then you had better examine your sermons again, and you had better make sure that you really are preaching the salvation that is offered in the New Testament to the ungodly, to the sinner, to those who are dead in trespasses and sins, to those who are enemies of God.

Isn't Grace Risky?

There is this kind of dangerous element about the true presentation of the doctrine of salvation.[1]

To Martyn Lloyd-Jones grace was not only risky, it was downright dangerous. He was clearly convinced it could be easily misunderstood. Meaning what? Well, some people will take advantage of it. They will misrepresent it. They will go to such an extreme that they will promote the erroneous idea that you can go on sinning as much as you like. To all fellow ministers I must add my voice to that of Martyn Lloyd-Jones: If you claim to be a messenger of grace, if you think you are really preaching grace yet no one is taking advantage of it, maybe you haven't preached it hard enough or strong enough. I can assure you of this: Grace-killing ministers will never have that charge brought against them. They make sure of that!

THE REALITY OF THE RISK

All this brings me to the reality of the risk. I ask again, Is grace risky? You bet your life it is. There is great risk in the book I am writing. I am well aware that this issue of grace is indeed controversial, especially when I am calling for a new awakening to the freedom Christians have in Christ. A few will take what I write and go crazy with it. Others will misread what I write and misquote me, misunderstand me, and charge me with caring little about the holiness of God because (they will say) I give people the freedom to sin. On the other hand, some in the camp of carnality will thank me for relieving their guilt, because in their misunderstanding they now think it is okay for them to continue in their loose and carefree lifestyle. I wish these things would not occur, but that is the chance I'm willing to take by holding nothing back in order that the full message of grace be set forth. Yes, grace that is presented in all its charm and beauty is risky. It brings grace abusers as well as grace killers out from under the rocks!

Statement of Clarification

Let's return to a verse of Scripture we looked at in the previous chapter, Romans 5:1: "Therefore having been justified by faith, we have peace with God through our Lord Jesus Christ."

In order for anyone to stand securely and be at peace before a holy and just God, that person must be righteous. Hence, our need for justification. Remember the definition of justification? It is the sovereign act of God whereby He declares righteous the believing sinner while still in his sinning state. It doesn't mean that the believing sinner stops sinning. It doesn't even mean that the believing sinner is *made* righteous in the sense of suddenly becoming perpetually perfect. The sinner is *declared* righteous. God sovereignly bestows the gift of eternal life on the sinner at the moment he believes and thereby declares him righteous while the sinner still lives a life marked by periodic sinfulness. He hasn't joined a church. He hasn't started paying tithes. He hasn't given up all to follow Christ. He hasn't been baptized. He hasn't promised to live a sacrificial, spotlessly pure life. He has simply taken the gift of eternal life. He has changed his mind toward Christ (repentance) and accepted the free gift of God apart from works. Period. Transaction completed. By grace, through faith alone, God declares the sinner righteous (justification), and from that moment on the justified sinner begins a process of growth toward maturity (sanctification). Day by day, bit by bit, he learns what it means to live a life that honors Christ. But immediately? No way.

Please understand, to be justified does not mean "just as if I'd never sinned." I hear that often, and it always troubles me. In fact, that definition weakens the full impact of justification. Justification really means this: Even though I still sin periodically and have found myself unable to stop sinning on a permanent basis, God declared me righteous when I believed. And because I will continue to sin from time to time, I find all the more reason to be grateful for grace. As a sinner I deserve vengeance. As a sinner I'm afraid of justice. And so, as a sinner, my only hope for survival is grace. In its purest form, it makes no earthly sense!

Let's imagine you have a six-year-old son whom you love dearly. Tragically, one day you discover that your son was horribly murdered. After a lengthy search the investigators of the crime find the killer. You have a choice. If you used every means in your power to kill the murderer for his crime, that would be *vengeance*. If, however, you're content to sit back and let the legal authorities take over and execute on him what is proper—a fair trial, a plea of guilty, capital punishment—that is *justice*. But if you should plead for the pardon of the murderer, forgive him completely, invite him into your home, and adopt him as your own son, that is *grace*.

Now do you see why grace is so hard to grasp and to accept? Very few people (if any) who are reading this page right now would happily and readily do that. But God does it *every day*. He takes the guilty, believing sinner who says, "I am lost, unworthy, guilty as charged, and undeserving of forgiveness," and extends the gift of eternal life because Christ's death on the cross satisfied His demands against sin, namely, death. And God sees the guilty sinner (who comes by faith alone) as righteous as His own Son. In fact, He even invites us to come home with Him as He adopts us into His forever family. Instead of treating us with vengeance or executing justice, God extends grace.

Allow me to repeat my earlier statement: To believe grace to that extreme and to live grace at that extreme means some will take advantage of it. Count on it. Some of you have had wonderful experiences in your homes with your children as they were growing up. You've dealt with them graciously and maturely. You have given them room to learn, to grow, even room to fail, as you've loved them, taught them Scripture, and encouraged them. You have raised the kids by grace, as, hopefully, we have in the

Swindoll home. And yet some of you are going through desperate times right now, though you did many things right. You gave your child proper freedom and let out the reins when it seemed right to do so. And yet, when your youngster reached an age of independence, he or she turned on you and, surprisingly, still remains in that state of mind. The enormous battle you have is the guilt that goes with it. My prayer is that God might help every one of you going through such a time. I have observed that most parents have no reason whatsoever to live with such guilt. You may struggle with some shame and embarrassment as well, though it is undeserved and inappropriate. In reality, your grown child has made a decision and is living in the wake of the consequences, but unfortunately it impacts you. It grieves you. You fear you may have been too gracious.

It's that same fear that causes many a minister to stay away from grace lest the congregation misinterpret his or her message and think of it as "cheap grace," a term we learned from Dietrich Bonhoeffer. Frankly, I'm glad he introduced those words to us. But we need to understand exactly what he meant by them. "Cheap grace" justifies the sin rather than the sinner. True grace, on the other hand, justifies the sinner, not the sin. Let me encourage you not to be afraid of true grace because some have misrepresented it as cheap grace. In spite of the very real risks, grace is worth it all.

Alternatives to Grace

If I choose not to risk, if I go the "safe" route and determine not to promote either salvation by grace or a lifestyle of grace, what are the alternatives? Four come to my mind, all of which are popular these days.

1. *I can emphasize works over grace.* I can tell you that as a sinner you need to have a stronger commitment to Christ, demonstrated by the work

you do in His behalf, before you can say that you truly believe. My problem in doing so is this: A sinner cannot commit to anything. He or she is spiritually dead, remember? There is no capacity for commitment in an unregenerate heart. Becoming an obedient, submissive disciple of Christ follows believing in Christ. Works follow faith. Behavior *follows* belief. Fruit comes *after* the tree is well rooted. Martin Luther's words come to mind:

> No one can be good and do good unless God's grace first makes him good; and no one becomes good by works, but good works are done only by him who is good. Just so the fruits do not make the tree, but the tree bears the fruit. . . . Therefore all works, no matter how good they are and how pretty they look, are in vain if they do not flow from grace.[2]

2. *I can give you a list of dos and don'ts.* The list comes from my personal and/or traditional preferences. It becomes my responsibility to tell you what to do or not to do and why. I then set up the conditions by which you begin to earn God's acceptance through me. You do what I tell you to do or you don't do what I tell you not to do, and you're "in." You fail to keep the list, you're "out." This legalistic style of strong-arm teaching is one of the most prevalent methods employed in evangelical circles. Grace is strangled in such a context. To make matters worse, those in authority are so intimidating, their authority is unquestioned. Rare are those with sufficient strength to confront the list makers. I have much more to say about this alternative later in the book.

3. *I can leave no room for any gray areas.* Everything is either black or white, right or wrong. And as a result, the leader maintains strict control over the followers. Fellowship is based on whether there is full agreement. Herein lies the tragedy. This self-righteous, rigid standard becomes more

important than relationships with individuals. We first check out where people stand on the issues, and then we determine whether we will spend much time with them. The bottom line is this: We want to be *right* (as we see it, of course) more than we want to love our neighbor as ourselves. At that point our personal preferences eclipse any evidence of love. I am of the firm conviction that where grace exists, so must various areas of gray.

4. *I can cultivate a judgmental attitude toward those who may not agree or cooperate with my plan.* Grace killers are notorious for a judgmental attitude. It is perhaps the single most un-Christlike characteristic in evangelical circles today.

A quick glance back through the time tunnel will prove beneficial. Jesus found Himself standing before the brain trust of legalism, the Pharisees. Listening to Him were also many who believed in Him. He had been presenting His message to the crowd; it was a message of hope, of forgiveness, of freedom.

> As He spoke these things, many came to believe in Him. Jesus therefore was saying to those Jews who had believed Him, "If you abide in My word, then you are truly disciples of Mine; and you shall know the truth, and the truth shall make you free." (John 8:30–32)

He spoke of the liberating power of the truth. Even though the official grace killers rejected His message, He assured them it could make them free. All who embrace grace become "free indeed" (John 8:36).

Free from what? Free from oneself. Free from guilt and shame. Free from the damnable impulses I couldn't stop when I was in bondage to sin. Free from the tyranny of others' opinions, expectations, demands. And free to what? Free to obey. Free to love. Free to forgive others as well as myself. Free to allow others to be who they are—different from me! Free to live beyond the limitations of human effort. Free to serve and glorify

Christ. In no uncertain terms, Jesus Christ assured His own that His truth was able to liberate them from every needless restriction: "If therefore the Son shall make you free, you shall be free indeed." I love that. The possibilities are unlimited. Return with me to Romans 6, where we started this chapter:

> Knowing this, that our old self was crucified with Him, that our body of sin might be done away with, that we should no longer be slaves to sin; for he who has died is freed from sin. Now if we have died with Christ, we believe that we shall also live with Him, knowing that Christ, having been raised from the dead, is never to die again; death no longer is master over Him. For the death that He died, He died to sin, once for all; but the life that He lives, He lives to God. Even so consider yourselves to be dead to sin, but alive to God in Christ Jesus.
>
> Therefore do not let sin reign in your mortal body that you should obey its lusts, and do not go on presenting the members of your body to sin as instruments of unrighteousness; but present yourselves to God as those alive from the dead, and your members as instruments of righteousness to God. For sin shall not be master over you, for you are not under law, but under grace.
>
> What then? Shall we sin because we are not under law but under grace? May it never be! (Rom. 6:6–15)

When we were without Christ, we were like ancient slaves on the slave block, consumed by the hopelessness of our depravity, lost, chained to sin, joyless, empty, spiritually bankrupt. All we could do was say to God, "Have mercy. Guilty as charged. I am enslaved to my passions. I am not free to obey my Savior." But once Christ took charge, He overthrew our old master and freed us to obey. Before conversion, all of us were in bondage to sin. After conversion, we were set free . . . free to obey. That is grace.

THE INESCAPABLE TENSION

All that discussion brings us back to that same issue of risk. Because of grace we have been freed from sin, from its slavery, its bondage in our attitude, in our urges, and in our actions. But having been freed and now living by grace, we can actually go too far, set aside all self-control, and take our liberty to such an extreme that we again serve sin. But that isn't liberty at all; that's license. And knowing of that possibility, many opt for legalism lest they be tempted to live irresponsibly. Bad choice. How much better to have such an awesome respect for the Lord we voluntarily hold back as we apply self-control.

I remember when I first earned my license to drive. I was about sixteen, as I recall. I'd been driving off and on for three years (scary thought, isn't it?). My father had been with me most of the time during my learning experiences, calmly sitting alongside me in the front seat, giving me tips, helping me know what to do. My mother usually wasn't in on those excursions because she spent more of her time biting her nails (and screaming) than she did advising. My father was a little more easygoing. Loud noises and screeching brakes didn't bother him nearly as much. My grandfather was the best of all. When I would drive his car, I would hit things . . . *boom!* He'd say stuff like, "Just keep on going, Bud. I can buy more fenders, but I can't buy more grandsons. You're learning." What a great old gentleman. After three years of all that nonsense, I finally earned my license.

I'll never forget the day I came in, flashed my newly acquired permit, and said, "Dad, look!" He said, "Whoa! Look at this. You got your license. Good for you!" Holding the keys to his car, he tossed them in my direction and smiled. "Tell you what, Son . . . you can have the car for two hours, all on your own." Only four words, but how wonderful: "all on your own."

I thanked him, danced out to the garage, opened the car door, and shoved the key into the ignition. My pulse rate must have shot up to 180 as I backed out of the driveway and roared off. While cruising along "all on my own," I began to think wild stuff—like, *This car can probably do 100 miles an hour. I could go to Galveston and back twice in two hours if I averaged 100 miles an hour. I can fly down the Gulf Freeway and even run a few lights. After all, nobody's here to say, "Don't!"* We're talking dangerous, crazy thoughts! But you know what? I didn't do any of them. I don't believe I drove above the speed limit. In fact, I distinctly remember turning into the driveway early . . . didn't even stay away the full two hours. Amazing, huh? I had my dad's car all to myself with a full gas tank in a context of total privacy and freedom, but I didn't go crazy. Why? My relationships with my dad and my granddad were so strong that I couldn't, even though I had a license and nobody was in the car to restrain me. Over a period of time there had developed a sense of trust, a deep love relationship that held me in restraint.

After tossing me the keys, my dad didn't rush out and tape a sign on the dashboard of the car: "Don't you dare drive beyond the speed limit" or "Cops are all around the city, and they'll catch you, boy, so don't even think about taking a risk." He simply smiled and said, "Here are the keys, Son. Enjoy it." What a demonstration of grace. And did I ever enjoy it! Looking back, now that I'm a father who has relived the same scene on four different occasions with my own children, I realize what a risk my father took.

There are many joys of being liberated that some of you have never known because you haven't given yourself permission to operate under grace. I don't mean this to sound insulting, but I am convinced that some Christians would be terrified if they were completely on their own. Because they have been told what to do for so many years, freedom is frightening. There are people who want to be told what to do and when . . . how to believe and why. And the result is tragic—perpetual adolescence. Without being trusted, without being freed, maturity never happens. You never learn to think on your own.

Someone on our staff at our *Insight for Living* office informed me several months ago that a woman had called the ministry office to find out what my "official position" was on a certain gray area. When she was told that it's not my policy to make "official" public statements on such issues, she was bewildered . . . actually, a little irritated. She asked, "How are we to know what to decide on this issue if Chuck doesn't tell us?" Some may find her question amusing. Frankly, I find it a little frightening. I thought, *Have we created that kind of Christian, where the minister must make statements in areas that are a matter of personal preference?* There is a fine line between responsible leadership and dogmatic control. All risks notwithstanding, people need to be informed and then released to come to their own convictions. Why must a minister constantly issue public edicts and decrees? Seems awfully pope-like to me. Have we wandered that far from grace?

You will never grow up as long as you must get your lists and form most of your opinions from me or some Christian leader. It is not my calling as a minister of the gospel to exploit a group of loyal listeners or dictate to everyone's conscience. It is my responsibility to teach the truths of Scripture as accurately as I am able and to model as best I can a lifestyle that pleases God (regardless of whether it pleases others) and allow others the freedom to respond as God leads them. That has worked well for me, and I plan to continue doing so. Seems to me that was the style Joshua modeled when he told the Hebrews they needed to decide where they stood when he said, "But as for me and my house, we will serve the Lord." Pretty risky, but it worked.

It still does.

I like the way some saint of old once put it: "Love God with all your heart . . . then do as you please." The healthy restraint is in the first phrase, the freedom is in the second. That's how to live a grace-oriented, liberated life. Some of the joyous benefits of such a life? I can think of several. You are:

- no longer helplessly bound by impulse and desires.
- free to make your own choices.
- able to think independently without the tyranny of comparison or the need to control.
- able to grow more rapidly toward greater maturity and flexibility, becoming the person you were meant to be.

And while I mention growing up, perhaps this is a good time to say to all parents, I hope you aren't continuing to look for ways to control your adult children. Release them. Toss 'em the keys. Let them be. Most therapists I know spend too many hours of their day dealing with people's struggles with their parents' messages that have them all bound up. Let's give our grown kids a lot of room, parents, and let's give them a break. In fact, I would suggest writing each one of them a letter stating their independence, saying, "Now that you're on your own, I want you to know that my trust is in you. My confidence is in God to guide you. And I respect you. You're an adult."

One of the best ways to handle the tension of letting go is to maintain a balance, realizing that some will take their liberty to an unwise extreme. We all admit that grace is risky. Let's also admit that some will live irresponsibly. You can detect such irresponsibility rather quickly.

1. There is a lack of love for others . . . little care about anybody else.
2. There is rationalization of out-and-out sin.
3. There is an unwillingness to be accountable.
4. There is a resistance to anyone's getting close enough to give them wise advice.
5. There is a disregard for one who is a new convert and therefore weak in the faith.

Scripture calls such a person a "weaker brother." (We need to be careful here; some people are "professional weaker brothers." Those folks are not weaker brothers at all; they are hardcore legalists who play the role of weaker brothers.)

A balance is necessary. Because grace is risky, self-imposed restrictions are important. It is necessary that we monitor those two things, isn't it? You can't be afraid of the heights if you're going to walk on the tightrope of grace. But at the same time you have to watch out for the strong gusts of wind that will occasionally blow like mad.

PRACTICAL SUGGESTIONS FOR GUARDING AGAINST EXTREMES

Three suggestions come to mind as I think about living with risks and putting all this into balanced living.

First, *guard against extremes if you want to enjoy the freedom grace provides*. Try your best to keep balanced, then enjoy it. No reason to feel guilty. No reason to be afraid. Try this first: Simply give yourself permission to be free. Don't go crazy . . . but neither should you spend time looking over your shoulder, worrying about those who "spy out your liberty" and wondering what they will think and say. I will write more about that in chapter 5.

Second, *treat grace as an undeserved privilege rather than an exclusive right*. This will also help you keep a balance. Live gratefully, not arrogantly. Have fun, but don't flaunt. It is all in one's attitude, isn't it? It has nothing to do with financial status or where you live or what clothes you prefer or which car you drive. It has everything to do with attitude.

Third, *remember that while grace came to you freely, it cost the Savior His life*. It may seem free, but it was terribly expensive when He purchased it for us. And who wouldn't want to be free, since we have been purchased from the horrors of bondage?

The Killing Fields is quite a movie. It is the true story of a *New York Times* reporter who was working in Cambodia during a time of awful bloodshed. His closest assistant was a Cambodian who was later captured by the Marxist regime, the Khmer Rouge, a totalitarian group known for its torturous cruelty. What the Cambodian assistant endured while trying to find freedom is beyond belief. If you reacted as I did when you watched the film, there were times you couldn't help but gasp.

The plot of the story revolves around the assistant's escape from the bondage of that terrible regime. It isn't a movie for the squeamish. There are things he sees and endures that defy the imagination. He is brutally beaten, imprisoned, and mistreated. Starving, he survives by sucking the blood from a beast in the field. He lives in the worst possible conditions. Finally he plans his escape. He runs from one tragic scene to another. On one occasion, while fleeing, he sinks into a bog only to discover it is a watery hellhole full of rotting flesh and human bones and skulls that foam to the top as he scrambles to climb out. It's enough to make you sick! Fleeing from one horror to another, he is surprised as he stumbles into a clearing.

Having endured the rigors of the jungle while being chased by his captors, he finally steps out into a clearing and looks down. To his utter amazement, he sees the Cambodian border. Down below him is a small refugee camp. His eyes catch sight of a hospital and a flag. And on that flag, a cross. There, at long last, hope is awakened! At that point the music builds to a climax. Light returns to his weary face, which says in a dozen different ways, "I'm free. I'm free!" The joys and the delights of his long-awaited freedom are his once again. Ultimately, he makes it to America and enjoys a tearful reunion with his friend—all because he is free. Free at last!

Grace is God's universal good news of salvation. The tragedy is that some continue to live lives in a deathlike bog because they have been so turned off by a message that is full of restrictions, demands, negativism, and legalism. You may have been one of those held in bondage, victimized by a system that has stolen your joy and snuffed out your hope. If so, I have some wonderful news. You've gotten very close to the border. There's a flag flying. And on that flag is a cross. And if you come into this camp of grace beneath the cross, you'll never have to be in that awful bog again.

You will be free . . . *free at last.*

4

Undeserving, Yet Unconditionally Loved

TO MANY PEOPLE, grace is nothing more than something to be said with heads bowed before dinner. But that idea, simple and beautiful as it may be, is light-years removed from the depth of meaning presented in Scripture regarding grace. This biblical concept of grace is profound, and its effects are both far-reaching and life changing. Were we to study it for a full decade, we would not come close to plumbing its depths.

I never knew Lewis Sperry Chafer, the founder of the seminary I attended. He had died a few years before I began my theological studies in 1959. Some of my mentors and professors, however, knew him well. Without exception they remembered him as a man of great grace. He was an articulate defender of the doctrine and an authentic model of its application throughout his adult life, especially during his latter years. I sincerely regret never having known Dr. Chafer.

I love the story one of my mentors tells of the time when this dear man of God had concluded his final lecture on grace. It was a hot afternoon in Dallas, Texas, that spring day in 1952. The aging professor (who taught that particular semester from a wheelchair) mopped the perspiration from his brow. No one in the class moved as the session ended. It was as though the young theologues were basking in what they had heard, awestruck with their professor's insights and enthusiasm about God's matchless grace. The gray-haired gentleman rolled his chair to the door, and as he flipped the light switch of the projector off, the class spontaneously broke into thunderous applause. As the beloved theologian wiped away his tears, head bowed, he lifted one hand, gesturing them to stop. He had one closing remark as he looked across the room with a gentle smile. Amid the deafening silence, he spoke softly, "Gentlemen, for over half my life I have been studying this truth . . . and I am just beginning to discover what the grace of God is all about." Within a matter of three short months, the stately champion of grace was ushered into his Lord's presence at the age of eighty-one.

I seldom sing John Newton's eighteenth-century hymn "Amazing Grace" without remembering those final words of that giant of grace:

> Amazing grace! how sweet the sound
> That saved a wretch like me!
> I once was lost, but now am found,
> Was blind, but now I see.[1]

Nobody—not Lewis Sperry Chafer, not even John Newton—ever appreciated grace more than Paul, the first-century apostle. From a past of Pharisaic pride, cruel brutality, and religious unbelief, he was changed from a zealous persecutor of the church to a humble servant of Christ. And what was the reason? The grace of God. Hear his own testimony:

> For I am the least of the apostles, who am not fit to be called an apostle, because I persecuted the church of God. But by the grace of God I am what I am, and His grace toward me did not prove vain; but I labored even more

than all of them, yet not I, but the grace of God with me. Whether then it was I or they, so we preach and so you believed. (1 Cor. 15:9–11)

REAFFIRMING THE TRUTH OF GRACE

Whatever he became, according to his own statement, Paul owed it all to "the grace of God." When I ponder the words from that grand apostle, I come up with what we might call his credo. We can reduce it to three statements with only single-syllable words, the first consisting of only eight words; the second, ten words; and the third, twelve. Occasionally, it helps to take a profound, multifaceted theological truth and define it in simple, nontechnical terms.

First statement: *God does what He does by His grace.* Paul's first claim for being allowed to live, to say nothing of being used as a spokesman and leader, was "by the grace of God." Paul deserved the severest kind of judgment, but God gave the man His grace instead. Humanly speaking, Paul should have been made to endure incredible suffering for all the pain and heartache he had caused others. But he didn't, because God exhibited His grace.

That leads us to the second statement: *I am what I am by the grace of God.* It is as if he were admitting, "If there is any goodness now found in me, I deserve none of the glory; grace gets the credit."

In our day of high-powered self-achievement and an overemphasis on the importance of personal accomplishments and building one's own ego-centered kingdom, this idea of giving grace the credit is a much-needed message. How many people who reach the pinnacle of their career say to the *Wall Street Journal* reporter or in an interview in *BusinessWeek*, "I am what I am by the grace of God"? How many athletes would say that kind of thing at a banquet in his or her honor? What a shocker it would be today if someone were to say, "Don't be impressed at all with me. My only claim to fame is the undeserved grace of God." Such candor is rare.

There's a third statement, which seems to be implied in Paul's closing remark: *I let you be what you are by the grace of God.* Grace is not something simply to be claimed; it is meant to be demonstrated. It is to be shared, used as a basis for friendships, and drawn upon for sustained relationships.

Jesus spoke of an abundant life that we enter into when we claim the freedom He provides by His grace. Wouldn't it be wonderful if people cooperated with His game plan? There is nothing to be compared to grace when it comes to freeing others from bondage.

Some, it seems, are like the cartoon character I saw recently. A dominant, aggressive type is philosophizing alongside his friend, who happens to be quieter and more passive. With unhesitating boldness, the stronger one says to the weaker one, "If I were in charge of the world, I would change Everything!" A bit intimidated, the friend who is forced to listen says rather meekly, "Uh, that wouldn't be easy. Like . . . where would you start?" Without a hesitation the stronger one looks directly back and says, "I would start with YOU!" No grace. You and I have been around a few grace killers like that, haven't we? With that notorious "No" face, they frown and say, "You need changing, so I'm going to start with you."

There are those who seem to be waiting for the first opportunity to confront. Suspicious by nature and negative in style, they are determined to find any flaw, failure, or subtle weakness in your life and to point it out. There may be twenty things they could affirm; instead, they have one main goal: to make sure you never forget your weaknesses. Grace killers are big on the "shoulds" and "oughts" in their advice. Instead of praising, they pounce!

Jackie Hudson is a good friend. She is the talented lady who has the dubious distinction of trying to teach me to snow ski, and she has the scars to prove it. What a beautiful model of patience! She wrote a book called *Doubt: A Road to Growth*, from which the article "People Grow Better in Grace" was adapted by *Worldwide Challenge* magazine in April 1988. In it she illustrates what I'm getting at:

Early in my career, I had a boss who held to numerous spoken and unspoken rules. One was that I needed to have my lights out by 11 p.m. so I wouldn't be tired on the job the next day. His house wasn't far from mine, and if he noticed my lights on after 11, I heard about it the next morning.

I remember my first compliment from him—a full year after I'd been on the job. I'd been given a project, and I worked night and day to make it perfect and, thus, win his approval.

The day of the event he wanted all the other employees to arrive an hour early to help with the preparations. Even after I explained that it wouldn't be necessary, he insisted. After the employees stood around for an hour with nothing to do, the program began. I couldn't have been more pleased with the event. The project was flawless.

Afterwards, my boss walked up to me, looked down at the floor, and out of his mouth came the long-awaited words: "Well done, Miss Hudson." My year in this environment brought on a remarkable response: rebellion. I was hardly growing in grace. Grace is fertile soil. . . .

Grace focuses on who God is and what He has done, and takes the focus off ourselves. And yet it's so easy to think we need to do something to earn God's favor, as though grace is too good to be true.[2]

Many (dare I say, most?) Christians live their lives as though they're going to be graded once a year by a God who stands there frowning with His hands stuck in the pockets of His robe. (I don't know why, but probably most people usually think of God with a robe on, never in sweats or cutoffs or a swimsuit . . . He's always wearing a beard and this white robe.) Glaring, He says, "Well, Johnson, that gets a C-." And, "Dorothy, you ought to be ashamed!" And, "Smith? Not bad. Could've been better, though." What heretical imaginations we have.

Why do we think like that? Who is responsible for such horror images of the Almighty? Where did we pick up the idea that God is mad or irritated?

Knowing that *all* of God's wrath was poured out on His Son at His death on the cross, how can we think like that? As a matter of fact, the reason He brought Jesus back from the grave is that He was satisfied with His Son. Ponder this: If the Father is satisfied with His Son's full payment for sin, and we are in His Son, by grace through faith, *then He is satisfied with you and me.* How long must Christians live before we finally believe that? Perhaps our problem is that we will forever have bosses and friends and pastors and parents who will give us lists. There will always be those who will give us more and more and more to live up to. These are grace killers whether they know it or not. By using guilt trips, shame techniques, and sneaky manipulations, they virtually drive us to distraction! But never God. He's the One who assures us that if we are anything, it is by His marvelous, infinite, matchless grace. And once we truly get hold of it for our own lives—once we experience the grace awakening—it's amazing how we want to share it. We delight in letting others be what they are by the same grace of God.

In a fine little book titled *The Liberty of Obedience*, Elisabeth Elliot writes about a young man eager to forsake the world and to follow Christ closely. *What is it I must forsake?* he asks himself.

She records the following response and in doing so illustrates the foolishness of trying to please God by keeping man-made rules and legalistic regulations. What must he give up? Try not to smile:

> Colored clothes, for one thing. Get rid of everything in your wardrobe that is not white. Stop sleeping on a soft pillow. Sell your musical instruments and don't eat any more white bread. You cannot, if you are sincere about obeying Christ, take warm baths or shave your beard. To shave is to lie against Him who created us, to attempt to improve on His work.[3]

"Does this answer sound absurd?" she asks. Then she surprises us with this statement:

It is the answer given in the most celebrated Christian schools of the second century! Is it possible that the rules that have been adopted by many twentieth-century Christians will sound as absurd to earnest followers of Christ a few years hence?[4]

Before we cluck our tongues or laugh out loud at second-century grace killers, we had better ask ourselves questions like: What message are we delivering to our brothers and sisters in the family of God? What list of dos and don'ts have we concocted and now require of others? What must they do to earn their way into the circle of our conditional love so that they can feel more accepted? And I must add this final question: Who gave us the right to give someone else the rules to live by?

If the great apostle had no list, if he was what he was by the grace of God, considering himself undeserving, I can assure you, we are all in the same camp, equally unqualified, undeserving, yet unconditionally loved by our Father. For there to be true maturity, people must be given room to grow, which includes room to fail, to think on their own, to disagree, to make mistakes. Grace *must* be risked, or we will be stunted Christians who don't think, who can't make decisions, who operate in fear and without joy because we know nothing but someone else's demands and expectations. When will we ever learn? God *delights* in choosing those most unworthy and making them the objects of His unconditional acceptance.

CONSIDERING AN EXAMPLE OF GRACE

For the next few minutes let's leave our modern world and step into the time tunnel. Travel back with me three thousand years as we return to the days of ancient dynasties and the kings of Israel. It's a brutal era when all those in the family of the previous king were exterminated once a new dynasty took control. Naturally, all members of the former monarch's family had every reason to live in fear once the new king took the throne.

In the case I'm thinking of, King Saul and his son Jonathan had died following a battle. When word of the dual tragedy reached David's attention, it grieved him; nevertheless, he was the Lord's choice as Saul's successor. Knowing that David was now Israel's new king, the members of Saul's family fled for their lives, erroneously thinking that David would treat them like all the other monarchs of eastern dynasties. The scene portrayed in Scripture is one of pandemonium and panic:

> Now Jonathan, Saul's son, had a son crippled in his feet. He was five years old when the report of Saul and Jonathan came from Jezreel, and his nurse took him up and fled. And it happened that in her hurry to flee, he fell and became lame. And his name was Mephibosheth. (2 Sam. 4:4)

In the haste of escape, Saul's little grandson suffered a permanent injury. Not having medical help available and not knowing where to turn for such assistance, the boy never recovered from the fall. He lived the balance of his life lame in both his feet. We leave him as a five-year-old on the pages of the ancient record. Nothing more is said regarding Mephibosheth for fifteen to twenty years.

A Question Asked

Chapter 9 of 2 Samuel provides a link to the continuing story. Years have passed. Mephibosheth is now an adult, living out his days with a severe handicap. He is still crippled in both his feet. David has not only taken the throne, he has won the hearts of the people. The entire nation is singing his praises. As yet there is not a blemish on his integrity. He has expanded the boundaries of the United Kingdom of the Jews in Palestine from approximately six thousand to sixty thousand square miles. The military force of Israel is stronger than ever in its history. Enemy nations now respect this powerful new country. David is healthy and happy. He has not known defeat on the battlefield, which means his immediate world is relatively peaceful. His economy and diplomacy are a refreshing change from Saul's. There is not only a chicken in every pot, there are grapes on every vine. It is a rare scene of incredible prosperity and God-given peace.

Overwhelmed by the Lord's goodness and grace, the middle-aged king muses over all his blessings. While doing so, he must have enjoyed a nostalgic moment, remembering his former friendship with Jonathan, which prompts him to ask:

> Is there yet anyone left of the house of Saul, that I may show him kindness for Jonathan's sake? (2 Sam. 9:1)

It's a question of grace asked by a grateful man.

Those of you who find yourself at a similar time in your own life know there are occasions when you will do that kind of reflecting. You think back and remember with fondness some pleasant relationship . . . some individual who played a significant role in your being where you are today. You smile, you wish there were some special way you could show your appreciation, but perhaps your longtime friend or mentor is dead.

This is precisely where we find David. Most likely he remembers the tender moment in his past when he and Jonathan agreed to preserve and protect one another, no matter what:

> "And may the Lord be with you as He has been with my father. And if I am still alive, will you not show me the lovingkindness of the Lord, that I may not die? And you shall not cut off your lovingkindness from my house forever, not even when the Lord cuts off every one of the enemies of David

from the face of the earth." So Jonathan made a covenant with the house of David, saying, "May the Lord require it at the hands of David's enemies." And Jonathan made David vow again because of his love for him, because he loved him as he loved his own life. (1 Sam. 20:13–17)

While lost in his memory, David has a flashback. Recalling that promise, he seeks a way to make it good. I don't want you to miss the importance of one term David used:

Is there yet anyone left of the house of Saul, that I may show him kindness for Jonathan's sake? (2 Sam. 9:1)

It's the Hebrew word *chesed*, often rendered *mercy, lovingkindness,* or *grace* in the Old Testament. *Is there anyone still living in the family of Saul to whom I could demonstrate the same kind of grace that God has demonstrated to me?* That's the idea turning over in David's mind.

I love the question for what it does not ask. It does not ask, "Is there anyone who is deserving? Is there anyone who is qualified? Is there anyone who is sharp, whom I could use in government matters . . . or in good shape, whom I could add to my army?" No, he simply asks, "Is there anyone?" It is an unconditional desire, a question dripping with grace. "I'm wondering if there is *anybody* out there."

David has a "Yes" face at this nostalgic moment, but something tells me that the servant he calls in has a "No" face. His name is Ziba. Listen to his answer and feel the "No" in his voice:

Now there was a servant of the house of Saul whose name was Ziba, and they called him to David; and the king said to him, "Are you Ziba?" And he said, "I am your servant." And the king said, "Is there not yet anyone of the house of Saul to whom I may show the kindness of God?" And Ziba said to

the king, "There is still a son of Jonathan who is crippled in both feet."
(2 Sam. 9:2–3)

Can't you feel the "No" in his response, even though it was affirma-
tive? Of course. "King David, I know of someone, but I really doubt that
you'd want him around. You see, he's crippled. He just doesn't fit in. He
isn't kingly." Which, being interpreted in unmasked pride, sniffs, "He's
not like the rest of us."

I love the response of King David. Rather than "Oh, really? How badly
is the man crippled?" David responds, "Where is he? If there's somebody,
anybody . . . let's get him in here." What grace! Perhaps a bit surprised,
"Ziba said to the king, 'Behold, he is in the house of Machir the son of
Ammiel in Lo-debar'" (2 Sam. 9:4).

Lo-debar, interestingly, in Hebrew means "a barren place." In English,
the name of the place could be translated "no pastureland." It's as if the
servant is saying that Jonathan's son is living in a place of stark barrenness,
a place where there are no crops, a wilderness . . . a wasteland. There is
not a moment's hesitation. David has heard enough to put a plan into
action.

A Straggler Sought

Then King David sent and brought him from the house of Machir the son
of Ammiel, from Lo-debar. And Mephibosheth, the son of Jonathan the son
of Saul, came to David and fell on his face and prostrated himself. And
David said, "Mephibosheth." And he said, "Here is your servant!" And
David said to him, "Do not fear, for I will surely show kindness to you for
the sake of your father Jonathan, and will restore to you all the land of your
grandfather Saul; and you shall eat at my table regularly." (2 Sam. 9:5–7)

The disabled man was obviously frightened when he arrived at the king's palace in Jerusalem. The watchword of his life since he was a little boy had been anonymity. He never wanted to be found, certainly not by the king who succeeded his grandfather. To do so would mean sure death. And yet there was no way he could say no when David sent for him. Before he knew it, he was whisked away in a chariot provided for him, and before he could believe it, there he stood before the king.

All that explains why David's words must have stunned Mephibosheth. They fit David, however. When grace is in your heart, your hope is to release others from fear, not create it.

Let me interrupt this wonderful story to ask you a question about Jesus, the One who was "full of grace and truth." Do you know what was the most often-repeated command from His lips? Most people I ask are unable to answer that question correctly. Our Lord issued numerous commands, but He made this one more than any other. Do you happen to know what it was? It was this: "Fear not." *Isn't that great?* "Do not fear." Naturally, the most common reaction when someone stood before the perfect Son of God would have been fear. And yet Jesus, great in grace, repeatedly said, "Do not be afraid." He didn't meet people with a deep frown, looking down on them and swinging a club. He met them with open arms and reassuring words: "Don't be afraid." Those are the words David used before Mephibosheth. They drip with grace.

Mephibosheth's first reaction must have been the fear of a spear in his belly. Small wonder he says, "Here is your servant!" as he falls on his face before the king. "Don't be afraid," says David, but the crippled man cannot stop shaking. It is as if David wants to say, "I haven't sought for you to punish you for something you've done or not done. I have good in mind for you, not harm. I want to lift you up, not tear you down." The secret of David's entire message to the man could be stated in seven words: "I will surely show kindness to you."

A Privilege Provided

Don't miss something that's terribly important in the overall message of grace. David wanted to show kindness not because of Mephibosheth (he didn't even know the man before they met that day) but "for the sake of your father Jonathan." Mephibosheth still can't believe what's happening. "Again he prostrated himself and said, 'What is your servant, that you should regard a dead dog like me?'" (2 Sam. 9:8). In calling himself "a dead dog," he uses the most descriptive words he can think of for a contemptuous, despicable, worthless creature. "I'm just a dead dog, living in Lo-debar. Why not just leave me alone in my misery?"

Remember when you said that to God? Has it been that long since you and He met? Or could you have already forgotten? Candidly, this is one of my all-time favorite stories in the Old Testament because its portrayal of grace is so powerful. Here is a man who is unknown, of no consequence to the king, and is crippled in both his feet. He can give nothing of benefit to the kingdom so far as physical strength is concerned. There is absolutely zero personal appeal, but David stoops in grace. Due to a relationship David had with his longtime friend Jonathan, the king is going to provide Mephibosheth the privileges and benefits he would have given his own son.

Swiftly and completely, the king kept his word. Watch it transpire . . . it's wonderful!

> Then the king called Saul's servant Ziba, and said to him, "All that belonged to Saul and to all his house I have given to your master's grandson." (2 Sam. 9:9)

Ziba must have shaken his head in amazement.

> And you and your sons and your servants shall cultivate the land for him, and you shall bring in the produce so that your master's grandson may have

food; nevertheless Mephibosheth your master's grandson shall eat at my table regularly." (2 Sam. 9:10)

Four separate times in the biblical account we read that the cripple would eat at the king's table—verses 7, 10, 11, and finally verse 13: "So Mephibosheth lived in Jerusalem, for he ate at the king's table regularly. Now he was lame in both his feet" (2 Sam. 9:13).

What a scene! What grace! From that time on he was welcome at the king's table of continual nourishment and uninterrupted provisions. Undeserving . . . yet unconditionally loved. Mephibosheth's head must have swirled for days as he forced himself to believe his new situation wasn't a dream.

Imagine a typical scene several years later. The dinner bell rings through the king's palace, and David comes to the head of the table and sits down. In a few moments Amnon—clever, crafty Amnon—sits to the left of David. Lovely and gracious Tamar, a charming and beautiful young woman, arrives and sits beside Amnon. And then across the way, Solomon walks slowly from his study—precocious, brilliant, preoccupied Solomon. The heir apparent slowly sits down. And then Absalom—handsome, winsome Absalom with beautiful flowing hair, black as a raven, down to his shoulders—sits down. That particular evening Joab, the courageous warrior and David's commander of the troops, has been invited to dinner. Muscular, bronzed Joab is seated near the king. Afterward, they wait. They hear the shuffling of feet, the clump, clump, clump of the crutches as Mephibosheth rather awkwardly finds his place at the table and slips into his seat . . . and the tablecloth covers his feet. I ask you: Did Mephibosheth understand grace?

Were he living today, I think he would quickly identify with the words from the hymn by John Newton:

> Through many dangers, toils, and snares
>> I have already come;
> 'Tis grace hath brought me safe thus far,
>> And grace will lead me home.[5]

SEEING THE GRACE ANALOGIES

Maybe you have already noticed some of the analogies between the grace demonstrated to Mephibosheth and the grace extended to you and me. I find no fewer than eight:

1. Once Mephibosheth enjoyed fellowship with his father. And so did the original couple, Adam and Eve, in the lovely Garden of Eden.
2. When disaster struck, fear came, and Mephibosheth suffered a fall that crippled him for the rest of his life. And so it was when sin came, humanity suffered a fall which has left us permanently disabled on earth.
3. David, the king, out of unconditional love for his beloved friend Jonathan sought out anyone to whom he might extend his grace. In like manner, God the Father, because of His unconditional acceptance of His one and only Son's death on the cross, continues to seek anyone to whom He might extend His grace.
4. The disabled man had nothing, did nothing, and deserved nothing. He didn't even try to win the king's favor. All he could do was humbly accept it. So we—sinners without hope and totally undeserving, in no way worthy of our God's favor—humbly accept it.
5. The king restored the cripple from his miserable existence—a place of barrenness and desolation—to a place of fellowship and honor. God, our Father, has done the same for us. From our own

personal "Lo-debar" of brokenness and depravity, He rescued us and brought us into a place of spiritual nourishment and intimate closeness.

6. David adopted Mephibosheth into his royal family, providing him with uninterrupted provisions, nourishment, and blessings. We, too, have been adopted as sons and daughters into His royal ranks, surrounded by ceaseless delights.

7. The adopted son's limp was a constant reminder of the king's grace. Our imperfect state keeps us from ever forgetting that where sin abounds, grace *super* abounds.

8. When Mephibosheth sat at the king's table, he was treated as one of David's own sons—no less than Absalom or Solomon. When we feast one day with our Lord, the same will be true.

There we shall sit alongside Paul and Peter, Lydia and Priscilla, Mary and Phoebe, James, John, Barnabas, and Luke . . . martyrs, monks, reformers and evangelists, seminary presidents and professors, ministers and missionaries, authors and statesmen alike, with no emphasis on rank or title . . . no special regard for high achievement. Why? Because we are all so undeserving, every one of us. Disabled all! And oh, how we'll sing God's praise.

> When we've been there ten thousand years,
>   Bright shining as the sun,
> We've no less days to sing God's praise
>   Than when we first begun.[6]

All our praise will go to the One who came and died, arose and lives. His name is Jesus; His message is grace. Few have ever pictured Him and His message more clearly than John Bunyan:

Thou Son of the Blessed,

what grace was manifested in Thy condescension

Grace brought Thee down from Heaven;

   grace stripped Thee of Thy glory;

   grace made Thee poor and despised;

   grace made Thee bear such burdens of sin,

      such burdens of sorrow,

      such burdens of God's curse as are unspeakable.

O Son of God!

Grace was in all Thy tears;

   grace came out of Thy side with Thy blood;

   grace came forth with every word of Thy sweet mouth;

   grace came out where the whip smote Thee,

      where the thorn pricked Thee,

      and where the nails pierced Thee.

Here is grace indeed!

Grace to make angels wonder,

   grace to make sinners happy,

   grace to astonish devils.[7]

As we are gathered with the people of God at that great marriage feast of the Lamb, the tablecloth of His grace will cover all our disabilities and limitations.

5

Squaring Off Against Legalism

LIBERTY IS ALWAYS WORTH FIGHTING FOR. It is the main reason Americans have laid down their lives for their country. If we were to interview any of those people who have fought in battle and ask, "Why did you live in those miserable and dangerous conditions?" or, "What was it that kept you out there fighting for your country?" the response would probably include words like, "Well, our liberty was at stake. I love my country, and our freedom was being threatened by the enemy. I wanted to defend it, and if necessary, I would still fight to the death for it."

Back in our earliest days as a nation, a determined thirty-nine-year-old radical-thinking attorney addressed the Virginia Convention. It was on March 23, 1775, a time of great patriotic passion. And his patriotism refused to be silenced any longer. Sounding more like a prophet of God than a patriot for his country, he announced,

> If we wish to be free we must fight! . . . I repeat it, sir, we must fight! An appeal
> to arms, and to the God of hosts, is all that is left us. It is vain, sir, to extenuate

the matter. The gentlemen may cry "Peace, peace!" but there is no peace. The war has actually begun! . . . Our brethren are already in the field. Why stand we here idle? . . . Is life so dear or peace so sweet as to be purchased at the price of chains and slavery? Forbid it, Almighty God. I know not what course others may take, but as for me, give me liberty or give me death![1]

What a soul-stirring speech! We applaud the courageous passion of Patrick Henry to this day. Because of it, he remains in our minds as one of our national heroes.

Not quite ninety years later we were fighting one another in our country's worst bloodbath. And again I remind you, it was for the cause of liberty. The issue was slavery versus freedom. The black people of our nation were not free. It was the conviction of the United States government that they should be free and, if necessary, to take up arms against those who opposed liberation from slavery.

Charles Sumner did a masterful job of summing up the issue of the Civil War in a speech he made on November 5, 1864: "Where Slavery is, there Liberty cannot be; and where Liberty is, there Slavery cannot be."[2]

I find it more than strange. Actually, I find it amazing that we as a nation will fight other nations for our national liberty and that we as a people will, if necessary, fight one another for the freedom of those within our borders, but when it comes to the living out of our Christianity, we will give up our liberty without a fight. We'll go to the wall and square off against any enemy who threatens to take away our national freedom, but we won't be nearly so passionate as Christians under grace to fight for our rightful liberty. Let enough legalists come aboard, and we will virtually give them command of the ship. We will fear their frowns, we will adapt our lives to their lists, we'll allow ourselves to be intimidated, and for the sake of peace at any price (even though it may lead to nothing short of slavery), we will succumb to their agenda.

This is nothing new. As far back as 1963, S. Lewis Johnson, one of my seminary professors, wrote an excellent article titled "The Paralysis of Legalism." In it he put his finger on the crux of the problem.

> One of the most serious problems facing the orthodox Christian church today is the problem of legalism. One of the most serious problems facing the church in Paul's day was the problem of legalism. In every day it is the same. Legalism wrenches the joy of the Lord from the Christian believer, and with the joy of the Lord goes his power for vital worship and vibrant service. Nothing is left but cramped, somber, dull, and listless profession. The truth is betrayed, and the glorious name of the Lord becomes a synonym for a gloomy kill-joy. The Christian under law is a miserable parody of the real thing.[3]

Though he wrote decades ago, Dr. Johnson described the church of the 1990s and the early twenty-first century. If you want to find a group of "cramped, somber, dull, and listless" individuals, just visit many (I'm trying hard not to write most) evangelical churches today. It is with a deep heartache and great disappointment that I write these words. If I were asked to name the major enemies of vital Christianity today, I'm not sure but what I would name legalism first! As I have stated from the beginning of this book, legalism is a killer. It kills congregations when a pastor is a legalist. It kills pastors when congregations are legalistic. Legalistic people with their rigid dos and don'ts kill the spirit of joy and spontaneity of those who wish to enjoy their liberty. Strict legalistic people in leadership drain the very life out of a church, even though they may claim they are doing God a service.

If you have never been under the thumb of legalism, you are rare. You don't know how blessed you have been. If you have been under bondage and have broken free (as I have), you know better than most what a treasured privilege freedom really is. It's worth fighting for!

I have my Bible beside me opened to the fifth chapter of the letter to the Galatians. Galatians is what some have correctly called the Magna Carta of Christian liberty. In fact, the first verse in this chapter contains the single command that, if believed and obeyed, would go a long way in putting a stop to legalism:

> It was for freedom that Christ set us free; therefore keep standing firm and do not be subject again to a yoke of slavery. (v. 1)

Nothing disturbs the legalist like the liberating truth of grace. Paul, far back in the first century, is writing to Christians who knew better than to let it happen, but they had allowed themselves to fall under the paralyzing spell of grace killers. J. B. Phillips, in a paraphrase of Galatians 5:1, renders it:

> Do not lose your freedom by giving in. . . . Plant your feet firmly therefore within the freedom that Christ has won for us, and do not let yourselves be caught again in the shackles of slavery.

If Patrick Henry had the courage to say, "Give me liberty or give me death," then the Christian ought to have the courage to say, "Give me freedom because of Christ." Bondage is bondage, whether it be political or spiritual. Give me the liberty that He won at Calvary, or I am still enslaved. Death is to be preferred to bondage . . . so grant me the liberty He won, or I should die! To live in slavery is to nullify the grace of God.

DEFINING TWO SIGNIFICANT TERMS

Without becoming needlessly academic, I want to define a couple of the terms that I've been tossing around. First of all, what do I mean when I declare that the Christian has *liberty*? And second, what does it mean to say that *legalism* puts people under bondage?

Liberty

Essentially, liberty is freedom . . . freedom from something and freedom to do something.

Liberty is freedom from slavery or bondage. It is initially freedom from sin's power and guilt. Freedom from God's wrath. Freedom from satanic and demonic authority. And equally important, it is freedom from shame that could easily bind me, as well as freedom from the tyranny of others' opinions, obligations, and expectations.

There was a time in my life without Christ when I had no freedom from the urges and impulses within me. I was at the mercy of my master Satan, and sin was my lifestyle. When the urges grew within me, I had nothing to hold me in check, nothing to restrain me. It was an awful bondage.

For example, in my personal life I was driven by jealousy for many miserable years. It was consuming. I served it not unlike a slave serves a master. Then there came a day when I was spiritually awakened to the charming grace of God and allowed it to take full control, and almost before I knew it, the jealousy died. And I sensed for the first time, perhaps in my whole life, true love—the joy, the romance, the spontaneity, the free-flowing creativity brought about by the grace of a faithful wife, who would love me no matter what, who was committed to me in faithfulness for all her life. That love and that commitment motivated me to love in return more freely than ever. I no longer loved out of fear that I would lose her, but I loved out of the joy and the blessing connected with being loved unconditionally and without restraint.

Now that Christ has come into my life and I have been awakened to

His grace, He has provided a freedom from that kind of slavery to sin. And along with that comes a freedom that brings a fearlessness, almost a sense of invincibility, in the presence of adversity. This power, keep in mind, is because of Christ, who lives within me.

In addition, He has also brought a glorious freedom from the curse of the Law. By that I mean freedom from the constancy of its demands to perform in order to please God and/or others. It is a freedom from the fear of condemnation before God as well as from an accusing conscience. It is freedom from the demands of other people, from all the *shoulds* and *oughts* of the general public.

Such freedom is motivated—motivated by unconditional love. When the grace of Christ is fully awake in your life, you find you're no longer doing something due to fear or out of shame or because of guilt, but you're doing it through love. The dreadful tyranny of performing in order to please someone is over . . . forever.

Grace also brings a freedom *to do* something else—a freedom to enjoy the rights and the privileges of being out from under slavery *and* allowing others such freedom. It's freedom to experience and enjoy a new kind of power that only Christ could bring. It is a freedom to become all that He meant me to be, *regardless of how He leads others.* I can be me—fully and freely. It is a freedom to know Him in an independent and personal way. And that freedom is then released to others so they can be who they are meant to be—different from me!

You see, God isn't stamping out little cookie-cutter Christians across the world so that we all think alike and look alike and sound alike and act alike. The body has variety. We were never meant to have the same temperaments and use the same vocabulary and wear the same syrupy smile and dress the same way and carry on the same ministry. I repeat: God is pleased with variety. This freedom to be who we are is nothing short of magnificent. It is freedom to make choices, freedom to know His will, freedom to walk in it, freedom to obey His leading me in my life and you in your life. Once you've tasted such freedom, nothing else satisfies.

Perhaps I should reemphasize that it is a liberty you will have to fight for. Why? Because the ranks of Christianity are full of those who compare and would love to control and manipulate you so you will become as miserable as they are. After all, if they are determined to be "cramped, somber, dull, and listless," then they expect you to be that way too. "Misery loves company" is the legalists' unspoken motto, though they never admit it.

Legalism

Now is a good time for us to become better acquainted with the staunch enemy of liberty. Legalism is an attitude, a mentality based on pride. It is an obsessive conformity to an artificial standard for the purpose of exalting oneself. A legalist assumes the place of authority and pushes it to unwarranted extremes. As Daniel Taylor states so well, it results in illegitimate control, requiring unanimity, not unity:

> The great weapon of authoritarianism, secular or religious, is legalism: the manufacturing and manipulation of rules for the purpose of illegitimate control. Perhaps the most damaging of all the perversions of God's will and Christ's work, legalism clings to law at the expense of grace, to the letter in place of the spirit.
>
> Legalism is one more expression of the human compulsion for security. If we can vigorously enforce an exhaustive list of dos and don'ts (with an emphasis on external behavior), we not only can control unpredictable human beings but have God's favor as well. . . .
>
> Legalistic authoritarianism shows itself in the confusion of the Christian principle of unity with a human insistence on unanimity. Unity is

a profound, even mystical quality. It takes great effort to achieve, yet mere effort will never produce it; it is a source of great security, yet demands great risk.

Unanimity, on the other hand, is very tidy. It can be measured, monitored, and enforced. It is largely external, whereas unity is essentially internal. Its primary goal is corrected behavior, while unity's is a right spirit. Unanimity insists on many orthodoxies in addition to those of belief and behavior, including orthodoxy of experience and vocabulary. That is, believers are expected to come to God in similar ways, to have similar experiences with God, and to use accepted phrases in describing those experiences.[4]

In so many words, legalism says, "I do this or I don't do that, and therefore I am pleasing God." Or, "If only I could do this or not do that, I would be pleasing to God." Or perhaps, "These things that I'm doing or not doing are the things I perform to win God's favor." They aren't spelled out in Scripture, you understand. They've been passed down, or they have been dictated to the legalist and have become an obsession to him or her. Legalism is rigid, grim, exacting, and lawlike in nature. Pride, which is at the heart of legalism, works in sync with other motivating factors. Like guilt. And fear. And shame. It leads to an emphasis on what should *not* be and what one should *not* do. It flourishes in a drab context of negativism.

Few people have ever described legalism better than Eugene Peterson does in his fine book *Traveling Light*, where he contrasts the healthy walk of faith with legalism:

The word *Christian* means different things to different people. To one person it means a stiff, uptight, inflexible way of life, colorless and unbending. To another it means a risky, surprise-filled venture, lived on tiptoe at the edge of expectation.

Either of these pictures can be supported with evidence. There are numberless illustrations for either position in congregations all over the world. But if we restrict ourselves to biblical evidence, only the second image can be supported: the image of the person living zestfully, exploring every experience—pain and joy, enigma and insight, fulfillment and frustration—as a dimension of human freedom, searching through each for sense and grace. If we get our information from the biblical material, there is no doubt that the Christian life is a dancing, leaping, daring life.

How then does this other picture get painted in so many imaginations? How does anyone get the life of faith associated with dullness, with caution, with inhibition, with stodginess? We might fairly suppose that a congregation of Christians, well stocked with freedom stories—stories of Abraham, Moses, David, Samson, Deborah, Daniel—would not for a moment countenance any teaching that would suppress freedom. We might reasonably expect that a group of people who from infancy have been told stories of Jesus' setting people free and who keep this Jesus at the center of their attention in weekly worship would be sensitive to any encroachment on their freedom. We might think that a people that has at the very heart of its common experience release from sin's guilt into the Spirit's freedom, a people who no longer lives under the tyranny of emotions or public opinion or bad memories, but freely in hope and in faith and in love—that these people would be critically alert to anyone or anything that would suppress their newly acquired spontaneity.

But in fact the community of faith, the very place where we are most likely to experience the free life, is also the very place where we are in most danger of losing it.[5]

Be honest, how many congregations do you know who are "dancing, leaping, daring" congregations—congregations whose individual grace awakenings are motivating people to live out their freedom in Christ? I'm afraid the number is much fewer than we might guess. Let's get specific.

How many Christians do you know who exercise the joy and freedom to be a person full of life, living on tiptoe, enjoying spontaneous delight—as opposed to the hundreds of thousands who take their cues from the legalists and live life accordingly? Isn't it surprising to anyone who has been set free that anybody would ever want to return to bondage? I suggest that you ponder the final sentence in Peterson's quote once more. As usual, he is right on target. The one place on earth where we would most expect to be set free is, in fact, the very place we are most likely to be placed into slavery: the church. Surely, that grieves our God.

What happened in the first century can surely happen in the twenty-first. Paul writes the Galatians of his surprise: "You were running well; who hindered you from obeying the truth?" (5:7).

Allow me to amplify his thought. "When I was with you, some of you were into the 100-meter dash, others were doing the 440 with ease. Still others were into much longer distances . . . you were marathoners. The truth freed you, and I distinctly recall how well you were running as well as how much joy you demonstrated. Who cut in on your stride? Who took away your track shoes? Who told you that you shouldn't be running or enjoying the race? Some of you have stopped running altogether" (Swindoll paraphrase).

That isn't all. Back in chapter 3, verses 1–3, Paul is even more assertive. His opening salutation is borderline insulting: "You foolish Galatians." (You won't like to read this, but J. B. Phillips calls them "idiots.") He writes:

O you dear idiots of Galatia, who saw Jesus Christ the crucified so plainly, who has been casting a spell over you? I shall ask you one simple question: Did you receive the Spirit of God by trying to keep the Law or by believing the message of the Gospel? Surely you can't be so idiotic as to think that a man begins his spiritual life in the Spirit and then completes it by reverting to outward observances?

The apostle says, in effect, "When I was there, teaching you the truth, I presented a Savior who paid the full penalty for your sins. The death that He died and His subsequent resurrection from the grave was God's final payment for sin. *Paid in full!* All you have to do is believe that He died and rose again from the dead for you. He was publicly displayed for all to see and now the truth can be declared for all to believe. You believed that once upon a time, and you were gloriously free. Not now. Who bewitched you? Who caused you to transfer allegiance from the glory of God to the opinions of man, from the work of the Spirit to the deeds of the flesh? When did you start running scared?" It's that idea.

The Living Bible renders this first verse: "Oh, foolish Galatians! What magician has hypnotized you and cast an evil spell upon you?" In other words, "Have you gone completely crazy? Who stole your minds?" Paul is beside himself. Who had hypnotized the once fully "awake" Galatians?

Earlier, in Galatians 1:6, he admits his amazement: "I am astonished that you are so quickly deserting the one who called you by the grace of Christ and are turning to a different gospel" (NIV).

It could be compared to your rearing your children in a healthy environment. They grow up in your home, and because it is a good home, they develop a security and a stability as they pick up your authenticity and unguarded lifestyle. They communicate openly and freely. They learn how to confront and handle problems. In short, they learn the basics of real living . . . which include knowing Christ and loving God and walking with Him and relating well to one another—all those things that represent integrity, vulnerability, authenticity.

Once they grow up, they move far away. Time passes and you begin to miss them, so after three or four years you go visit them. You're shocked! You find them living cramped, closed, dirty, and emotionally crippled lives. You're amazed to find them struggling with problems, evidencing negative attitudes; they're even suicidal. Naturally you ask, "Who got to you? Who twisted your mind? What's happened over these past few years?" It is with that same kind of passion that Paul writes his concern to his Galatian friends.

Think, now . . . what's he fighting for? Liberty! "You were once freed. But now, my friends in Galatia, you are enslaved. I want to know what's gone wrong." The answer is not complicated: the grace killers had invaded and conquered.

IDENTIFYING THREE TOOLS OF LEGALISM

Let's get down to brass tacks. What are the inroads most legalists make on a life, on a church, on a missionary outreach, or on a denomination? How do legalists get in? Who are they? Furthermore, why are they effective? As a result of studying the first and second chapters of Galatians, I'm prepared to identify at least three different tools used by century-one legalists: doctrinal heresy, ecclesiastical harassment, and personal hypocrisy.

First, let's consider *those who disturb and distort by interjecting doctrinal heresy.* Scripture says it plain and simple; legalists were twisting truth among the Galatian assembly:

> I am amazed that you are so quickly deserting Him who called you by the grace of Christ, for a different gospel; which is really not another; only there are some who are disturbing you, and want to distort the gospel of Christ. But even though we, or an angel from heaven, should preach to you a gospel contrary to that which we have preached to you, let him be accursed. As we have said before, so I say again now, if any man is preaching to you a gospel contrary to that which you received, let him be accursed. For am I now seeking the favor of men, or of God? Or am I striving to please men? If I were still trying to please men, I would not be a bond-servant of Christ. (Gal. 1:6–10)

Legalists were disturbing others and distorting the truth as they spread doctrinal heresy. Their heretical message was that the Galatian Christians should let Moses finish what Christ began. In other words, salvation is not by faith alone; it requires works. Human achievement must accompany sincere faith before you can be certain of your salvation. We continue to hear that "different gospel" to this day, and *it is a lie.* A theology that rests its salvation on one ounce of human performance is not good news; it is bad information. It is *heresy.* It is antithetical to the true message that lit the spark to the Reformation: *sola fide*—faith alone.

A salvation that begins with God's love reaching down to lost humanity and is carried out by Christ's death and resurrection results in all the praise going to God. But a salvation that includes human achievement, hard work, personal effort, even religious deeds distorts the good news because man gets the glory, not God. The problem is, it appeals to the flesh. Paul's twice-repeated reaction to the one who introduced that doctrinal heresy is, "Let him be accursed!" This is Paul's way of saying the person is *doomed!* The original word is *anathema!* It is the strongest single Greek term for condemnation.

Nevertheless, the heresy goes on. Most every cult you could name is a cult of salvation by works. It appeals to the flesh. It tells you, if you will stand so long on a street corner, if you will distribute so much literature, if you will sacrifice so much of life, if you will be baptized, if you will contribute your money, if you will pray or attend numerous meetings, then your good works and hard effort will cause God to smile on you. Ultimately, when the good is weighed against the bad on the Day of Judgment, you will finally earn His favor. The result in that, I say again, is man's glory, because you added to your salvation.

Grace says you have nothing to give, nothing to earn, nothing to pay. You couldn't if you tried! Remember what we learned in chapter 2? Salvation is a free gift. You simply lay hold of what Christ has provided.

Period. And yet the heretical doctrine of works goes on all around the world and always will. It is effective because the pride of men and women is so strong. We simply *have* to *do* something in order to feel right about it. It just doesn't make good humanistic sense to get something valuable for nothing.

Please allow me to be straightforward with you: Stop tolerating the heretical gospel of works! It is legalism. Wake up to the fact that it will put you into a bondage syndrome that won't end. The true gospel of grace, however, will set you free. Free forever.

Let's take a closer look at Galatians 1:10: "For am I now seeking the favor of men, or of God? Or am I striving to please men? If I were still trying to please men, I would not be a bond-servant of Christ."

You wonder what Paul's life was like before Christ? He tells us: he was a man-pleaser. He says, "If I were *still* trying to please men . . ." He was a legalist back in his years as a Pharisee. His goal, among other things, was to please people.

When he realized Christ was who He claimed to be and His death was effective and sufficient to provide the complete payment for sin, he was crushed to the bone when he realized the enormity of his guilt before God. He was stunned in meeting Christ on the road to Damascus. He learned then (and in subsequent years) that you cannot try to please people or live your life being afraid of people. There is only One to please and to fear on this earth, and that is God.

I want to add something here especially for pastors and Christian leaders. Those who seek to please God only are invincible from within. Not only that, but when we stop striving to please people, we are also unintimidated from without. The church of Jesus Christ needs more invincible, unintimidated pastors. We put a lot of effort into training men and women for ministry, but there isn't equal effort in training congregations for ministers. That is most unfortunate. Church congregations need to know when to let a pastor lead, how to respect his judgment, and the importance of following a pastor with confidence. Yes, pastors need to be deserving of such respect, and they need to be accountable . . . no question. But the tragedy is that there are numerous ministers who "seek the favor" and "strive to please" at any price. I don't know of a quicker way to ruin a ministry or, for that matter, to be consumed with anxiety. True spiritual leadership cannot occur as long as the leader runs scared of what people may think or say.

I can remember an experience that taught me this lesson permanently. I was pastoring a church in another state over thirty years ago. A particular issue arose that divided the leadership right down the middle. It was a volatile issue, and I realized it had the possibility of splitting the church. Adding to my pressure was the inescapable reality that my vote on the board of elders was the "swing vote." Our board of strong-minded men was equally divided on each side, and my vote was needed to break the tie. All eyes would ultimately be on me. The climactic meeting was set for a Thursday evening. I was relatively young, and looking back, I was still too interested in pleasing people—I now admit to my own embarrassment.

I told Cynthia I had to be alone overnight to think everything through. I got into my 1969 Volkswagen early Wednesday morning, turned onto the highway that led out of town, and rested my New Testament on the steering wheel as I drove along. I opened to Galatians, chapter 1, and began reading aloud, glancing up onto the road then back down at my Bible. Suddenly, verse 10 leaped off the page like a tiger with sharp claws: "Am I striving to please men?" Yes, it was the same verse of Scripture we have been analyzing, but that day I saw it for the first time. I immediately pulled to the side of the highway, turned off the engine, and read the words aloud again and again and again. *What a rebuke!* I not only had my answer, I had stumbled upon a life-changing principle. Within a very few minutes, confidence replaced fear. I lost the nagging desire to please a group of men. My one goal was to please God. I was freed from the awful clutches of "striving to please men."

I did a U-turn, drove back home to the surprise of my wife, who was not expecting to see me until the next day, and told her of the discovery. She smiled in agreement. She had noticed my insecurity earlier that morning. The following night I openly declared my convictions, which displeased some of the board members but resulted in what proved to be the best decision. A few left the church (thankfully!) . . . yet for the first time in my ministry I experienced a fresh surge of freedom. Invincible and unintimidated, I displayed a calm assurance in my leadership style that has stayed with me; thank God. And what a difference it has made. I was liberated from the bondage of striving to please people.

Perhaps that is one of the reasons I write with such passion about the importance of being free — why I plead with you so earnestly to allow the quickening power of God's grace to awaken within you a hunger for liberty. Those who let freedom be taken from them not only embrace heresy, they live under the thumb of grace killers who love to control and intimidate.

The second tool I find legalists using is ecclesiastical harassment; they are *those who spy and enslave.*

Then after an interval of fourteen years I went up again to Jerusalem with Barnabas, taking Titus along also. And it was because of a revelation that I went up; and I submitted to them the gospel which I preach among the Gentiles, but I did so in private to those who were of reputation, for fear that I might be running, or had run, in vain. But not even Titus who was with me, though he was a Greek, was compelled to be circumcised. But it was because of the false brethren who had sneaked in to spy out our liberty which we have in Christ Jesus, in order to bring us into bondage. But we did not yield in subjection to them for even an hour, so that the truth of the gospel might remain with you. But from those who were of high reputation (what they were makes no difference to me; God shows no partiality)—well, those who were of reputation contributed nothing to me. (Gal. 2:1–7)

I know of few scriptures that more boldly expose the damaging style of legalism. Earlier we analyzed those who disturb and distort the gospel. Now we are considering those who spy on and enslave individuals who wish to be free. In a few sentences, let me give you the background to what Paul wrote about here in Galatians 2.

Fourteen years earlier, the apostle Paul had been given a direct revelation from God that he was called to minister especially to the Gentiles. Peter, you may remember, was called to minister especially to the Jews. A great question grew out of Paul's reaching out to Gentiles: Should a Gentile be circumcised in order for him to be a Christian? There were related questions. Does he need to maintain a certain diet? Does he need to fulfill the requirements of the Mosiac Law? Does he need to become "somewhat Jewish"? In other words, was it necessary for Moses to complete what Christ had begun? Paul emphatically said no. In doing so, he presented the gospel of Christ based on the message of grace. Not surprisingly, the Gentiles responded by the thousands. This caused some of the Jewish believers to get a little nervous, especially those who held to a more legalistic position of salvation. The influx of so many Gentile converts disturbed them no little bit.

The apostle Paul's response was commendable: "Let's let the distinguished church fathers, the pillars of the church, answer this one. We need their seasoned wisdom." And so off he went to Jerusalem, where the meeting would be held, taking along with him Barnabas (a circumcised Jew) and Titus (an uncircumcised Gentile), both of whom had believed in the Lord Jesus Christ as Savior. Paul tells us what he did when he arrived: "I submitted to them the gospel which I preach among the

Gentiles, but I did so in private to those who were of reputation, for fear that I might be running, or had run, in vain" (v. 2).

This assures us that he came with an open attitude. He said, in effect, "Men, I want you to know that I have been teaching the good news of Christ according to grace. Am I right, or do I need to be corrected?" Their answer, in brief, was, "You're right. We approve of this message." Don't miss the third verse: "But not even Titus who was with me, though he was a Greek, was compelled to be circumcised."

You think the legalists took that sitting down? No way:

> But it was because of the false brethren who had sneaked in to spy out our liberty which we have in Christ Jesus, in order to bring us into bondage. But we did not yield in subjection to them for even an hour. (vv. 4–5)

Good for him! Why didn't Paul tolerate their disagreement and submit to their legalistic demands? Because liberty is worth fighting for! The sneaking legalists were making their move, and he refused to submit to them even for sixty minutes.

We need to pause and analyze the words "spy out our liberty." The Greek term *kataskopos* is translated "spy out." A. T. Robertson says it means "to reconnoitre, to make a treacherous investigation."[6] Why? That's not difficult to answer: To enslave! There were those who not only disliked Paul's freedom but who also wanted others to live in the same bondage they did. (By the way, people like that still exist.)

In verse 4 Paul says they "sneaked in" to bring them into bondage. In verse 5 he states, "I didn't submit, to make sure you kept free." Good principle: When there is a sneaking in of legalism, there will also be the need for those in leadership to stand fast. The strong must defend the weak. Paul was undaunted, unintimidated, unrelenting in his determination. With confidence, he pursued the freedom each one of those Gentile converts had every right to claim. He withstood legalism, and so must we. Trust me, legalists don't get the message if you're unsure and soft with them. There is no need to be mean-spirited, but there is the need to be firm.

Earlier I quoted Eugene Peterson. Because his words fit what I am trying to communicate, let's return to one further paragraph:

> There are people who do not want us to be free. They don't want us to be free before God, accepted just as we are by his grace. They don't want us to be free to express our faith originally and creatively in the world. They want to control us; they want to use us for their own purposes. They themselves refuse to live arduously and openly in faith, but huddle together with a few others and try to get a sense of approval by insisting that all look alike, talk alike and act alike, thus validating one another's worth. They try to enlarge their numbers only on the condition that new members act and talk and behave the way they do. These people infiltrate communities of faith "to spy out our freedom which we have in Christ Jesus" and not infrequently find ways to control, restrict and reduce the lives of free Christians. Without being aware of it, we become anxious about what others will say about us, obsessively concerned about what others think we should do. We no longer live the good news but anxiously try to memorize and recite the script that someone else has assigned to us. In such an event we may be secure, but we will not be free. We may survive as a religious community, but we will not experience what it means to be human, alive in love and faith, expansive in hope. Conforming and self-congratulatory behavior is not free. But Paul "did not yield in submission even for a moment, that the truth of the gospel might be preserved for you." Every free person who benefits from Paul's courage will continue vigilant in the resistance movement he formed.[7]

Some years ago I was conversing with a man I greatly admire. He is a Christian leader in a position that carries with it heavy and extensive responsibilities. He said he was grieved on behalf of a missionary family he and his wife had known for years. The legalism they had encountered again and again on the mission field from fellow missionaries was so petty, so unbelievably small-minded, they had returned to the States and no longer planned to remain career missionaries. He said it was over a jar of peanut butter. I thought he was joking, to which he responded. "No, it's no joke at all." I could hardly believe the story.

The particular place they were sent to serve the Lord did not have access to peanut butter. This particular family happened to enjoy peanut butter a great deal. Rather creatively, they made arrangements with some of their friends in the States to send them peanut butter every now and then so they could enjoy it with their meals. The problem is they didn't know until they started receiving the supply of peanut butter that the other missionaries considered it a mark of spirituality that you *not* have peanut butter with your meals. I suppose the line went something like this: "We believe since we can't get peanut butter here, we should give it up for the cause of Christ," or some such nonsense. A basis of spirituality was "bearing the cross" of living without peanut butter.

The young family didn't buy into that line of thinking. Their family kept getting regular shipments of peanut butter. They didn't flaunt it; they just enjoyed it in the privacy of their own home. Pressure began to intensify. You would expect adult missionaries to be big enough to let others eat what they pleased, right? Wrong. The legalism was so petty, the pressure got so intense, and the exclusive treatment became so unfair, it finished them off spiritually. They finally had enough. Unable to continue against the mounting pressure, they packed it in and were soon homeward bound, disillusioned and probably a bit cynical. What we have here is a classic modern-day example of a group of squint-eyed legalists spying out and attacking another's liberty. Not even missionaries are exempted.

Would you please give up your list of dos and don'ts for everybody else? Just keep it for yourself. If you're not into peanut butter, that is fine. That's great! In fact, you have every right to avoid it. If that's your thing, you shouldn't eat it! But don't tell me or someone else we can't enjoy it. And don't judge us because we do.

The examples of such harassment are legion. Recently I heard about a fellow who attended a legalistic college where students were to live according to very strict rules. They weren't supposed to do any work on Sundays. None! Guess what? He spied on his wife and caught her hanging out a few articles of clothing she had washed on Sunday afternoon. Are you ready? The guy turned in his wife to the authorities! I'll bet she was fun to live with the next day or two. Candidly, there are days in my life when the pettiness of some people makes me want to scream.

In one of his more serious moments, Mike Yaconelli, editor of *The Wittenburg Door*, wrote strong words concerning pettiness in the church:.

Petty people are ugly people. They are people who have lost their vision. They are people who have turned their eyes away from what matters and focused, instead, on what doesn't matter. The result is that the rest of us are immobilized by their obsession with the insignificant. It is time to rid the church of pettiness. It is time the church refused to be victimized by petty people. It is time the church stopped ignoring pettiness. It is time the church quit pretending that pettiness doesn't matter. . . . Pettiness has become a serious disease in the Church of Jesus Christ—a disease which continues to result in terminal cases of discord, disruption, and destruction. Petty people are dangerous people because they appear to be only a nuisance instead of what they really are—a health hazard.[8]

Yaconelli may be blunt, but he is correct. Now is the time for the church (that's you and me, my friend) to acknowledge the need for a "grace awakening" in the land—a new reformation of freedom that proclaims that liberty is worth fighting for.

The third grace killer identified in the book of Galatians is *hypocrisy—those who lie and deceive* (Gal. 2:11–14). This is one of those rare accounts in Scripture where two important church leaders clash. The two are Paul, the apostle, and Peter, here called Cephas. "But when Cephas came to Antioch, I opposed him to his face, because he stood condemned" (v. 11). Question: Why would Paul rebuke Peter? He tells us:

> For prior to the coming of certain men from James, he used to eat with the Gentiles; but when they came, he *began* to withdraw and hold himself aloof, fearing the party of the circumcision. (v. 12)

The New English Bible says, "He was in the habit of eating his meals with the Gentiles." That went on until the Jews showed up. And when they did . . . "Oh, no thanks, I never eat ham," lied Peter, hoping to make the Jews smile in approval. The problem was that before James and his Jewish friends arrived, ol' Peter could be heard saying to his Gentile cronies, "Sure, serve it up. Add a little bacon while you're at it. I love the taste!" Hypocrite!

I like Ralph Keiper's contemporary paraphrase of Paul's strong rebuke:

> "Peter, I smell ham on your breath. You forgot your Certs. There was a time when you wouldn't eat ham as part of your hope of salvation. Then after you trusted Christ, it didn't matter if you ate ham. But now when the no-ham eaters have come from Jerusalem you have gone back to your kosher ways. But the smell of ham still lingers on your breath. You are most inconsistent. You are compelling Gentile believers to observe Jewish law which can never justify anyone."

Peter, by returning to the law, you undercut strength for godly living."[9]

Paul saw through the duplicity and exposed the hypocrisy in Peter. In effect, he scolds, "The very idea, Peter, that you would fake it in front of Jews and then turn around and fake it in front of Gentiles. You're talking freedom, Peter, but you're not living it. Then out of the other side of your mouth, you're talking law, but you don't live that either. Get off the fence, Peter."

The problem intensified as others saw their leader and modeled his hypocritical lifestyle:

> And the rest of the Jews joined him in hypocrisy, with the result that even Barnabas was carried away by their hypocrisy. But when I saw that they were not straightforward about the truth of the gospel, I said to Cephas in the presence of all, "If you, being a Jew, live like the Gentiles and not like the Jews, how is it that you compel the Gentiles to live like Jews?" (vv. 13–14)

Why would Paul be so strong? Because people take their cues from their leaders. Sheep follow shepherds. And since legalistic hypocrisy never quietly dies on its own, it must be confronted. Again I remind you, liberty is always worth fighting for.

I knew a man approaching seventy years of age who was still haunted by the memory of being raised by hypocritical parents. It has taken him most of his adult life to face the full truth that he was emotionally and spiritually abused by their deception. Throughout his childhood his family attended a church where they were taught you shouldn't go to the movies. This was so firmly enforced that in Sunday church services people would be called to come forward to an altar and confess that they had done that or some other "sins." The problem is, his family usually went to movies on Friday or on Saturday night, always in secret. But they made it very clear that he shouldn't say anything about it. They drilled it into him, "Keep your mouth shut." Here he is, a little boy, being lectured on the

way home from the theater, week after week, "Don't tell anybody on Sunday that we did this." Of course, they went to see the film miles away from the church so church folks wouldn't know. Not until recently had the man come to realize how damaging that hypocrisy was to his walk with Christ. Because they were not straightforward about the truth, no one should be surprised he picked up a lifestyle of deception and lying. Only through the help of a fine Christian therapist has he been able to sort through his confusion.

You want to mess up the minds of your children? Here's how—guaranteed! Rear them in a legalistic, tight context of external religion, where performance is more important than reality. Fake your faith. Sneak around and pretend your spirituality. Train your children to do the same. Embrace a long list of dos and don'ts publicly but hypocritically practice them privately . . . yet never own up to the fact that it's hypocrisy. Act one way but live another. And you can count on it—emotional and spiritual damage *will* occur. Chances are good their confusion will lead to some sort of addiction in later years.

By the way, before you're tempted to think that you'll never be guilty of hypocrisy, that you're above that sort of temptation, remember what Paul exposed in this letter to the Galatians. A spiritual leader as strong and stable as Peter fell into it. And with him, many others as well, "even Barnabas." Legalism is so subtle, so insidious. I have found that it's especially tempting to those whose temperament tends toward pleasing people, which brings us back to that wonderful verse that frees us, Galatians 1:10:

> For am I now seeking the favor of men, or of God? Or am I striving to please men? If I were still trying to please men, I would not be a bond-servant of Christ.

SPECIFYING FOUR STRONG STRATEGIES

Killers cannot be mildly ignored or kindly tolerated. You can no more allow legalism to continue than you could permit a rattlesnake to slip into your house and hide. Before long, somebody is going to get hurt. So then, since liberty is worth fighting for, how do we do it? Where can our personal grace awakening begin? I can think of four strong strategies:

1. *Keep standing firm in your freedom.* I'm reminded of what Paul wrote in Galatians 5:1: "It was for freedom that Christ set us free; therefore keep standing firm and do not be subject again to a yoke of slavery." Stand your ground. Ask the Lord to give you courage.

2. *Stop seeking the favor of everyone.* This may be a stubborn habit to break, but it is really worth all the effort you can muster. If you're in a group where you feel you are being coerced to do certain things that are against your conscience or you're being pressured to stop doing things that you see no problem with, get out of the group! You're unwise to stay in situations that your conscience tells you are not right. That is nothing more than serving men, not God. I don't care how spiritual sounding it may be, stop seeking the favor of everybody.

3. *Start refusing to submit to bondage.* Call it what it is: slavery. It's trying to be "spiritual" by performance. Think of how delightful it would be to get rid of all the anxiety that comes with the bondage to which you have submitted yourself; think how clean you could feel by being real again or, perhaps, for the first time in your adult life.

4. *Continue being straightforward about the truth.* That means live honestly. If you don't agree, say so kindly but firmly. If you are the only one, be true to yourself and stand alone. When you blow it, say, "I blew it." If you don't know, admit the truth. It's okay not to know. And the next time your kids spot hypocrisy, even though you may feel embarrassed, agree with them, "You know what, kids? You're right. I was a first-class hypocrite. What

you saw and pointed out is exactly right." Tell them that. It may sound embarrassing to you now, but they will admire and respect your admission. And they won't grow up damaged. Best of all, they will learn to model the same kind of vulnerability and honesty, even if you are in vocational Christian work . . . *especially if you're in vocational Christian work.* Nobody expects perfection, but they do and they should expect honesty.

We need affirmation and encouragement to be all we're meant to be, and because so many people are rather delicate within, they need those who are strong to assist them in their fight for liberty. If for no other reason, liberty is worth fighting for so others can breathe freely.

Paul Tournier writes of this in *Guilt and Grace:*

> In all fields, even those of culture and art, other people's judgment exercises a paralyzing effect. Fear of criticism kills spontaneity; it prevents men from showing themselves and expressing themselves freely, as they are. Much courage is needed to paint a picture, to write a book, to erect a building designed along new architectural lines, or to formulate an independent opinion or an original idea.[10]

If fighting for liberty sounds too aggressive to you, perhaps too selfish, then think of it as fighting so others can be set free—so others can be awakened to the joys and privileges of personal freedom. Those who fight like that on real battlefields are called patriots or heroes. With all my heart, I believe those who square off against legalism should be considered the same.

6

Emancipated?
Then Live Like It!

I HAVE NEVER WITNESSED SLAVERY, not in raw reality. I have read about it, and I have seen films, plays, and television docudramas where slavery was portrayed in all its cruelty, but I have never seen it first-hand. I'm glad I haven't. I know of nothing more unjust or ugly. As an American I find it amazing—perhaps a better word is *confusing*—to think that my forefathers were willing to fight for their own freedom and win our country's independence yet turned around and enslaved others. The triangles of such twisted logic are not mentally congruent—free citizens owning slaves.

It took a civil war to break that yoke. It called for a courageous, clear-thinking president to stand in the gap . . . to be misunderstood and maligned and ultimately killed for a cause that was, to him, not only worth fighting for but worth dying for.

At Abraham Lincoln's second inaugural in 1865, only weeks before he was assassinated, he spoke of how both parties "deprecated war," and yet a war had come. He continued,

Neither party expected for the war, the magnitude, or the duration, which it has already attained. . . . Each looked for an easier triumph. . . . Both read from the same Bible, and pray to the same God, and each invokes His aid against the other.[1]

At that point the reelected sixteenth president's voice broke, his feelings showing through. And he spoke of how strange it was "that any men should dare to ask a just God's assistance in wringing their bread from the sweat of other men's faces."[2]

Ultimately, with the adoption of the Thirteenth Amendment of the United States Constitution, slavery was legally abolished. It was then that black slaves all across America were officially set free. Long before that, however, and even before his second inaugural address, the president had stated his antislavery convictions in a proclamation that won him no favor in the South. It was on New Year's Day 1863 when the Emancipation Proclamation was publicly stated, but it was not until December 18, 1865, that the Constitution made those convictions official. Though dead by then, Lincoln still spoke. At last his dream was realized. The word swept across Capitol Hill and down into the valleys of Virginia and the back roads of the Carolinas and even deeper into the plantations of Georgia, Alabama, Mississippi, and Louisiana. Headlines on newspapers in virtually every state trumpeted the same message: "Slavery Legally Abolished."

And yet something happened that many would have never expected. The vast majority of the slaves in the South who were legally freed continued to live as slaves. Most of them went right on living as though nothing had happened. Though free, the former slaves lived virtually unchanged lives throughout the Reconstruction period.

Shelby Foote, in his monumental three-volume work *The Civil War*, verifies this surprising anomaly:

. . . the Negro—locked in a caste system of "race etiquette" as rigid as any he had known in formal bondage . . . every slave could repeat with equal validity, what an Alabama slave had said in 1864 when asked what he thought of the Great Emancipator whose proclamation went into effect that year. "I don't know nothing bout Abraham Lincoln," he replied, "cep they say he sot us free. And I don't know nothing bout that neither."[3]

I call that tragic. A war had been fought. A president had been assassinated. An amendment to the Constitution had now been signed. Once-enslaved men, women, and children were now legally emancipated. Yet amazingly, many continued living in fear and squalor. In a context of hard-earned freedom, slaves chose to remain as slaves. Cruel and brutal though many of their owners were, black men and women chose to keep serving the same old master until they died. There were a few brave exceptions, but in many parts of the country you'd never have known that slavery had been officially abolished and that they had been emancipated. That's the way the plantation owners wanted it. They maintained the age-old philosophy, "Keep 'em ignorant and you keep 'em in the field."

Now if you think that is tragic, I can tell you one far worse. It has to do with Christians living today as slaves. Even though our Great Emancipator, Christ the Lord, paid the ultimate price to overthrow slavery once for all, most Christians act as though they're still held in bondage. In fact, strange as it is, most seem to prefer the security of slavery to the risks of liberty. And our slave master, Satan, loves it so. He is delighted that so many have bought into that lie and live under the dark shadow of such ignorance. He sits like the proverbial fat cat, grinning, "Great! Go right on livin' like a slave!" even though he knows we have been liberated from his control. More than most in God's family, the adversary knows we are free, but he hates it. So he does everything in his power to keep us pinned down in shame, guilt, ignorance, and intimidation.

REVIEWING SOME BASIC THOUGHTS ON SLAVERY

Though some are well informed about these facts I want to mention regarding slavery in the spiritual realm, most aren't. Therefore, I believe a brief review of some basics is necessary. Let's begin in the "emancipation letter" of Romans.

> As it is written,
> "There is none righteous, not even one;
> There is none who understands,
> There is none who seeks for God;
> All have turned aside, together they have become useless;
> There is none who does good,
> There is not even one."
> "Their throat is an open grave,
> With their tongues they keep deceiving,"
> "The poison of asps is under their lips;"
> "Whose mouth is full of cursing and bitterness;"
> "Their feet are swift to shed blood,
> Destruction and misery are in their paths,
> And the path of peace have they not known."
> "There is no fear of God before their eyes."
> Now we know that whatever the Law says, it speaks to those who are under the Law, that every mouth may be closed, and all the world may become accountable to God; because by the works of the Law no flesh will be justified in His sight; for through the Law comes the knowledge of sin. (Rom. 3:10–20)

I find in Romans at least three analogies regarding slavery. The first analogy is grim: *All of us were born in bondage to sin.* You wonder how bad our slavery really was in our unsaved condition? Look back over those words and observe for yourself:

- No one righteous
- No spiritual understanding
- No worthwhile achievements before God
- No purity, no innocence, no peace, no hope

On top of all that, we had no escape . . . we were unable to change our enslavement to sin. In that unsaved condition the lost person truly knows nothing about liberty.

The second analogy is glorious: *A day came when Christ set us free.* There came a day when an eternal Emancipation Proclamation was made known throughout the heavens and all the way to the pit of hell—"The sinner is officially set free!" It is the announcement that originated from Christ's empty tomb on that first Easter, the day our Great Emancipator, Christ, set us free. Doctrinally, the word is *redemption.* He redeemed us.

> But now apart from the Law the righteousness of God has been manifested, being witnessed by the Law and the Prophets, even the righteousness of God through faith in Jesus Christ for all those who believe; for there is no distinction. (Rom. 3:21–22)

I love those last two words—"no distinction." To qualify for freedom, you don't have to be born in a certain country. You don't have to speak a certain language. Your skin doesn't have to be a certain color. You don't have to be educated or cultured or make a certain amount of money or fulfill some list of requirements. There is absolutely no distinction. Why? Because we were all slaves, slaves of our master and slaves of sin. "For all have sinned and fall short of the glory of God" (v. 23). Therefore, all sinners are "savable," if I may use that word. How? "Being justified as a gift by His grace through the redemption which is in Christ Jesus" (v. 24).

Let me explain this in nontechnical terms, staying with our word picture of slavery. Christ came on the scene, and He saw every one of us on the slave block—lost, miserable, spiritually useless, and unable to change ourselves or escape from the bondage of our master. Moved by compassion and prompted by love, He, in grace, paid the price to free us. The price was His death. By doing so, He said to every one of us, in effect, "You don't have to live under your former master any longer. You're free. You're free to serve Me for the rest of your life."

Before Christ came into our lives, we were hopelessly lost in our lust, helpless to restrain our profanity, our glandular drives, our insatiable greed, our continual selfishness, or our compulsions either to please people or to control and manipulate others. While some of those things may have brought us feelings of pleasure and periodic satisfaction, our inability to control them was not without its complications. We were slaves! We were chained to the slave block, and we had to serve the old master. There was insufficient strength within us to live any other way. By "redeeming" us, Jesus set us free. When God raised Jesus from the dead (the crucial act of triumph over Satan), He said, in effect, "No one else need ever live as a victim of sin. All who believe in Jesus Christ, My Son, will have everlasting life and will have the power to live in Me." How could it be that wicked slaves could be given such standing before God? We're back to our favorite word: *grace*. To use terms everyone can understand, President Grace legally freed us from our lifelong master, Sin, and his wife, Shame. Theoretically, we were freed when we believed in Christ, but practically speaking, our plantation owners do everything in their power to keep us ignorant, afraid, and thinking like a slave.

The third analogy I find in Romans 3 is tragic: *Many Christians still live as though they are enslaved.* When told they are free, some could easily respond like the Alabama slave: "I don't know anything about grace, except they say it set us free. And I don't know anything about that either." As a result of choosing to ignore the freedom Christ won for His own, many still live with a sin-oriented mentality. Most do, in fact.

It comes out in words like, "You know, I just can't help myself. I'm really not worth much; I'm only human." Instead of living above those constant references to failure and inadequacy and shamefulness, Christians too often resemble frightened and unsure religious slaves. Sometimes it emerges in other manifestations. We rationalize our sin; we act hypocritically; occasionally we lie and cheat and steal. Then with a shrug we say, "Well, you know, man, nobody's perfect." In effect, we are saying, "I'm still enslaved. Sin still overpowers me. I'm so ashamed. But I just can't help it." Nonsense! When will we start living like those who are free? God says to every one of us, "Where sin abounded, grace super-abounded. You were once enslaved to a passion, yes, but no longer . . . Now you're free from that. You can live above it." Grace awakens, enlivens, and empowers our ability to conquer sin.

Are you ready for a maverick thought? Once we truly grasp the freedom grace brings, we can spend lengthy periods of our lives without sinning or feeling ashamed. Yes we can! And why not? Why should sin gain the mastery over us? Who says we cannot help but yield to it? How unbiblical! You see, most of us are so programmed to sin that we wait for it to happen.

To tell the truth, most Christians have been better trained to expect and handle their sin than to expect and enjoy their freedom. The shame and self-imposed guilt this brings is enormous, to say nothing of the "I'm defeated" message it reinforces. We begin the day afraid of sin. We live ashamed. We go to bed with a long list, ready to confess. If it isn't very long, we fear we've overlooked several "hidden sins." Maybe we've gotten proud.

What in the world has happened to grace? Furthermore, where is the abundant life Christ offered? Are freed people supposed to live such a frightened existence? Are we emancipated or not? If so, let's live like it! That isn't heresy; it's the healthiest kind of theology imaginable.

I can assure you, your old master doesn't want you to read this or think like this. He wants you to exist in the shack of ignorance, clothed in the rags of guilt and shame, and afraid of him and his whip. Like the cruel slave owner, he wants you to think you "gotta take a beatin' every now 'n' then" just so you will stay in line. Listen to me today: *That* is heresy! Because our Savior has set us free, the old master—the supreme grace killer—has no right whatsoever to put a whip to your back. Those days have ended, my friend. You're free. Those of us who are a part of the grace awakening refuse to live like slaves. We've been emancipated!

UNDERSTANDING THE THEMES OF LIBERTY

Turning a few pages further in the liberating letter of Romans, we arrive at Romans 6, one of the great chapters in all the Word of God. Having spent months studying this one chapter (and loving every minute of it!), I have come to realize it contains the Christian's Emancipation Proclamation. Here, as in no other section of Scripture, is the foundational truth of our liberty—freedom from Satan's intimidation and sin's domination. It is here all young Christians should spend their first hours in the Bible . . . not passages that tell us what to do once we sin (like 1 John 1:9) or how to restore our fellowship, important as those scriptures may be. No, it is *here* the believer discovers his or her freedom from sin's control and how to live on that victorious level above fear, guilt, shame, and defeat.

For the next few minutes, graze gently over the first fifteen verses of Romans 6. Take plenty of time; there is no hurry:

> What shall we say then? Are we to continue in sin that grace might increase? May it never be! How shall we who died to sin still live in it? Or do you not know that all of us who have been baptized into Christ Jesus have been bap-

tized into His death? Therefore we have been buried with Him through baptism into death, in order that as Christ was raised from the dead through the glory of the Father, so we too might walk in newness of life. For if we have become united with Him in the likeness of His death, certainly we shall be also in the likeness of His resurrection, knowing this, that our old self was crucified with Him, that our body of sin might be done away with, that we should no longer be slaves to sin; for he who has died is freed from sin. Now if we have died with Christ, we believe that we shall also live with Him, knowing that Christ, having been raised from the dead, is never to die again; death no longer is master over Him. For the death that He died, He died to sin, once for all; but the life that He lives, He lives to God. Even so consider yourselves to be dead to sin, but alive to God in Christ Jesus.

Therefore do not let sin reign in your mortal body that you should obey its lusts, and do not go on presenting the members of your body to sin as instruments of unrighteousness; but present yourselves to God as those alive from the dead, and your members as instruments of righteousness to God. For sin shall not be master over you, for you are not under law, but under grace.

What then? Shall we sin because we are not under law but under grace? May it never be!

Even a casual reading of these thoughts reveals two questions that get the same answer from the apostle. The questions may appear to be the same, but they are not.

What shall we say then? Are we to continue in sin that grace might increase? May it never be! (vv. 1–2)

What then? Shall we sin because we are not under law but under grace? May it never be! (v. 15)

These two questions introduce two themes related to liberty. The first question addresses *those who fail to claim their liberty and continue to live like slaves*—those who *nullify* grace. (That theme is developed in the opening fourteen verses of Romans 6.)

The second question is addressed to *those who take their freedom too far* (vv. 15–23). In other words, they take advantage of their liberty. They live irresponsibly. Those who do that *abuse* grace (a subject I will address in the following chapter). Now, go back and read Romans 6 again and see if that doesn't make sense and help you understand the chapter better.

Paul, the writer, answers both questions with identical words: "May it never be!" Frankly, he is horrified. We could say what he says in similar ways:

- "By no means!"
- "Away with such a notion!"
- "Perish the thought!"
- "Never, never, never!"
- "What a ghastly thought!"

Paul's summary answer to the first question comes in the form of another question: "How shall we who died to sin still live in it?" (v. 2).

All it takes to appreciate that question is a brief mental trip back to our unsaved days. Many of you may recall that time with misery. Remember how you couldn't get control of your desires? Perhaps you helplessly dropped into bed night after night a victim of a habit that you couldn't conquer for the life of you. You recall the feeling that there was no hope at the end of a tunnel—no light. No matter what, you could not change, not permanently. Your slavery was an addiction at its worst. It was a prison from which no one could escape on his own. Remember how the shame increased and, at times, overwhelmed you? Others may have lived in the realm of freedom so long they've forgotten what it was like to be enslaved in the lost estate. If so, the following words will help:

> It is my earnest conviction that everyone should be in jail at least once in his life and that the imprisonment should be on suspicion rather than proof; it should last at least four months; it should seem hopeless; and preferably the prisoner should be sick half of the time. . . . Only by such imprisonment does he learn what real freedom is worth.[4]

Imagine being thrown into jail on suspicion of a charge, left there, virtually forgotten, while the system, ever so slowly, caught up with you. You get sick. You're treated harshly. Abused. Assaulted. Would you begin to entertain that feeling of lostness and hopelessness?

Back to the question: "How shall we who died to sin still live in it?" Who would volunteer to be dumped in a jail for another series of months, having been there and suffered the consequences of such a setting? His point: Then why would emancipated slaves who have been freed from sin and shame return to live under that same domination any longer?

"Yes, master. Yes, master. Don't hit me, ma'am . . . I'll be a good slave." Why, those words should make one gag, especially former slaves. You say, "I would never say such a thing!" Oh yes you would! We do every time we see ourselves as helpless victims of our urges and sin's tempting thoughts. I call it running scared of a master who no longer has any rights over us. How much better to say, "I refuse to live like that any longer. By the grace of Christ, I will live as a victor, not as a victim." Yes, you can live like that. Most, however, have been programmed to live another way.

I would venture to say that many who are Christians know 1 John 1:9 from memory: "If we confess our sins, He is faithful and righteous to forgive us our sins and to cleanse us from all unrighteousness." And yet how few could quote Romans 6:13:

And do not go on presenting the members of your body to sin as instruments of unrighteousness; but present yourselves to God as those alive from the dead, and your members as instruments of righteousness to God.

We have been programmed to think, *I know I am going to sin, to fail . . . to fall short today. Since this is true I need to be ready to find cleansing.* You have not been programmed to yield yourself unto God as those who have power over sin.

How much better to begin each day thinking victory, not defeat; to awake to grace, not shame; to encounter each temptation with thoughts like, *Jesus, You are my Lord and Savior. I am Your child—liberated and depending on Your power. Therefore, Christ, this is Your day, to be lived for Your glory. Work through my eyes, my mouth, and through my thoughts and actions to carry out Your victory. And, Lord, do that all day long. When I face temptations, I will present myself to You and claim the strength You give to handle it. Sin has no authority over me any longer.*

Yes, I know there will be times when we may momentarily fail, but they will be the exceptions rather than the rule of our day. We are under new ownership. Prompted by love, we serve a new master, Christ, not the old one who mistreated us. There is something exciting about enjoying a relationship with our new Friend. But we won't until we put our "old man" in his place.

The late J. Vernon McGee told a memorable story when I was a student at Dallas Theological Seminary. He was bringing the Bible lectures on the letter to the Romans. His humorous illustrations were unforgettable, especially this one.

I was sitting in Chafer Chapel as Dr. McGee was waxing eloquent on Romans 6. He told the story of a lady who lived in the Deep South and had a close relationship with her childhood sweetheart. She fell in love with him and ultimately married him. Their life together was not perfect, but it was rewarding. There was faithfulness, and there were times of joy. This continued for years, until he was suddenly taken from her side by a heart attack. Not being able to part with him visibly, she decided to have him embalmed, put in a chair, sealed up in a glass case, and placed immediately inside the front door of their large plantation home. Every time she walked through the door, she smiled, "Hi, John, how are you?" Then she would walk right on up the stairs. Things rocked along as normally as possible month after month. There he sat day after day as she acknowledged his presence with a smile and friendly wave.

A year or so later she decided to take a lengthy trip to Europe. It was a delightful change of scenery. In fact, while in Europe she met a fine American gentleman who was also vacationing over there. He swept her off her feet. After a whirlwind romance, they got married and honeymooned all over Europe. She said nothing about ol' John back on the farm.

Finally they traveled together back to the States. Driving up the winding road to her home, her new husband decided, *This is my moment to lift my bride over the threshold and to carry her back into her home . . . this wonderful place where we'll live together forever.* He picked her up, bumped the door open with his hip, and walked right in. He almost dropped his bride on the floor!

"Who is this?"

"Well, that is John. He was my old man from —"

"He is *history*; he's dead!"

The new husband immediately dug a big hole and buried her former old man in it, case and all.

That's exactly what Christ has done! However, without realizing the effect, many Christians put the old man in a case and greet him every morning and cater to him every day of their lives. We live as though our "old man" is alive, even though we are dead to him. He has no right to be in our conscious thinking. We serve a new Master who has walked us across the threshold, who has awakened us to new life, new love, a new relationship, and an entirely different future.

Being creatures of habit, we still prefer the security of slavery to the risks of liberty. That is why those former slaves stayed on the plantation, and that's why we continue to be sin-conscious . . . even more than Savior-conscious. We know down deep that He lives within us, that He has redeemed us; but most are at a loss to know how to get beyond the fear-failure-shame-confession syndrome. How is it possible to break the habit of serving the old master and start enjoying the benefits of being free under the new One?

CLAIMING OUR FREEDOM FROM SIN'S CONTROL

In this wonderful sixth chapter of Romans, Paul presents three techniques for living by grace, above sin's domination. I find each one linked to a particular term he uses:

Know—"Or do you not know that all of us who have been baptized into Christ Jesus have been baptized into His death? . . . knowing this, that our old self was crucified with Him, that our body of sin might be done away with, that we should no longer be slaves to sin; . . . knowing that Christ, having been raised from the dead, is never to die again; death no longer is master over Him" (vv. 3, 6, 9).

Consider—"Even so consider yourselves to be dead to sin, but alive to God in Christ Jesus" (v. 11).

Present—"And do not go on presenting the members of your body to sin as instruments of unrighteousness; but present yourselves to God as those alive from the dead, and your members as instruments of righteousness to God" (v. 13).

In order for us to live free from sin's control, free from the old master, with the power to walk a new kind of life, we have to *know* something, we have to *consider* something, and we have to *present* something.

Romans 6 is not easy and entertaining. Understanding it is not Saturday-morning cartoons on the tube; we will have to think. So for the next few minutes I'll do my best to make it clear and keep it interesting as we answer three questions in the balance of this chapter. What is it that you and I have to know? What is it that you and I have to consider? And what is it that you and I have to present?

Let's start with *knowing*.

> Or do you not know that all of us who have been baptized into Christ Jesus have been baptized into His death? Therefore we have been buried with Him through baptism into death, in order that as Christ was raised from the dead through the glory of the Father, so we too might walk in newness of life. For if we have become united with Him in the likeness of His death, certainly we shall be also in the likeness of His resurrection, knowing this, that our old self was crucified with Him, that our body of sin might be done away with, that we should no longer be slaves to sin; for he who has died is freed from sin. (vv. 3–7)

To understand what this is all about, we have to set aside the concept of water baptism and understand that this is a reference to dry baptism. Some baptisms in the New Testament are *wet*, and some of them are *dry*. This one is in the latter category.

The word *baptizo* primarily has to do with identification. It was a term that was used in the first century for dipping a light-colored garment into a dye that was, let's say, scarlet. Once the fabric was dipped into the scarlet dye, it would be changed in its identity from its original color to scarlet. The act of dipping it, resulting in changing its identity, was called *baptizo*. It is the Greek term from which we get our English word *baptism*.

Christ died for us on the cross. He was raised from the dead for us at the tomb. When we believed in the Savior's death and resurrection, we were "dipped" into the same scene. Our identity was changed. We didn't feel it, we didn't see it, we didn't hear it, but it occurred nevertheless. When we came to Christ, we were placed into Him as His death became ours, His victorious resurrection became ours, His "awakening" to new life became our "awakening," and His powerful walk became our powerful walk. Before we can experience the benefits of all that, we have to *know* it. The Christian life is not stumbling along, hoping to keep up with the Savior. He lives in me, and I live in Him. And in this identification with Him, His power becomes mine. His very life becomes my life, guaranteeing that His victory over sin is mine to claim. I no longer need to live as a slave to sin.

> Now if we have died with Christ, we believe that we shall also live with Him, knowing that Christ, having been raised from the dead, is never to die again; death no longer is master over Him. For the death that He died, He died to sin, once for all; but the life that He lives, He lives to God. (vv. 8–10)

You will meet well-meaning Christians who teach about crucifying oneself. But I have good news for you: that has already been done. You are in Christ. He was crucified once for all. He died for you, so you never need to die again. Because we have our identification with Him, we have all the power needed to live the rest of our lives above the drag and dregs of slavery. Death to sin is an accomplished act, a finished fact. Theoretically, it has all been taken care of. A victorious walk begins with our *knowing* this fact. Christ's Emancipation Proclamation has put to death the whole idea of slavery to sin. Having died to sin's power, we are now free to serve our new Master.

I love the story of the missionary who sailed from Liverpool to serve Christ along the African coast. He changed vessels at Lagos. He boarded a coastal tugboat to make his way into a fever-infested region where he would invest the rest of his life. While changing vessels, he came upon a cynical old slave trader who looked critically on the man's decision by saying, "If you go to that place, you will die." The missionary, a devoted Christian, replied softly, "I died before I ever left Liverpool."[5]

Not until you and I *know* that we are dead to sin's control and alive to God's power through Christ will we live like victors, not victims.

Next, Romans 6:11 tells us there is something we must *consider*: "Even so consider yourselves to be dead to sin, but alive to God in Christ Jesus." The word *consider* is crucial. It is from a Greek word that means "to calculate, to take into account, to figure." It is a financial term, an accounting term. Rather than meaning "act like it is so," it means "reckon it true. Enter it in the ledger. Record it in the creases of your brain." What exactly are we to calculate? Namely this: We are *in Christ*, dead to sin's power. And Christ is in us, releasing God's *new* power.

And the result of such calculating? "Therefore do not let sin reign in your mortal body that you should obey its lusts" (v. 12).

By calculating (considering) all of this and by taking into account the truth we know to be a fact, we *dethrone* sin and refuse to obey our lusts any longer. The flip side of this truth is equally liberating. Even when we do sin, when we occasionally fail, God's interest is not in flailing us as slaves, screaming, "You ought to be ashamed!" but in forgiving us as His dear children.

While speaking at a weeklong conference some years ago, I was introduced to a twenty-four-year-old woman. She was visibly uneasy and tearful. As we talked, it was obvious that she was riddled with guilt, overcome with shame. She could hardly maintain eye contact. I soon learned she had been promiscuous in her past. A couple or three years prior to our meeting, she had become a Christian. As she became increasingly more interested in spiritual things, her past returned to haunt her. In recent weeks she had begun to be tortured with shame and the accompanying fear that either God would judge her or she would fall back into that old lifestyle.

The more we talked, the clearer it became that she genuinely believed in and loved the Lord . . . but she knew nothing of the truth of Romans 6. Her major problem? She failed to understand grace. She did not realize that her secure position in Christ left her with nothing to fear, absolutely nothing to be ashamed of. I turned to this great section of Scripture and read it to her, pausing periodically and explaining what she needed to "know" and what she needed to "reckon as true." Time and again she interrupted and reminded me of her past, which intensified her feelings of shame. Her face reflected an inner battle. Her old master didn't want to let her go. He stubbornly clung to her, using fear to immobilize her. Each time, I reminded her of God's forgiveness in Christ . . . of her new position by grace . . . and of her need to see herself as free, no longer enslaved. I must have said those words a half-dozen times. Finally the light dawned. She forgave herself (a giant step toward accepting grace), and she claimed her freedom. The woman was aglow with radiance the rest of the week. She had been transformed in her mind from a slave, full of shame and disgrace, to one who was free, liberated from the enemy's oppressive desire to keep her defeated. Instead of beginning each day in dreadful fear, she began to focus on being free from her old master. Rather than thinking, *My sin, my shame, my failure,* she remembered, *His forgiveness, His grace, His life.* The change in her countenance was nothing short of remarkable. By Friday she had the most obvious "Yes" face at the conference.

In the state of California there are many picturesque roads and highways through mountainous areas. Though some are narrow and a bit treacherous, all of them lead through sites that are breathtakingly beautiful. Those who have driven the Pacific Coast Highway, Highway 1, can never forget the incredible natural scenes that stretch along the craggy coastline from Los Angeles to San Francisco. A few of the curves are especially dangerous and must be driven slowly and with great care. There are treacherous drop-offs, which add both to the beauty and to the danger of the journey.

It occurred to me that California could offer two options to travelers along those dangerous mountain roads. First, the state could build very well-equipped clinics at the bottom of those high elevations where the narrow roads twist and turn. Every sharp curve could be provided with a clinic down below. When speeding drivers went over the side and tumbled down the cliff, those in the clinic would be there to rescue and treat them. Second, the state could erect very clear, well-placed signs before each sharp curve, reading "Danger! Curve Ahead. Drive Slowly." You are probably not surprised to know that the highway department chose the second option, not the first. Smart plan.

We should learn from that decision. First John 1:9 is the corrective clinic at the bottom of the hill. It rescues and treats us, which is wonderful, but it's not the best alternative. Romans 6, on the other hand, is preventive counsel, providing the signs: "No need to crash . . . slow down . . . danger ahead." We must calculate the importance of these spiritual "signs" and reckon them as true.

This brings us to the third crucial term: *present.*

And do not go on presenting the members of your body to sin as instruments of unrighteousness; but present yourselves to God as those alive from the dead, and your members as instruments of righteousness to God. For sin shall not be master over you, for you are not under law, but under grace. (vv. 13–14)

111

Not only must there be intelligent calculation ("consider") based on true information ("know"), there has to be a conscious *presentation* of ourselves to God. Paul spells that out in two simple commands.

Negatively: "Do not go on presenting the members of your body to sin as instruments of unrighteousness." Why? Because we aren't slaves anymore. Our bodies are not helpless victims of lustful urges and uncontrollable weaknesses. Those days ended when we became Christians. Remember, we've been emancipated!

Positively: "But present yourselves to God as those alive from the dead. . . . For sin shall not be master over you." Since we have been emancipated, it is high time we start living like it. I remind you that our adversary doesn't want us to think like this. He would erase grace immediately if he could. But since he cannot, his strategy is to do everything in his power to deceive us into thinking like slaves. Why? Because when we start operating like free men and women, our old "master" can no longer control us.

A NECESSARY WARNING

I would love to tell you that change is easy, but I cannot. Old habits are terribly difficult to break. Thinking correctly takes courage. Furthermore, our adversary, Satan, won't back off easily. Neither will the legalists he uses. If you think the plantation slave owners following the Civil War were determined to keep their slaves, I'm here to tell you that today's grace killers are even more stubborn than they were. Count on it, the enemies of our souls despise this message of freedom. They hate grace, so be warned. In order for you to leave the security of slavery and of ignorance and walk out into the new, risky fields of freedom and grace, you will need courage and inner resolve. My prayer is that God will give you an abundance of both. You're not alone in your quest for freedom. There are a lot of us taking this journey with you. A "grace awakening" has begun in the hearts of God's people.

The sixteenth president made a comment shortly after the Emancipation Proclamation was passed by Congress early in 1863. Sounding more like Captain Ahab in Melville's novel *Moby Dick* than Abraham Lincoln delivering a speech, he warned:

> We are like whalers who have been on a long chase. We have at last got the harpoon into the monster, but we must now look how we steer, or with one flop of his tail he will send us all into eternity.[6]

The president proved himself a prophet with those words. His proclamation resulted in an escalation of the Civil War. He was absolutely correct. The declaration of freedom brought on even greater struggles and more bloodshed.

Such a warning is necessary. Who knows what battles you will encounter now that you have determined to live emancipated rather than enslaved. But the good news for many of you is this: at last we have gotten the harpoon into the monster. Now we must steer carefully and watch out for that wicked tail.

7

Guiding Others to Freedom

AN UNEXPECTED SHIFT OF ATTENTION occurred during the presidential campaign back in the fall of 1988. Instead of the evening news focusing on the Democratic and the Republican candidates, all eyes were on two California whales up in Alaska, trapped in a breathing hole many miles from the ocean.

Strange as it may seem, Bush and Dukakis were upstaged by "Bonnett" and "Crossbeak," the names biologists gave the whales.

It all started when the gentle giants of the sea overlooked the fact that winter arrived early that year in northern Alaska. This mistake left them trapped, stranded inland by the ever-increasing covering of solid ice that prevented them from swimming to freedom.

At first few bothered to notice . . . only a few compassionate Eskimos who decided the creatures needed help. In a rather primitive fashion they hauled their chain saws and dragged long poles to the site and began to gouge out ice holes, enabling the whales to breathe en route to open water. Crude, rugged, and tiresome though the work was, the Eskimos were determined to work their way toward the open ocean.

The weather wasn't cooperating. During some of the days, the temperature dropped below zero. That meant the small band of rescuers had to add some water-churning devices to keep the surface of the water from freezing over, especially during the screaming winds of the night. Interest in the project intensified once it caught the attention of the media. Other volunteers joined in the rescue efforts. Because the original plan wasn't moving along fast enough, in rolled an "Archimedean Screw Tractor," an enormous eleven-ton vehicle that rode on two screw-shaped pontoons, resembling something taken from a sci-fi movie set. That clumsy behemoth would clear away the ice after it was broken up and push it aside inch by inch, slowly grinding out a pathway to the sea. But that was also too slow and tedious. Next came the National Guard, who brought in two CH-54 Skycrane helicopters that systematically dropped five-ton concrete bashers onto the ice, mile after mile, so the journey to freedom could be accelerated.

If you can believe it, the Soviets arrived next, having dispatched two of their ships to the scene. One was a mammoth twenty-ton, eleven-story-tall icebreaker, and the other a smaller vessel with similar equipment. Interestingly, two flags flew on the stern of the Russian ships. Perhaps for the first and only time, the United States' Stars and Stripes flew alongside the familiar hammer and sickle. All political contrasts, economic differences, and military conflicts were set aside for this unusual mission . . . so a couple of whales could be free. Eureka! It finally happened at Point Barrow, Alaska. The world cheered as the exhausted creatures silently slipped out to sea.

Frankly, I found it a nice diversion from the presidential race. We got a chance to look at two new faces and see some unusual scenery. Instead of mudslinging, there was ice gouging. Rather than caustic comments, there was mutual cooperation. We felt good inside. There was something gallant and clean and beautiful about the whole thing. Even though it evolved into an expensive project—over $1.5 million during a three-week period—and even though the sixty-mile pathway was grueling, to make the shift in emphasis was refreshing.

It occurred to me a few days after the rescue project ended that we had been observing a strange phenomenon. I thought of the contrast between what we are willing to do as human beings for whales and yet what we're not willing to do for one another. There they were, two huge denizens of the deep, with whom we cannot intelligently communicate, yet we will risk life and limb, spend an enormous amount of money, and expend tireless energy in subzero weather for as long as it takes so that they can go free—and that is all well and good. What stunned me was how little effort we are willing to put forth to help another human being find freedom in God's family.

When it comes to providing personal freedom so others can breathe free and enjoy an ocean of endless possibilities, we're not nearly so cooperative. Isn't it strange? Most seem to prefer restricting and resisting someone's getting to freedom rather than helping that person along. Nations are willing to set aside vast ideological differences and cooperate in a joint effort to do whatever is necessary to help the natural world breathe free, but when it comes to the Christian community's assisting one of its own to find true freedom, well, that's another story. Cruel as it may sound, there are grace killers throughout this world who are plugging up breathing holes and trapping people under the ice pack of their manipulations and rigid controls. What is so unbelievably tragic is that they continue doing so, even if it cripples or kills the spirit of a fellow human being. We'll free the whales but not one another.

With all this talk about grace and liberty, perhaps it's time for me to clarify something. Some may be asking: Doesn't liberty have its limits?

Shouldn't folks restrain their freedom and occasionally hold themselves in check? Yes, without question. Grace can be—and sometimes is—abused. By that I mean exercising one's liberty without wisdom . . . having no concern over whether it offends or wounds a young and impressionable fellow believer. But I must hasten to add that I believe such restraint is an individual matter. It is not to be legislated, not something to be forced on someone else. Limitations are appropriate and necessary, but I fail to find in Scripture any place where one is to require such restraint from another. To do so is legalism. It plugs up breathing holes. It kills grace. The best restraint is self-restraint that comes from the inner prompting of the Holy Spirit through the person and presence of Jesus Christ in each individual life. It's been my observation over the last forty years that the vast majority of believers need to be freed, not restrained. Our job is to free people; God's job is to restrain them. God is doing His job much better than we are doing ours.

WONDERFUL TRUTHS REGARDING FREEDOM

I like to think of certain verses in Scripture as those that help us breathe. By that I mean they encourage true freedom. They liberate! I suggest that all who wish to be free—truly free from bondage traps and legalistic prisons—read these verses again and again and again. I would suggest you type them on three-by-five cards and tape them to your bathroom mirror. Read them aloud each morning. They will help awaken grace within you on a daily basis. Here are a few that I often quote and claim.

It was for freedom that Christ set us free. (Gal. 5:1)

For he who has died is freed from sin. (Rom. 6:7)

For the law of the Spirit of life in Christ Jesus has set you free. (Rom. 8:2)

What then shall we say to these things? If God is for us, who is against us? He who did not spare His own Son, but delivered Him up for us all, how will He not also with Him freely give us all things? (Rom. 8:31–32)

And you shall know the truth, and the truth shall make you free. (John 8:32)

If therefore the Son shall make you free, you shall be free indeed. (John 8:36)

More such verses will come to your attention as you begin to see the subject of freedom emerging from Scripture. For example, Paul writes Timothy that God "richly supplies us with all things to enjoy" (1 Tim. 6:17). I can't think of a greater mission in life than helping others know how to *enjoy* the life God has supplied. To be honest, that is one of my life goals . . . to help others *enjoy* life.

Some of you are engaged in a counseling ministry. And unless I miss my guess, helping others relax and enjoy living is one of your constant assignments and delights. I commend you and encourage you to help your counselees find the freedom that they need. Once they have dealt with their sins correctly, urge them to lift the veil of guilt and draw in the rusty anchor of shame that has ensnared them long enough. Such weights become galling, unbearable. They smother. They strangle. They stifle. They ultimately bury. Don't stop opening those breathing holes! No matter how long it takes, stay at it, fellow Christian.

You don't have to be a professional counselor to help others. Make it your aim to help your trapped friends to freedom. You may be their only defense and protection from the grace killers. I can tell you without hesitation that one of my major goals for the rest of my years in ministry is to provide more and more breathing holes for fellow ministers who have lost the joy of freedom, who know little of the charm of grace. If anybody needs to breathe free, to join the grace awakening, those in vocational Christian service do!

There are breathing holes throughout God's Word. I'm thinking of that huge hole Paul broke open in his letter to the Corinthians:

> Eat anything that is sold in the meat market, without asking questions for conscience' sake; FOR THE EARTH IS THE LORD'S AND ALL IT CONTAINS. If one of the unbelievers invites you, and you wish to go, eat anything that is set before you, without asking questions for conscience' sake. But if anyone should say to you, "This is meat sacrificed to idols," do not eat it, for the sake of the one who informed you, and for conscience' sake; I mean not your own conscience, but the other man's; for why is my freedom judged by another's conscience? If I partake with thankfulness, why am I slandered concerning that for which I give thanks? (1 Cor. 10:25–30)

First Corinthians 10 centers attention on eating meat. In those days the premier taboo was not going to the movies or wearing cosmetics or dancing or playing cards. Back then the major question was this: Should Christians eat meat that had been offered to idols? That needs some explanation.

In ancient pagan worship, portions of meat were offered to idols. Some of the carcass, however, was left over and was sold in a meat market. It was perfectly good meat. There were Christians back then who had no qualms about buying that meat in the meat market. Others who were young and recently converted out of an idol-worshiping lifestyle felt they should not do that. They reasoned like this: "That is meat that has been offered to idols. We shouldn't buy it or eat it. Its association with an idol temple and pagan worship contaminates the meat." Paul writes to say, in effect, "Meat isn't contaminated because the other part of the animal was sacrificed on a pagan altar. There's no way that some idol of wood or stone could contaminate a piece of meat." Which explains why he says, "Eat anything that is sold in the meat market." The apostle felt free to eat it even though others did not.

Look again at verse 27: "If one of the unbelievers invites you, and you wish to go, eat anything that is set before you." Paul is digging an ice hole. He is setting believers free. They don't have to worry about the meat served in an unbeliever's home. If the unbeliever is going to have barbecued steak, great! Eat up and don't ask questions.

Paul also makes some wise comments about times when it is best to restrain, but the overall general rule is to eat the meat. "The grace of God says you can eat it," implies the Apostle of Grace. So enjoy! Some, however, don't feel the same freedom, but they have no reason to slander those who eat.

And Paul says the same thing here. Look at verse 30: "If I partake with thankfulness, why am I slandered concerning that for which I give thanks?" That's a great question. In asking it he breaks open another breathing hole, and he states his case rather boldly: "Why do you slander me because I happen to enjoy eating the meat that is served? Some go for certain kinds of meat, others for another."

A funny thing happened to me at a previous church. One of the sound-and-light people at the church (a real character!) heard me teach on this subject. A couple of weeks later he pulled a gag on me. With an impish grin he said, "You had a birthday recently, didn't you?" I nodded yes. He said, "You're originally from Texas, right?" By now I knew I was in for something! "Yep," I answered. He said, "Well, I have something for you." He put a small can in my hand about the size of a can of snuff. It was a can of armadillo meat. I groaned. The label read, "Pure Texas Armadillo—sun-dried and road-tenderized." The ingredients were printed on the other side: "Pure sun-dried armadillo, run over by a log truck three miles south of Pollok, Texas. Not over twenty percent hair and gravel. May contain foreign matter."

He told me that since I was such a believer in grace, I was free to eat it. I thought, *Whoa! This will gag a maggot!* My point? Because of grace, my friend can eat armadillo, and I can eat armadillo. It's okay. It's fine if he wishes to, but it so happens that God has led me *not* to eat armadillo. (It's that "foreign matter" that concerns me.) But if you want to eat armadillo, that's great! Personally, I have my own list of dietary don'ts (which includes armadillo). You may not have that on your list, so in good Texas fashion, "git at it." I promise, I will not slander you or judge you as you munch on all that hair and gravel.

What in the world is all this about? Let me give it to you straight. Don't give me your personal list of dos and don'ts to live by! And you can count on this: I will never give you my personal list of dos and don'ts to follow! Being free means you have no reason whatsoever to agree with my personal list, nor should you slander me because it isn't exactly like yours. That is one of the ways Christians can live in harmony. It is called living by grace . . . and it is the only way to fly.

Now you say, "Well, what if we find a list in Scripture?" That is a very different issue! Any specified list in Scripture is to be obeyed without hesitation or question. That's an inspired list for all of us to follow, not someone's personal list. Let me encourage you to guide your life by any and all Scripture with all of your heart, regardless of how anyone else may respond. But when questionable things aren't specified in Scripture, it then becomes a matter of one's personal preference or convictions. I'll say more about that later.

God has given His children a wonderful freedom in Christ, which means not only freedom from sin and shame but also a freedom in lifestyle so that we can become models of His grace. Being free, enjoying your liberty, and allowing others the same enjoyment are hard to do if you're insecure. It is especially hard to do if you were raised by legalistic parents and led by legalistic pastors with an oversensitive conscience about pleasing everyone. Those kinds of parents and pastors can be ultra-controlling, manipulative, and judgmental. Frequently they use the Bible as a hammer to pound folks into submission rather than as a guide to lead others into grace. Sometimes it takes years for people who have been under a legalistic cloud to finally have the courage to walk freely in the grace of God. Unfortunately, some who finally grasp this freedom go so far in it they abuse the grace of God by flaunting their liberty.

That can be just as tragic as those who don't go far enough. To return to one of my favorite words, we need *balance*.

In the previous chapter, I referred to the first part of Romans 6. Let's focus on the second part of that chapter. But first I'd like to look again at the two questions around which Romans 6 revolves. The questions may sound alike, but they are not the same.

First Question

What shall we say then? Are we to continue in sin that grace might increase? (Rom. 6:1)

Earlier, in Romans 5:20, we read "where sin increased, grace abounded all the more." The question that would logically follow such a statement is the one Paul asks in 6:1, which could be paraphrased, "Should we continue living under the domination of sin so that grace might super-abound more and more?" And he answers with gusto: "Perish the thought!"

As we've already discovered, the first question has to do with those who fail to live in freedom. They choose sin as their dominating master. Those Christians who live like that every day are overly conscious and sensitive to sin. They fear failing. Shame dominates their thinking. In essence, they focus so clearly on sin that they set themselves up for failure. Instead of concerning themselves with the positive benefits of serving Christ and enjoying the liberty He has provided, they continue living under the domination of their old nature.

By living like that, we develop a worst-case mentality. That is like my taking my keys and handing them over to one of my teenagers who just got a driver's license and saying, "Now let me remind you, you're going to have a wreck. So the first thing you need to do is memorize the phone number of our car insurance agent. That way, when you have an accident, you can be sure to call the right number. But here are the keys. Hope you enjoy the drive."

What a weird, negative piece of counsel. Yet that's what we do with young Christians. "Listen, you need to know *you're going to sin*. And so you've really got to watch out. Memorize 1 John 1:9, okay? That way *when* you sin, you'll know what to do." How seldom (if ever) young believers are told, "You know what? You no longer have to serve sin. You can actually live several days without it, perhaps a week or more. The reason is, you've got a new Master—Christ. And you know what else? You have a power down inside of you, one you never had before, called the Holy Spirit. And you have a set of keys called the Scriptures. So when you engage the key in the ignition correctly, you can enjoy a life like you've never enjoyed before. There may be times when you have an accident. There will be times when sins do occur. When they do, let me tell you how to handle it. But remember: That's not the norm; that's the exception. The good news is that you have freedom from the old master because of Christ." Grace has set us free! We have been emancipated.

Talk about opening up breathing holes! What if someone had told us that? Could we have grown? Would we have found the ocean? I mean, with people cutting holes like that for us, we would have been swimming free, out in the depths, within a matter of months! When grace awakens, hope and joy dominate our days.

Second Question

> What then? Shall we sin because we are not under law but under grace? May it never be! (Rom. 6:15)

This question may look the same, but it is quite different from the first. This one asks, "Shall we deliberately sin now because we're not under law but under grace?" In other words, why not just go full-bore? Pull out all the stops? "Not under law" must mean "I'm strictly on my own. Why not eat, drink, and have a blast? I'm under grace!" Some have misread it to mean just that. As a result, they rationalize their way around deliberate acts of disobedience. I have seen folks go off the deep end so far that they convince themselves it is okay to disobey specific scriptural statements or principles, dissolve their marriages, walk away from prior commitments, and choose another partner. When asked how they could justify such irresponsible behavior, almost without exception they refer to grace, as though it were the God-given, pervasive covering for whatever they please. Twisting Scripture to accommodate our desires has nothing to do with grace.

Such rationalization is freedom gone to seed, liberty without limits, which is nothing more than disobedience in another dress. Some may see it as amazing grace; I call it abusing grace. Those who do so not only live confused and get hurt, they confuse and hurt others. And that's what the latter half of Romans 6 is about: being so determined to fly free that you abuse the very freedom you've been given. We are wise to think of grace as a privilege to be enjoyed and protected, not a license to please ourselves.

CAREFUL WARNING TO ALL WHO ARE FREE

Even those who live in a free country need warnings. So we shouldn't be surprised that God gives His own a few warnings lest we abuse our privileges as people under grace. These warnings are set forth in verses 16 through 23 of Romans 6. None of them is complicated, but to grasp each one we'll need to concentrate. For some reason, this information is not commonly heard in many churches today, so we must be taught to handle grace rather carefully.

An overall principle is woven into the words of verse 16:

> Do you not know that when you present yourselves to someone as slaves for obedience, you are slaves of the one whom you obey, either of sin resulting in death, or of obedience resulting in righteousness?

If you were to ask me to give you in one sentence what the balance of chapter 6 is teaching, it would be this: *How we live depends on the master we choose.* "Do you not know that when you present yourselves to someone as slaves for obedience, you are slaves of the one whom you obey?" Why, of course! Submission to a master is tantamount to slavery to the same master. And what are the results?

There are only two: "either of sin resulting in death, or of obedience resulting in righteousness." Every day we live we have a choice to do what is right or what is wrong. When we send our young children off to school, we tell them, "Now, sweetheart, you need to know that Mom and Dad won't be there to make your decisions. You will find some kids at school who will encourage you to do what is right, and you'll find others who will lead you to disobey and do what is wrong. Make the right choice. Select your friends carefully. Be smart."

We would say in terms of Romans 6, "Serve the right master. Link up with righteousness." You see, before the Savior was present in our lives, we had no choice. We were all trapped under the ice. Breathing free wasn't an option. There was no way we could find freedom, no way to enjoy the ocean depths of righteousness. We were enslaved to wrong, lawlessness, selfishness, wicked choices, and impure motives. When Christ came, He freed us, leaving us with a choice. We can choose Him to be our Master, or we can go back and choose sin to master us.

As J. B. Phillips states it: "You belong to the power which you choose to obey." It's that simple. Each moment of every day we choose whom we wish to follow. If it's the Savior, the benefits are many. If it is sin, the consequences are destructive and miserable. Then where does grace enter in to this equation? Quite simply, grace makes the choice possible.

Before Christ, we had no choice. Sin was our one and only route. All of life was marked by unrighteousness. But once we came to the Cross and gave the Lord Jesus the right to rule our lives, we were granted a choice we never had before. Grace freed us from the requirement to serve sin, allowing us the opportunity to follow Christ's directives voluntarily. So as long as we do this, *we will not sin!* But as soon as you or I compromise with His mastery over us, the old master stands ready to lure us into sin.

I wish I could guarantee all of us full freedom from sin 365 days a year, but that is not possible—not so long as we are earthbound. Perpetual sinlessness (theologians call it "sinless perfection") will not be ours to enjoy until we are given glorified bodies and we are at home in heaven. The good news is that we don't have to sin on a constant, day-after-day basis. Grace has freed us to obey Christ:

> But thanks be to God that though you were slaves of sin, you became obedient from the heart to that form of teaching to which you were committed, and having been freed from sin, you became slaves of righteousness. (vv. 17–18)

Wonderful, magnificent truth! Choosing righteousness, we enjoy a lifestyle marked by God's blessings, stability, and strength. All of which seem to multiply. But have you discovered, as I have, that when you choose wrong, you adopt a lifestyle that gets increasingly worse? Let me show you from Scripture how true that is. Proverbs 5:21 states: "For the ways of a man are before the eyes of the Lord, / And He watches all his paths."

Let's imagine that Frank is a Christian. Though he knows better, Frank chooses to fall under the dominating sway and authority of his own nature—sinfulness. He deliberately decides to disobey, which he's free to do. Even though the Lord could intervene, He permits Frank, in grace, the freedom to choose. Look at what happens.

> His own iniquities will capture the wicked,
> And he will be held with the cords of his sin.
> He will die for lack of instruction,
> And in the greatness of his folly he will go astray. (Prov. 5:22–23)

What a word picture! We usually think of this situation as applicable only to an unbeliever. But it could just as easily be applied to a Christian who deliberately chooses to disobey his Lord. Instead of seeing the error of his way, he stays in a state of carnality, which grieves the Spirit of God living within him. Carnality occurs when a believer deliberately operates in the strength of his or her own will . . . stubbornly refusing to acknowledge wrong and choosing to walk contrary to the teachings of Scripture. The promptings of God's Spirit are ignored as disobedience becomes a lifestyle. Choosing to live like that is like getting caught in a whirlpool. The wickedness intensifies. It gets more treacherous as Frank goes deeper into it, until he finds himself less sensitive to it, and before long he is sucked into a kind of black hole of waywardness. Like the prodigal son, he winds up in misery and filth. And that is exactly where some Christians find themselves today. There aren't many places on earth more miserable. Actually, Frank could die in that condition, tragic as it may be. Some in Corinth did: "For this reason many among you are weak and sick, and a number sleep" (1 Cor. 11:30). Yes, some refused to return by confession and repentance, and their rebellion resulted in physical death.

Admittedly, many carnal Christians excuse such a lifestyle by saying, "It's all under grace. I can leave my wife and walk away from our children and marry someone else who is more attractive and will love me more passionately. It may not be accepted by some in the Christian community, but under grace I am free to do that. After all, the lady I'm marrying is a Christian too. We're both under grace!" Or, "My preference is to live with this person, not marry him. I'm not into a long-term commitment and vows. Grace gives me the liberty to do as I please!" Wrong! That isn't what grace is about. That is an abuse of grace.

Grace never means we're free to live any way we wish, whatever the consequences. Grace does not mean God will smile on me, regardless. It means I'm free to choose righteousness or disobedience. If I choose the latter, I will have to take the consequences: mental anguish, a guilty conscience, hurting and offending others in the Christian community, and bringing reproach to the name of Christ. If righteousness is spurned, sin can multiply much the same way as it did in our unsaved days. The Christian can be temporarily addicted to sin. As I have mentioned before, it is called carnality. I would encourage you to make a serious study of carnality because you will encounter it throughout your Christian life, and you will discover how easy it is to get caught in its trap:

Sin begets sin. The first time we do a wrong thing, we may do it with hesitation, and a tremor and a shudder. The second time we do it, it is easier;

and if we go on doing it, it becomes effortless; sin loses its terror. To start on the path of sin is to go on to more and more.[1]

I am emphasizing this not to be negative but to sound a necessary warning. We need to pass it on to those we wish to guide into freedom. As we begin to stretch our wings in grace, enjoying new freedom, new depths, and new heights, we will be wise never to forget our primary goal in life: to glorify and please God. God grants you grace:

So that you may walk in a manner worthy of the Lord, to please Him in all respects, bearing fruit in every good work and increasing in the knowledge of God; strengthened with all power, according to His glorious might, for the attaining of all steadfastness and patience; joyously giving thanks to the Father, who has qualified us to share in the inheritance of the saints in light. (Col. 1 :10–12)

Before we came to the Cross by faith, we couldn't please God. Now that the Cross has cast its shadow over our lives and Christ's blood has cleansed us from our sin, we are gloriously free—free to please Him. But we don't have to. And when we don't, we can get caught in the cords of our sin.

One writer describes the path of continued sin quite vividly:

One lie has to be covered by a dozen more. . . .

The downward cycle of sin moves from a problem to a faulty sinful response, thereby causing an additional complicating problem which [is] met by . . . additional sinful response. . . .

Sinful habits are hard to break, but if they are not broken they will bind [you] ever more tightly. [You will be] held fast by these ropes . . . in a downward cycle. . . . At length, [you] become sin's slave.[2]

Need a good warning? A healthy reminder? Never give yourself permission to hide behind grace as a cover for disobedience. Scripture calls that presumption. I've noticed that increasingly more Christians are prone to do that. In the past twenty years I have heard and seen grace abused in this manner more than ever before in my ministry. One more voice deserves to be heard on the subject. John Henry Jowett wrote words many years ago that still sting with relevance:

> Sin is a blasting presence, and every fine power shrinks and withers in the destructive heat. Every spiritual delicacy succumbs to its malignant touch. . . . Sin impairs the sight, and works towards blindness. Sin benumbs the hearing and tends to make men deaf. Sin perverts the taste, causing men to confound the sweet with the bitter, and the bitter with the sweet. Sin hardens the touch, and eventually renders a man "past feeling." All these are Scriptural analogies, and their common significance appears to be this— sin blocks and chokes the fine senses of the spirit; by sin we are desensitized, rendered imperceptive, and the range of our correspondence is diminished. Sin creates callosity. It hoofs the spirit, and so reduces the area of our exposure to pain.[3]

Life is like a menu in the Grace Restaurant. In this new establishment you are free to choose whatever you want. But whatever you choose will be served to you, and you must eat it. If you choose the wrong food and realize later just how badly your body reacted to it, don't think that grace will protect you from getting sick. There is good news, however. God's grace does hold out the hope of acceptance before the Father. He will welcome you back into His fellowship if you *deal with the wrong, repent of it, and get back on track.*

Since I am a brother in the same family, I may warn you of the harm it will cause you to make the wrong choice, but grace means I take my hands off and give you the freedom to choose. God is quite capable of guiding you. He will lead some to live one kind of lifestyle and others to live another . . . some to choose this occupation, others another . . . some, this career, others that one. He will direct some to rear their children this way and others to rear their children another way. You have the freedom to do whichever. You may prefer this kind of music; I may prefer a different kind of music. I may decide to emphasize this in my ministry; you may choose that. One of us may give this amount, another that. Some may live in this kind of house, others in another. Those options are all open to us. Because there are differences of taste or preference, grace frees us to choose. My counsel is this: Let people make their own choices. Accept them as they are. Let's uphold each other's right to have different opinions, convictions, and preferences. By doing so we keep opening up holes in the ice for one another. We all breathe easier.

I heard a fine group of singers several years ago who traveled around the country. They called themselves "Gospel State of Mind." Great harmony . . . good spirit . . . wonderful music, much of it original. One of their selections was about grace. As I listened to them and watched the joy with which they sang, I thought, *I like the name of their group. It fits.* As I write these pages on grace, I am reminded of their song, and it occurs to me that what I'm urging is not just tacking *grace* onto our vocabulary, but cultivating it in each other . . . encouraging a mental framework of grace in one another. My plea is for the body of Christ to have a "grace state of mind." As this transpires, an awakening will become obvious to all, even those outside the ranks of Christianity.

IMPORTANT REALIZATIONS

When we read through Romans 6:19–23, we come to several realizations that are important in cultivating this "grace state of mind."

First, we discover the indisputable fact that we need a master. Christ is the ideal one to choose. We don't do well with no one in authority over us. We cannot handle either life's pressures or life's temptations strictly on our own. God didn't create us to live isolated lives without a master. We need Him in charge.

Read the balance of the chapter slowly:

> For just as you presented your members as slaves to impurity and to lawlessness, resulting in further lawlessness, so now present your members as slaves to righteousness, resulting in sanctification. For when you were slaves of sin, you were free in regard to righteousness. Therefore what benefit were you then deriving from the things of which you are now ashamed? For the outcome of those things is death. But now having been freed from sin and enslaved to God, you derive your benefit, resulting in sanctification, and the outcome, eternal life. For the wages of sin is death, but the free gift of God is eternal life in Christ Jesus our Lord. (Rom. 6:19–23)

As I read those words and try to put what they are saying into simple terms, I come up with two statements. This passage is teaching us to *make the right choice.* Look again at the first three verses, this time from the New International Version: "I put this in human terms because you are weak in your natural selves. Just as you used to offer the parts of your body in slavery to impurity and to ever-increasing wickedness, so now offer them in slavery to righteousness leading to holiness. When you were slaves to sin, you were free from the control of righteousness. What benefit did you reap at that time from the things you are now ashamed of? Those things result in death!" (vv. 19–21).

And second, I believe it is telling us to *focus on the benefits of our current position in grace.* Again, from the New International Version, read the next two verses: "But now that you have been set free from sin and have become slaves to God, the benefit you reap leads to holiness, and the result is eternal life. For the wages of sin is death, but the gift of God is eternal life in Christ Jesus our Lord" (vv. 22–23).

- Because of God's grace we are freed from sin's mastery.
- By God's grace we are enslaved to God.
- Through God's grace there are benefits to be derived.

What benefits? I can think of at least three: an exciting process of growing up and maturing as a Christian; a guilt-free lifestyle characterized by creativity and freedom; and finally, enjoying the outcome—eternal life. The alternative? A sinful lifestyle that results in "death wages." Several come to mind:

- Instant breakdown of fellowship with God
- Removal of His hand of blessing
- Misery of a guilty conscience . . . knowing how much others were hurt
- Loss of personal integrity
- Sudden stoppage of spiritual growth
- Strained relationships with fellow Christians
- Reproach brought to one's family and to the name of Christ
- Injury to the testimony of your local church

Yes, in grace you are free to choose either path. It is wise to choose righteousness. If that is your selection, quality life can be yours to enjoy . . . called here "eternal life." The benefits are numerous, and all are delightful. But you can also choose the path of disobedience and start cashing in on some "death wages," all of which are awful. Before you yield to the temptation to abuse the grace God extends to you, spend some time considering the consequences. The scars of such a decision could mark you for life. Sins can be forgiven, but some scars cannot be erased.

I knew a fellow in high school who is now gone; he died of a sudden heart attack several years ago. What a guy! While in school, he was the toughest, vilest, most rebellious kid in the class. He played the meanest game of football imaginable. He was also on the wrestling team (he was never pinned . . . never lost a match), and he played catcher on the baseball team. One of his summer hobbies was racing speedboats in Galveston Bay. He was one of those wild guys who preferred to drive his boat full speed at night. Needless to say, the last thing on his mind was any interest in spiritual things. Nothing any of us could say interested him in the least—until the night God got his attention.

While speeding about sixty miles an hour under a summer moon, his boat hit a large wave near Galveston's west jetties. The boat flipped and soon sank. Although pretty banged up, he was able to swim to some rocks where he grabbed hold. The sharp barnacles began to cut into his arms, chest, stomach, and legs. The waves and swells pulled him up and down, slicing his skin into ribbons, which caused blood to flow rather freely into the water. Realizing that sharks might be near, he was scared for the first time in his life. This led him to do something he'd never done before: pray. He told God that he didn't deserve it, but he asked to be rescued. Without realizing it, he prayed for grace . . . God's unmerited favor. He told the Lord he would not only become a Christian, he would become a minister (which, to him, was the ultimate, drastic sacrifice—ugh!). God graciously intervened.

It wasn't five minutes before a Coast Guard vessel spotted him with a searchlight and soon had him on board. He looked like raw meat—his arms, belly, and legs were shredded from the razorlike barnacles. In the hospital he did a lot of thinking. During recovery he truly gave his heart to Christ. No conversion was more amazing to those of us who had known him through school. As he healed, long and ragged vertical scars remained on his body, never allowing him to forget his narrow escape from death.

As time passed, however, he forgot his words to God, and he chose to return to a carnal lifestyle—drinking heavily, chasing women, cursing, the whole ugly scene. He wasn't happy in his carnal state, but he never let on how miserable he was. Late one night, he was driving while intoxicated and struck head-on a concrete column of an underpass. He was thrown through the windshield, which left his face mutilated and permanently scarred.

Finally that got his attention. He went on to college, then seminary, and for the remaining years until his death he proclaimed the Savior whom he had ignored and whose grace he had abused. He told me many years ago that every time after a shower, as he stood in front of a mirror toweling off, those scars he bore silently shouted back at him . . . mute reminders of the wrong choices he had made both before and after his conversion. He was forgiven, but the scars didn't go away.

Yes, grace frees us to choose. We can decide to walk with God and draw strength from Him to face whatever life throws at us. Or we can decide to walk away from God, like my friend, and face the inescapable consequences. The next time you are tempted to yield to your old master, remember this: Grace invites you to return and find forgiveness, but it doesn't automatically erase the scars that accompany sin; some could stay with you for life.

In spite of the terrible consequences sins may bring, I still must emphasize that grace means we allow others the freedom to choose, regardless. To do otherwise is as much an abuser as those who use their freedom as a license to sin. I am a firm believer in mutual accountability, but grace means I will not force or manipulate or judge or attempt to control you, nor should you do those things to me. It means we will keep on helping others to freedom by providing breathing holes. It means we deliberately let go so each of us can grow and learn on our own; otherwise, we shall never enjoy the liberty of an open sea. For most of us, letting others go is neither natural nor easy. Because we care, it is more our tendency to give people hints or advice. The thought of letting them fail or fall is extremely painful to us, but God treats us like that virtually every day of our lives. We tend to clutch, not release . . . to put people in our frame and not allow them any breathing holes unless and until they accept the shape of our molds.

If you are like that, the following piece (source unknown) is written just for you. It will help you release your grip. Being a person of grace *requires* letting go of others.

LETTING GO

To let go doesn't mean to stop caring,
  it means I can't do it for someone else.
To let go is not to cut myself off,
  it's the realization that I can't control another.
To let go is not to enable,
  but to allow learning from natural consequences.
To let go is to admit powerlessness,
  which means the outcome is not in my hands.
To let go is not to try to change or blame another,
  I can only change myself.
To let go is not to care for,
  but to care about.
To let go is not to fix,
  but to be supportive.
To let go is not to judge,
  but to allow another to be a human being.

To let go is not to be in the middle arranging all the outcomes,
  but to allow others to effect their own outcomes.
To let go is not to be protective;
  it is to permit another to face reality.
To let go is not to deny,
  but to accept.
To let go is not to nag, scold, or argue,
  but to search out my own shortcomings and to correct them.
To let go is not to adjust everything to my desires,
  but to take each day as it comes.
To let go is not to criticize and regulate anyone,
  but to try to become what I dream I can be.
To let go is not to regret the past,
  but to grow and live for the future.
To let go is to fear less and love more!

8

The Grace to Let Others Be

GRACE COMES TO US IN TWO DIMENSIONS: vertical and horizontal. Vertical grace centers on our relationship with God. It is amazing. It frees us from the demands and condemnation of the Mosaic Law. It announces hope to the sinner—the gift of eternal life, along with all its benefits. Horizontal grace centers on our human relationships. It is charming. It frees us from the tyranny of pleasing people and adjusting our lives to the demands and expectations of human opinion. It gives relief—the enjoyment of freedom along with all its benefits. It silences needless guilt and removes self-imposed shame.

Few people realize better than non-Christians how guilt ridden many Christians are. A lady in a former congregation tells of a conversation she had with a fellow student while the two of them were students at the Berkeley campus of the University of California. He knew she was a Christian, and he made it painfully clear that he had no interest whatsoever in her faith. When she asked why, his answer bore the sting of reality: "Because the most guilt-ridden people I know are Christians. No thanks."

This is a good time for me to ask you two probing questions. Only you can answer them:

1. Do you add to others' guilt, or do you lessen it?
2. Are you the type who encourages another's liberty or restrains it?

Both questions have to do with attitude, don't they? We do what we do with others because of the way we think. Our attitude, therefore, is crucial. It is also at our mercy. We have full control of which attitude we shall have: charming and gracious, or restrictive and rigid. Liberty or legalism will be the result. Depending on our attitude, we are grace givers or grace killers.

Dr. Viktor Frankl survived three grim years at Auschwitz and other Nazi death camps. In his book *Man's Search for Meaning,* he reflected on those dark months and offers this insightful observation:

> We who lived in concentration camps can remember the men who walked through the huts comforting others, giving away their last piece of bread. They may have been few in number, but they offer sufficient proof that everything can be taken from a man but one thing: the last of the human freedoms—to choose one's attitude in any given set of circumstances.
>
> And there are always choices to make. Every day, every hour, offered the opportunity to make a decision . . . which determined whether you would or would not submit to those powers which threatened to rob you of your very self, your inner freedom; which determined whether or not you would become the plaything of circumstance, renouncing freedom and dignity to become molded into the form of the typical inmate. . . . Even though conditions such as lack of sleep, insufficient food and various mental stresses may suggest that the inmates were bound to react in certain ways, in the final analysis it becomes clear that the sort of person the pris-

oner became was the result of an inner decision, and not the result of camp influences alone.[1]

True words, and wise indeed. It's those inner decisions, not outer influences, that make us into the kind of people we are. One of my great hopes in writing this book is to encourage others to come to grips with the importance of maintaining a positive attitude that results in extending grace . . . the kind of grace that lets others be whoever and whatever God is leading them to be. Being that kind of person begins with an inner decision to release, to deliberately let go.

TWO STRONG TENDENCIES THAT NULLIFY GRACE

Located in the greatest doctrinal book of the Bible is a paragraph of intensely practical instruction. It is, in fact, a series of commands that, if obeyed, will turn us into some of the most affirming people imaginable:

> Let love be without hypocrisy. Abhor what is evil; cling to what is good. Be devoted to one another in brotherly love; give preference to one another in honor; not lagging behind in diligence, fervent in spirit, serving the Lord; rejoicing in hope, persevering in tribulation, devoted to prayer, contributing to the needs of the saints, practicing hospitality. Bless those who persecute you; bless and curse not. Rejoice with those who rejoice, and weep with those who weep. Be of the same mind toward one another; do not be haughty in mind, but associate with the lowly. Do not be wise in your own estimation. Never pay back evil for evil to anyone. Respect what is right in the sight of all men. (Rom. 12:9–17)

In a nutshell, those words represent the essence of authentic Christianity. Unless I miss my guess, I think every person who knows and loves Jesus Christ would respond to that list in words similar to these: "I would love to be like that. What a list of resolutions to claim at the beginning of every new year. My relationships with others would immediately improve. How I would wish all these things were true of me!"

Why don't we treat one another as the Lord instructs us to? Why do we love with such hypocrisy? What keeps us from being devoted to one another, from honoring one another, from contributing to each other's needs, from practicing hospitality? When others are promoted or receive special recognition or are able to enjoy a few luxuries we may not have, why don't we applaud their success and rejoice with them? Why do we pay back evil for evil, even though we know that retaliation will only create greater barriers? The list of why questions could continue for another page. The inescapable fact is that, more often than not, we nullify grace rather than magnify it. We resist it much more often than we release it. What is it within us that hinders an attitude of horizontal grace from flowing freely?

I thought about that for many years. While thinking, I not only examined my own life, I also observed others, most of them Christians. My findings were not pleasant, but they were revealing and I think reliable. Most of us fall short when it comes to letting others be, because of two strong and very human tendencies: We compare ourselves with others (which leads us to criticize or compete with them), and we attempt to control others (which results in our manipulating or intimidating them). For a few moments, let's dissect and examine both of those tendencies that keep grace from awakening.

To Compare

Christians seem especially vulnerable when it comes to comparison. For some reason, which I cannot fully discern, we are uneasy with differences. We prefer sameness, predictability, common interests. If someone thinks

differently or makes different choices than we do, prefers different enter-
tainment, wears different clothing, has different tastes and opinions, or
enjoys a different style of life, most Christians get nervous. We place far
too much weight on externals and the importance of appearances and not
nearly enough on individuality and variety. We have "acceptable norms"
in which we are able to move freely and allow others the freedom to do so.
But heaven help the poor soul who steps beyond those bounds!

We compare musical tastes. We compare financial incomes. We compare marital status. We compare spirituality on the basis of externals. If an
individual appreciates hymns and mellow songs, fine. If another prefers
jazz or rock, watch out. If someone makes about as much money as we do
(or less), we feel comfortable, relaxed, and accepting. If they make a great
deal of money, drive a luxury car or two, own their own airplane or a summer home, or take extensive vacations, we consider them extravagant . . .
even though we know next to nothing of their giving habits. If someone is
married, has several well-disciplined and intelligent children (like ours!),
we enjoy being around them. They are "in." If a person is living alone, or
is divorced, or is a single parent, or has never gotten married, well—
"something must be wrong with him (or her)." Actually, the only thing
wrong is the comparison!

Who wrote the "let's compare" rule book? Will you please show me
from Scripture where God is pleased with such negative attitudes? Why
can't a person be spiritual and enjoy expressions of music or art totally different from those you like? Who says it is carnal to have nice things or
enjoy a few extravagant luxuries, especially if one's generosity is also
extravagant? Why can't people drive any car they can afford or vacation
anywhere they please or live in whatever size home they enjoy or wear
whatever clothing they prefer? Just because you or I can't or don't choose
to or would prefer not to doesn't mean others can't or shouldn't.
Comparison fuels the fire of envy within people. It prompts the tendency

to judge . . . it makes us prejudiced people. The worst part of all is that it nullifies grace. It was never God's intention for all His children to look alike or embrace identical lifestyles. Look at the natural world He created. What variety! The buzzard and the butterfly . . . the dog and the deer . . . the zinnia and the orchid . . . the wriggling minnow and the sleek shark.

The church is not a religious industry designed to turn out mass-produced reproductions on an assembly line. The Bible wasn't written to change us into cookie-cutter Christians or paper-doll saints. On the contrary, the folks I read about in the Book are as different as Rahab and Esther, one a former prostitute and the other a queen . . . as unusual as Amos and Stephen, a fig picker turned prophet and a deacon who became a martyr. Variety honors God; predictability and mediocrity bore Him. And if there is proof that He prefers differences, take a look down the long hall of fame in church history. Some of those folks would never have been welcome in most evangelical churches today: "too extreme . . . too eccentric . . . too liberal!" Can you imagine fiery John Knox in one of today's sophisticated pulpits? Or how about Martin Luther on television! You're smiling if you are familiar with the man's uninhibited, provocative style. He was the one who once admitted that he never preached better than when he was angry.

Before we will be able to demonstrate sufficient grace to let others be, we'll have to get rid of this legalistic tendency to compare. (Yes, it is a form of legalism.) God has made each one of us as we are. He is hard at work shaping us into the image He has in mind. His only pattern (for character) is His Son. He wants each one of us to be unique . . . an individual blend and expression unlike any other person. That is by His design. There is only one you. There is only one me. And the same can be said of each member of His family.

Legalism requires that we all be alike, unified in convictions and uniform in appearance, to which I say, "Let me out!" Grace finds pleasure in differences, encourages individuality, smiles on variety, and leaves plenty of room for disagreement. Remember, it releases others and lets them be, to which I say, "Let me in!" I agree with and often quote the old saying, "Comparisons are odious." Not until we put a stop to them will horizontal grace flourish in the body.

To Control

Another attitude worth changing (if we hope to promote the grace awakening in our generation) is the tendency to control others. I find this especially prevalent among those who find their security in religious rigidity. They get their way by manipulating and intimidating. They use fear tactics, veiled threats, and oblique hints to get their way. If you have ever been around a controller, you know exactly what I'm trying to describe. Most often, controllers are insecure in themselves and do not know the first principle of being free, so naturally they are uneasy with your or my being free. Hence, they issue demands and force their will on others in no uncertain terms. You're not around controllers very long before you know it. Subtlety is not their long suit, which can be very intimidating.

I'm reminded of a dialogue between a couple of comic strip characters. One is sitting alone, watching television. In storms the other, demanding that he change the channel to the one she wants to watch, threatening him with her fat little fist in his face. Rather meekly he asks her what makes her think she can walk in and take over. She blurts out: "These five fingers!" which she tightens into a fist. It works. Without a protest the little guy responds by asking which channel she prefers.

Naturally, she gets to watch any channel she wants. Slowly he slips out of the room, feeling like a wimp. He looks at his own five fingers and asks, "Why can't you guys get organized like that?"

Controllers win by intimidation. Whether physical or verbal, they bully their way in as they attempt to manipulate us into doing their will. In Christian circles controllers usually are more insidious than the strong-willed little gal was with her wimpy friend. But they are equally determined, count on it. Whatever the method, controlling, like comparing, nullifies grace. If you are given to controlling others, grace is a foreign concept to you.

FOUR BIBLICAL GUIDELINES THAT MAGNIFY GRACE

Enough about things that nullify grace. What we want most is to magnify it . . . promote it . . . release it, right?

In his letter to the Romans, Paul goes into great detail regarding the issue of personal freedom—greater detail than almost anywhere else in his writings. In the fourteenth chapter, for example, he sets forth four very practical guidelines that can be followed by all who are serious about releasing others in grace. My hope is not only that we learn what they are but, equally important, that we spend our days following them.

The first guideline is based on Romans 14:1–4:

> Now accept the one who is weak in faith, but not for the purpose of passing judgment on his opinions. One man has faith that he may eat all things, but he who is weak eats vegetables only. Let not him who eats regard with contempt him who does not eat, and let not him who does not eat judge him who eats, for God has accepted him. Who are you to judge the servant of another? To his own master he stands or falls; and stand he will, for the Lord is able to make him stand.

Since we have already dealt with the issue of eating meat from a carcass offered to idols, there is no reason for me to explain the background again. But perhaps I should repeat the question that arose from the controversy: Should a Christian eat it or not? Some had no problem whatsoever, while others thought it was wrong to do so, feeling that the one who ate it would be spiritually contaminated by the association with pagan worship. Let's see how this situation can relate to magnifying grace:

Guideline 1: *Accepting others is basic to letting them be.* The problem was not a meat problem; it was a love problem, an acceptance problem. It still is. How often we restrict our love by making it conditional: "If you will (or won't), then I will accept you." Paul starts there: "Accept one another!" In other words, "Let's allow others the freedom to hold to convictions that are unlike our own . . . and accept them in spite of that difference." Those who didn't eat (called here "weak in faith") were exhorted to accept and not judge those who ate. And those who ate were exhorted to accept and not regard with contempt those who did not eat. The secret lies in accepting one another. All of this is fairly easy to read as long as I stay on the issue of eating meat. That one is safe because it isn't a current taboo. It's easy to accept those folks today because they don't exist!

How about those in our life who may disagree with us on issues that are taboos in evangelical Christian circles today? Here are a few:

- Going to the movies or live theater
- Wearing cosmetics
- Playing cards
- Watching television
- Going to the beach
- Not having a "quiet time" every morning or at least every day
- Going to a restaurant that sells liquor
- Wearing certain clothing
- Driving certain cars
- Wearing certain jewelry
- Listening to certain music

- Dancing . . . square, ballroom, disco—whatever
- Holding a certain job
- Wearing your hair a certain way (assuming you have hair)
- Having lovely and elegant possessions
- Getting a face-lift
- Drinking coffee
- Eating certain foods

There are a dozen other things I could list, some of which would make you smile. But believe me, in various areas of our country or the world, some or all of these things may be taboo, and if you cross that boundary, may God help you continue on in the church you're attending. Someone will probably say something. If not, you will be pounced upon by looks and reactionary treatment, revealing attitudes that lack grace. We are masters at that. If you hope to "survive," you had better learn the rules—fast. Don't assume that all areas are identical when it comes to taboos. The list changes from culture to culture even to this day.

I read about a pastors' conference where a group of German Lutherans had gathered. Part of their reception included serving beer. No one thought anything of it because in that culture a mug of beer is absolutely accepted. But if one of the men lit up a cigar, the place would go up in smoke! Strange, isn't it? They shouldn't smoke, but if they choose to enjoy a swig of beer, no problem.

I know of churches where you are frowned on if you go to live theater or attend a movie, no matter what the rating is. Members of these congregations even spy out those places. But some of those same people will sit up late into the night and watch movies on television. Some even have cable TV and may watch movies that are far worse than those at the theaters. Funny, to me movies are movies, no matter where they are viewed. But not to these folks!

One of my favorite stories comes from a man who used to be in our church. He and his wife were close friends of our family, but they moved to another part of the country. When he was a youth worker many years ago in an ethnic community, he attended a church that had Scandinavian roots. Being a rather forward-looking and creative young man, he decided he would show the youth group a missionary film. We're talking simple, safe, black-and-white, religious-oriented movie. That film projector hadn't been off an hour before a group of the leaders in the church called him in and asked him about what he had done. They asked, "Did you show the young people a film?" In all honesty he responded, "Well, yeah, I did." "We don't like that," they replied. Without trying to be argumentative, the youth worker reasoned, "Well, I remember that at the last missionary conference, our church showed slides—" One of the church officers put his hand up, signaling him to cease talking. Then, in these words, he emphatically explained the conflict: "If it's still, fine. If it moves, sin!" You can show slides, but when they start movin', you're gettin' into sin. My friend crossed the invisible line and got his hand slapped. He and I still laugh about the incongruity of that logic, but he does not look down on those leaders for their different understanding. (Remember, our goal is acceptance, the basis of a grace state of mind.)

In Romans 14 Paul mentions the two most common reactions to such conflicts. First he says, "Let not him who eats regard with contempt him who does not" (v. 3). The words "regard with contempt" mean "regard as nothing, utterly despise, to discount entirely." That is the normal response of those who feel the freedom to do whatever toward those who are more restrictive and rigid. It is easy to look down on them . . . to "regard as nothing."

The second reaction Paul mentions is that of the other side—"and let not him who does not eat judge him who eats." *Judging* means to criticize, to view negatively, to make assumptions that are exaggerated and erroneous and even damaging to character. No matter how strongly you may feel about a certain taboo, judging another who may disagree with you is going too far. That kind of thing has been going on for years, actually, ever since the *first* century.

William Barclay writes:

> The Jews had made a tyranny of the Sabbath, surrounding it with a jungle of rules, regulations and prohibitions.[2]

It became a fetish!

Can you imagine making the Sabbath into a fetish? Why, of course! Anything we make too much of easily becomes a fetish, which is the tragedy of it all.

Do you remember Paul's question? "Who are you to judge the servant of another? To his own master he stands or falls." When we truly accept another person, we remember that the Lord is perfectly capable of directing his or her life. That relieves us from having to be his or her conscience. It's our job to accept others; it's God's job to direct them.

What does acceptance mean? What does it include? Because I cannot say it better than what I read in a periodical many years ago, I'll return to that source for my answer to those two questions:

> Acceptance means you are valuable just as you are. It allows you to be the real you. You aren't forced into someone else's idea of who you really are. It means your ideas are taken seriously since they reflect you. You can talk about how you feel inside and why you feel that way—and someone really cares.
>
> Acceptance means you can try out your ideas without being shot down. You can even express heretical thoughts and discuss them with intelligent questioning. You feel safe. No one will pronounce judgment on you, even though they don't agree with you. It doesn't mean you will never be cor-

rected or shown to be wrong; it simply means it's safe to be you and no one will destroy you out of prejudice.[3]

Acceptance is basic to letting others be. Consider the next four verses of Romans 14 as we turn to a second guideline:

One man regards one day above another, another regards every day alike. Let each man be fully convinced in his own mind. He who observes the day, observes it for the Lord, and he who eats, does so for the Lord, for he gives thanks to God; and he who eats not, for the Lord he does not eat, and gives thanks to God. For not one of us lives for himself, and not one dies for himself; for if we live, we live for the Lord, or if we die, we die for the Lord; therefore whether we live or die, we are the Lord's. (vv. 5–8)

Guideline 2: *Refusing to dictate to others allows the Lord freedom to direct their lives.* I especially appreciate the statement at the end of verse 5: "Let each man be fully convinced in his own mind." Give people room to make up their minds. Do you have a few new converts who are a part of your life and ministry? Do you want to help them grow toward maturity? Here is how: Let them grow up differently. Let them learn at their own pace, just as you had to learn, including failures and mistakes. If you really want grace to awaken, be easier on them than others were on you. Don't make up their minds . . . let them! Don't step in and push your weight around . . . give them plenty of space. Whatever you do, don't control and manipulate them to get what you want.

Be an accepting model of grace. Refuse all temptations to be a brother basher or sister smasher. We already have too many of them roaming around the religious landscape. Nothing catches the attention of the unsaved world quicker than those times when we Christians beat up on one another. Don't think the unsaved world doesn't notice our cannibalism.

Leslie Flynn writes about the time when evangelist Jack Van Impe was closing a citywide crusade in Green Bay, Wisconsin. It was to end on a Sunday afternoon. The very same public arena also featured wrestling on Sunday night. Interestingly, on Monday evening (the following day), Rex Humbard was scheduled to begin a new series of evangelistic meetings. One wonders if the man who set up the sign didn't have his tongue in his cheek when he arranged the letters on the marquee,

JACK VAN IMPE

WRESTLING

REX HUMBARD[4]

Most Christians have a long way to go when it comes to releasing others to the Lord. I love the way Paul provides the right perspective—"We are the Lord's." Few things will keep us from directing others' lives like that reminder. Each one of us belongs to the same Lord. When we stop dictating, it is easier for others to mature as they follow the Lord's directing.

Let's press on to the next four verses in Romans 14:

For to this end Christ died and lived again, that He might be Lord both of the dead and of the living. But you, why do you judge your brother? Or you again, why do you regard your brother with contempt? For we shall all stand before the judgment seat of God. For it is written, "AS I LIVE, SAYS THE LORD, EVERY KNEE SHALL BOW TO ME, AND EVERY TONGUE SHALL GIVE PRAISE TO GOD." So then each one of us shall give account of himself to God. (vv. 9–12)

Guideline 3: *Freeing others means we never assume a position we're not qualified to fill.* This, in one sentence, is enough to stop any person from judging another. We're not qualified. We lack full knowledge. How often we have jumped to wrong conclusions, made judgmental statements, only to find out later how off-base we were . . . then wished we could cut out our tongue.

What keeps us from being qualified to judge?

- We do not know all the facts.
- We are unable to read motives.
- We find it impossible to be totally objective.
- We lack "the big picture."
- We live with blind spots.
- We are prejudiced and have blurred perspective.
- Most of all, we ourselves are imperfect and inconsistent.

In a Connecticut city, fifty-three residents of a certain neighborhood signed a petition to stop reckless driving on their streets. The police set a watch. A few nights later five violators were caught. All five had signed the petition.[5]

I will never forget what happened to me several years ago that illustrates how wrong I can be in judging another. I was speaking at a summer Bible conference for a week. Attending the same conference was a couple I had not seen before. We met briefly the first night. Both were friendly and seemed especially glad to be there. I began to notice as the week wore on that the man fell asleep in every one of the meetings. I mean every one. Normally, that doesn't bother me . . . I often talk in other people's sleep! But this time, for some strange reason, it began to bug me. By Wednesday I was irritated. As I mentioned, that has happened to me numerous times . . . but this guy was out within ten minutes after I started to speak. It made no difference if I spoke in the morning or evening—he slept. By the last meeting on Friday evening (through which he slept, of course), I had become convinced it was she who wanted to be there, not her husband. I sized him up as a fellow who talked one way but lived another. "Probably a carnal Christian," I mused.

She stayed after the crowd and her husband had left. She asked if she could speak with me for a few minutes. I figured she wanted to talk about how unhappy she was living with a man who didn't have the same interest in spiritual things as she. How wrong I was. She said their being there was his idea. It had been his "final wish." I didn't understand. She informed me he had terminal cancer and had only weeks to live. At his request they attended the conference where I was speaking even though the medication he was taking for pain made him sleepy—something that greatly embarrassed him. "He loves the Lord," she said, "and you are his favorite Bible teacher. He wanted to be here to meet you and to hear you, no matter what." I was sincerely stunned. She thanked me for the week and left. I stood there, all alone, as deeply rebuked as I have ever been. I had judged my brother, and I was as wrong as I could possibly have been.

Does this guideline mean we must always agree? It does not. That is the subject of my next chapter, so I'll not attempt to address it at length here. There are any number of people with whom you and I may not agree. That's fine . . . we can still be civil to each other, instead of spending our time putting each other's face on a dartboard. I'm a lot happier if I accept the fact that others won't always fall in line with my convictions. That's okay. But the main thing you and I must guard against is judging. I repeat, we are not qualified to fill that role. God alone is to be our Judge and Jury.

There is one more guideline that grows out of verses 13–18 in Romans 14:

Therefore let us not judge one another anymore, but rather determine this—not to put an obstacle or a stumbling block in a brother's way. I know and am convinced in the Lord Jesus that nothing is unclean in itself; but to him who thinks anything to be unclean, to him it is unclean. For if because of food your brother is hurt, you are no longer walking according to love. Do not destroy with your food him for whom Christ died. Therefore do not let what is for you a good thing be spoken of as evil; for the kingdom of God is not eating and drinking, but righteousness and peace and joy in the Holy Spirit. For he who in this way serves Christ is acceptable to God and approved by men.

Guideline 4: *Loving others requires us to express our liberty wisely.* In other words, love must rule. I'm not my own; I'm bought with a price. My goal is not to please me; it is to please my Lord Jesus, my God. It is not to please you; it is to please my Lord. The same is true for you. So the bottom line is this: I don't adapt my life according to what you may say; I adapt my life according to the basis of my love for you because I answer to Christ. And so do you.

To paraphrase those verses we just read from Romans: "Nothing that is not specifically designated as evil in Scripture is evil—but rather a matter of one's personal preference or taste. So let it be. Even if you personally would not do what another is doing, let it be. And you who feel the freedom to do so, don't flaunt it or mock those who disagree. We are in the construction business, not destruction. And let's all remember that God's big-picture kingdom plan is not being shaped by small things like what one person prefers over another, but by large things, like righteousness and peace and joy."

One of the marks of maturity is the ability to handle liberty without flaunting it. Mature folks don't flaunt their privileges. They enjoy them fully, yet quietly . . . privately . . . with those of like mind, who aren't offended by the liberty.

When our children began to grow up, we (like you) increased their privileges. One of the first privileges our oldest child enjoyed was not having to take a nap and not having to go to bed so early. He could miss his afternoon nap, and he could stay up later with his mom and dad. The problem was, the other three weren't old enough to have the same privilege. So he had to be mature about handling this new freedom. If he flaunted it, chaos would break out. In other words, he couldn't walk by their closed bedroom door and taunt them by shouting, "Na-na-na-na-na . . . I don't have to take a na-ap." Or "Ha! You've got to go to bed early—not me. I'm free to stay up reeeal late!" We warned him to stay quiet and handle his liberty very wisely. Paul cautions you and me to do the same. Otherwise, the grace killers will get ammunition and have reason to load up and fire in our direction. Grace never gives us the right to rub anyone's nose in our liberty. When I see that happening, I realize I'm watching religious childishness in action.

A FEW ACTIONS THAT SIGNIFY GRACE

I want to close this chapter by focusing on the concluding verses in Romans 14. Read verse 19 slowly and thoughtfully. "So then let us pursue the things which make for peace and the building up of one another." On the basis of that great statement, consider the first of four action steps.

1. *Concentrate on things that encourage peace and assist others' growth.* An idea that works for me is to filter whatever I do through a twofold "grid"—two questions that keep me focused: (a) Is this going to make a lot of waves, or will it encourage peace? (b) Is this going to hurt and offend, or will it help and strengthen my brother or sister? Let's commit ourselves anew to encouragement and affirmation.

2. *Remember that sabotaging saints hurts the work of God.* "Don't tear down the work of God for the sake of food" (v. 20). You sabotage the saints when you flaunt your liberty, knowing that they have convictions against it. That is not fair. Frankly, that is fighting dirty. Scripture calls it

"regarding with contempt" and counsels us against it. Enjoy your liberty with discretion.

3. *Exercise your liberty only with those who can enjoy it with you.* I repeat, that means to keep it private and personal. Remember my story about our oldest child. What others don't know can't hurt them. That's not deception; it's wise and necessary restraint. It isn't prompted by hypocrisy but by love.

4. *Determine where you stand and refuse to play God in anyone else's life.* That may sound simple and easy, but it is tougher than it may seem. Be absolutely sure you are right, then press on, regardless. By letting others be, you free yourself to give full attention to what God is trying to make of you. You have neither the time nor the energy to keep holding on. Love demands that you let go.

Some time ago *The American Scholar* magazine included a piece by Wyatt Prunty that illustrates rather well what I've been attempting to write in this chapter.

LEARNING THE BICYCLE
(for Heather)

The older children pedal past
Stable as little gyros, spinning hard
To supper, bath, and bed, until at last
We also quit, silent and tired
Beside the darkening yard where trees
Now shadow up instead of down.
Their predictable lengths can only tease
Her as, head lowered, she walks her bike alone
Somewhere between her wanting to ride
And her certainty she will always fall.
Tomorrow, though I will run behind,

The Grace Awakening

Arms out to catch her, she'll tilt then balance wide
Of my reach, till distance makes her small,
Smaller, beyond the place I stop and know
That to teach her I had to follow
And when she learned I had to let her go.[6]

9

Graciously Disagreeing and Pressing On

ONE OF THE MARKS OF MATURITY is the ability to disagree without becoming disagreeable. It takes grace. In fact, handling disagreements with tact is one of the crowning achievements of grace.

Unfortunately, the older we get the more brittle we become in our reactions, the more tedious and stubborn and fragile. For some strange reason, this is especially true among evangelical Christians. You would think that the church would be the one place where we could find tolerance, tact, plenty of room for disagreement, and open discussion. Not so! It is a rare delight to come across those in the family of God who have grown old in grace as well as in knowledge.

A friend told me of a beautiful example of this—a true story. The minister of a church of a different denomination contacted the pastor of a large downtown Baptist church and made an unusual request. He had several folks who had recently joined his church who preferred to be baptized by immersion rather than by sprinkling, the church's normal mode of baptism. The minister requested not only the use of their baptistry but

159

that the Baptist pastor himself baptize those who came. This posed a dilemma: What if those being baptized weren't born again? Since it was the pastor's conviction that only Christians should be baptized, he realized he couldn't with good conscience cooperate with the plan, but he wished to handle his answer with tact so as not to offend the other minister. I understand that he wrote a letter, a masterpiece of grace, in which he included this humorous statement: "We don't take in laundry, but we'll be happy to loan you our tub."

Would that all issues of that nature were handled that graciously.

Many a ministry lives on the edge of upheaval and borderline controversy simply because there is no room for disagreement . . . no freedom to negotiate . . . no open ear to those who hold to a different opinion. I know of some ministers who never read critical mail; it's all screened by their secretaries and quickly discarded. Another has publicly stated that he would have no one on his board who says "No." When I heard that, I couldn't help but wonder about two things: How in the world could he find enough people like that to form his board, and how does his wife handle her disagreements? Maybe she mails them in anonymously. Just kidding.

The other side of this matter of criticism needs to be addressed with equal vigor, namely, the importance of stating our disagreements graciously. Because I happen to read most of my critical mail, I am continually aware of how people declare their disagreements. There are a few beautiful exceptions, but the general rule is that criticisms are tactless, blunt, accusatory, and sometimes sarcastic. The most offensive ones are usually left unsigned (a cowardly act) and have little truth, if any. Talk about grace killers!

I've said for years that people should not read unsigned mail. My problem is that I usually do. I also have said people should not pay any attention to it—"Toss it in the trash!" My problem is that I usually *memorize* it.

I know, I know, it isn't healthy, but since when am I a model of perfection? Oh, to practice what one preaches!

All this is to say that I have read enough "hate mail" (strong term but occasionally true) to make this suggestion: *Think before you write your disagreements.* I have found that it helps to pause and put myself in the other person's place and imagine myself opening the letter and feeling the sting of those words. As a result of that little exercise, I have usually torn up my letter of criticism instead of sending it.

Trust me, bitter and harsh words stick like pieces of shrapnel in one's brain, even in those you might think of as strong and able to handle it. The critic may soon forget them, but seldom will the one being verbally assaulted. I love the old saying "Write your criticisms in dust, your compliments in marble."

The last four verses of Ephesians 4 come to mind:

> Let no unwholesome words proceed from your mouth, but only such a word as is good for edification according to the need of the moment, that it may give grace to those who hear. And do not grieve the Holy Spirit of God, by whom you were sealed for the day of redemption. Let all bitterness and wrath and anger and clamor and slander be put away from you, along with all malice. And be kind to one another, tender-hearted, forgiving each other, just as God in Christ also has forgiven you. (vv. 29–32)

No one could say it more succinctly than that. Just be nice, my Christian friend, in whatever you say or write. It costs no more, and it takes only a little more time to express your disagreements in tactful and gracious ways . . . when you don't get your way or when someone holds a different opinion or even when a correction should be made and reproof is in order. Rudeness is never appropriate. Without exception, kindness is.

THINGS WE AGREE ON REGARDING DISAGREEMENTS

As much as we may pursue peace, and as positive and tactful as we may be, there will still be occasions when disagreements arise. As one wag put it, "Life ain't no exact science," which brings me to the first of four facts with which everyone (well, most of us) would agree.

1. *Disagreements are inevitable.* Throughout this book, I have emphasized the value of variety and the importance of individuality. The downside of that is it leaves the door open for differing opinions. I say downside only because those inevitable differences can lead to strong disagreements. There will be opposing viewpoints and a variety of perspectives on most subjects. Tastes differ as well as preferences. That is why they make vanilla and chocolate and strawberry ice cream, why they build Fords and Chevys, Chryslers and Cadillacs, Hondas and Toyotas. That is why our nation has room for Democrats and Republicans, conservatives and liberals—and moderates. The tension is built into our system. It is what freedom is all about, including religious freedom. I am fairly firm in my theological convictions, but that doesn't mean you (or anyone) must agree with me. All this explains why I place so much importance on leaving "wiggle room" in our relationships. One's theological persuasion may not bend, but one's involvements with others must. Leaders are especially in need of leaving "wiggle room" if they hope to relieve steam from inevitable tensions.

2. *Even the godly will sometimes disagree.* When I was younger, I had difficulty with this one. I couldn't understand how two people who loved the Lord with equal passion and who believed the Bible with equal zeal could come to different conclusions. In my two-by-four mind I was convinced that all godly minds held to identical conclusions. Not so! To my amazement, I soon discovered that there were not only various opinions on the same subject but that God had the audacity to bless those who dis-

agreed with me. I believe it was Dr. Bob Cook, while he was president of The King's College, who wisely said, "God reserves the right to use people who disagree with me." I'll go one step further, for I am now convinced that God is not nearly so narrow as many of His people are. I find that God is much easier to live with than most of His followers . . . far more tolerant, certainly full of more grace and forgiveness than all of us are.

Unlike us, when He forgives, He forgets the transgression and removes it as far as east is from west. Perhaps you have heard of the man who loved the Lord, but he couldn't seem to conquer a particular sin. Time and again through the week he would come before the Lord and confess the same transgression. In all sincerity, he would tell God how much he hated what he had done and how grateful he was for God's grace in forgiving him. Wouldn't you know it, by Saturday of that same struggling week he was back on his knees: "Here I come again, Lord, with the same sin . . . asking Your forgiveness and claiming Your cleansing." To his surprise, he heard God's audible answer: "What sin?"

There will be no denominations in heaven, no categories of Christians—only the vast company of the saints, and only then will there be perfect harmony of heart and complete unanimity of agreement. Until then, count on it, even the godly will disagree.

3. *In every disagreement there are the same two ingredients:* (a) an issue, and (b) various viewpoints. The issue is usually objective and involves principles. The viewpoints are subjective and involve personalities. And therein lies the sum and substance of a clash, which could be defined as a disagreement over an issue because of opposing points of view. I will be candid with you: Every time I have remembered those two basic ingredients in the midst of a disagreement, I have been able to keep calm and think clearly. When I have forgotten them, almost without exception I have failed to negotiate my way through the clash with wisdom. Furthermore, I have regretted something I said in the heat of verbal

exchange. Those two simple ingredients have never failed to help me keep cool. Why? The next fact will explain.

4. *In many disagreements each side is valid.* As "liberal" as you may think that sounds, chew on it before you toss it aside. On numerous occasions when I have encountered a brother or sister who felt as strongly as I about the other side of the argument, I came to realize it was not so much an I-am-right-and-you-are-wrong matter as it was an I-see-it-from-this-perspective-and-you-from-that-perspective matter. Both sides of most disagreements have strengths and weaknesses, which means neither side is an airtight slam dunk. Nevertheless, any disagreement can lead to a serious, permanent rift in a relationship . . . and sometimes (this may surprise you) that is God's will. There are times God chooses to spread the good news of His Son rapidly in different directions by having two capable servants of His have a major disagreement. As they separate and minister effectively in two different locations, He accomplishes a greater objective than their being in agreement.

A DISAGREEMENT BETWEEN TWO GODLY LEADERS

That is exactly what happened between two men who had labored alongside each other for years. I am thinking of Paul, the godly apostle of grace, and Barnabas, the godly servant of compassion. Two more dedicated men could not be found in the first century. Both were effective, both spiritually minded. Neither was selfish or immature. But what an argument! Can you imagine what the media today would have done with the headlines?

RELIGIOUS COWORKERS CLASH HEAD-ON

or

EVANGELISTS FIGHT OVER TEAM MEMBER

. . . or some such nonsense. There are two things I have learned over the past few years regarding the media: be suspicious of the headlines, and never expect the media to get the whole story straight. If it can be garbled or exaggerated or slanted, they will do it.

Frankly, I am pleased to read of two men as respected and as full of integrity as Paul and Barnabas wrestling over an issue about which both felt strongly. Too often we Christians resemble the little toy dog sitting in the back window of a car always nodding in agreement. Too many fear that disagreement is tantamount to mutiny. But that's not true; grace leaves room for a few clashes. The late great G. Campbell Morgan agrees:

> I am greatly comforted whenever I read this [disagreement between Paul and Barnabas]. I am thankful for the revelation of the humanity of these men. If I had never read that Paul and Barnabas had a contention, I should have been afraid. These men were not angels, they were men.[1]

One more thought before we get into the specific clash between Paul and Barnabas. No matter how much good may come from such disagreements, they often hurt . . . and I mean hurt deeply. This is especially true when you have to take it on the chin and choose not to strike back. The more heated the disagreement, the more our inner steam tank builds to the breaking point, and it is all we can do to keep a level head through the whole explosive episode. Again, only God's grace can give us sufficient strength to restrain retaliation.

This reminds me of the Quaker who owned an ornery cow. Every time he milked her, it was a clash of two wills. This particular morning she was unusually irritable, but he was determined to endure the session without so much as a cross word. As the farmer began to milk her, ol' Bossy stepped on his foot with all her weight. He struggled silently, groaned a little under his breath, pulled his foot free, then sat back down on the stool. She then swished her tail in his face like a long-string whip. He merely leaned away so it wouldn't be able to reach him. Next she kicked over the bucket, by then half-full of warm milk. He started over, mumbling a few words to himself, but he never lost his cool. Once finished with the ordeal, he breathed a sigh of relief and picked up the bucket and stool, and as he was leaving she hauled off and kicked him against the barn wall twelve to fifteen feet away. That did it. He stood to his feet, marched in front of his cow, stared into those big eyes, and as he shook a long, bony finger in her face, he shouted, "Thou dost know that I am a Quaker. Thou dost also know that I cannot strike thee back . . . But I can sell thee to a Presbyterian!"

Let's look now into the biblical account and set the stage for how the disagreement arose between Paul and Barnabas. It all started when they took their first missionary journey together. Accompanying these two seasoned veterans of the faith was a young man named John Mark, who was neither seasoned nor strong. Perhaps because he was Barnabas's cousin and because he showed real promise as an up-and-coming young believer, they felt comfortable having him travel with them. For sure, they could use an extra set of hands to help them with what they carried by way of supplies and clothing, not knowing what they would encounter in the primitive and rugged places of their destination. Everything was fine at the start:

> And when they reached Salamis, they began to proclaim the word of God in the synagogues of the Jews; and they also had John as their helper. (Acts 13:5)

But when they crossed over to the difficult area of Pamphylia, they reached a region that was probably tougher to take than the Normandy coastline was in the Second World War. An imposing range of mountains stood before them like rugged giants of stone. It was a mosquito-infested, feverish coastline. To say the least, the honeymoon of adventure was over when they got to Perga in Pamphylia. The excitement and theoretical delight of missionary travel screeched to a halt as the three companions came upon hard times. Finally it became too much for John Mark, who lost the heart to go any farther. "Now Paul and his companions put out to sea from Paphos and came to Perga in Pamphylia; and John left them and returned to Jerusalem" (Acts 13:13).

Don't move too hurriedly over that last statement. The young man's drive weakened. His dream turned into a personal nightmare. No doubt embarrassed, he admitted, "I just can't go any further. I'm leaving." William Barclay calls him "the deserter."[2] Chrysostom says, "The lad wanted his mother."[3] More than a few New Testament scholars refer to him as "the defector." When the going got tough, John Mark up and quit. If my figuring is correct, this was also the time Paul got sick. It may have been a bout with malaria or the beginning of intense headaches connected with some form of eye disease. Whatever, it was the worst possible time to be deserted. If ever they needed to pull together, it was then. Nevertheless, Paul and Barnabas were faced with no other option than to slug it out on their own. Little did they know the pain awaiting them. It was on this trip, you may remember, that Paul was stoned and left to die. Ultimately, he and Barnabas endured the rigors of the trip, came back, and reported the wonderful results. I have often wondered if John Mark was there in the Antioch church when the report was given. If so, he probably sat back in the shadows out of sight, feeling terribly ashamed.

The Critical Issue

Some time later the thought dawned in Paul's mind, *Let's go back and look things over.* The Acts account picks up the story:

> And after some days Paul said to Barnabas, "Let us return and visit the
> brethren in every city in which we proclaimed the word of the Lord, and

see how they are." And Barnabas was desirous of taking John, called Mark, along with them also. (15:36–37)

"Let's take John Mark. Let's give him another chance." The next verse makes it clear that Paul disagreed: "But Paul kept insisting that they should not take him along." Remember my earlier comment? In every disagreement there are two ingredients: an objective issue and opposing viewpoints. The issue here? Should a person who defects from a mission be given a second chance? Should someone who leaves people in the lurch when they really need him be taken again on a similar mission? And the viewpoints? Paul said, "No, absolutely not." Barnabas said, "Yes, by all means."

The Opposing Viewpoints

There stood two men of God, each fully convinced in his own mind that he was right. Remember Barnabas? He is the model of compassion. I have heard my friend Howard Hendricks call him "the man with an oily disposition." Barnabas is the builder-up of men. He is the same one, in fact, who earlier had searched for and found Paul when the other disciples were suspicious of Paul's recent conversion. When one who had been persecuting Christians said, "I've become a Christian," the other Christians sneered, "No, we don't trust that." But it was Barnabas who found Paul, believed in him, vouched for him, and won a hearing for Paul. It was Barnabas who was responsible for introducing him to the Christian community. Giving people a chance was Barnabas's style. Naturally, he felt it would be best to give John Mark another chance.

Not Paul. His style was altogether different. He was a man of great conviction and strong commitment to the truth, the one who founded more churches than anyone in the history of Scripture. Paul was the trailblazer who set the pace for missionary ministries to this day, a man of discipline and determination . . . more of the shape-up-or-ship-out mentality. Paul looked at the issue from the viewpoint of the overall good of the ministry. Barnabas looked at the issue from the viewpoint of the overall good of the man. Barnabas saw it as the classic opportunity to restore John Mark's confidence. It is not an oversimplification to say that Paul was led by his head, Barnabas by his heart. That is why we read, "Barnabas was desirous of taking John, called Mark." He thought, *Why, he could become a great disciple of Christ. We can't leave him here with his memories, licking his wounds, feeling ashamed, and badgered by remorse. That would kill him! We've got to bring him along.* Paul strongly disagreed: "There is no way!"

A close reading of the next verse reveals the intensity of Paul's feelings: "But Paul kept insisting that they should not take him along who had deserted them in Pamphylia and had not gone with them to the work" (v. 38). The Greek term translated "deserted" is the term from which we get *apostasized.* In Paul's mind, Mark had done more than back off and bail out . . . the young man had apostasized. *He was unfaithful once, and I've learned in dealing with defectors that you can't trust them once they blow it, certainly not as royally as John Mark blew it.* Paul had no room in his future plans for John Mark . . . at least not now.

Unless I miss my guess, you are leaning in favor of Barnabas, right? I understand, and I am tempted to agree. However, I am reminded of a proverb we would be wise to consider: "Like a bad tooth and an unsteady foot is confidence in a faithless man in time of trouble" (Prov. 25:19).

Franz Delitzsch, the reliable and reasonable German scholar, amplifies the verse to say: "He who, in time of need, makes a faithless man his ground of confidence, is like one who seeks to bite with a broken tooth and one who supports himself on a shaking leg, and thus stumbles and falls."[4]

Before you start feeling too magnanimous and greathearted, let me ask you if you have ever loaned money to somebody who never paid it back. Let's say the debt is still outstanding. My question is this: Would you be desirous of loaning that person money again if you had a chance? Probably not. Suddenly the issue is clearer.

Why? Because confidence in an unfaithful man in time of trouble is a shaky thing. He stumbled and fell once . . . he's still not paid you back, and chances are good he will do the same again. Paul's reasoning is, "What if he defects again and one of us gets hurt . . . or it has an impact on the lost souls we're ministering to? What if his action gains public sentiment and several in the church begin to be persuaded that John Mark has a better plan, leaving the home church polarized?" It's risky, no doubt about it.

Paul has a point. If you see only Barnabas's side, chances are good you have never been in a rugged place in ministry and had a partner fail you. Nothing hurts quite like that. I am not saying I vote for Paul or that I vote for Barnabas. I am really saying I see both sides, which highlights my earlier comment that both sides have validity.

Was it really a severe argument? Verse 39 states that the conflict resulted in a "sharp disagreement." It is the Greek word *paroxysm*. Interestingly, our English word is a transliterated Greek word. "There arose such a paroxysm." One Webster's dictionary says a paroxysm is "a sudden attack, as in a disease." It is a convulsion, a violent emotion. There arose such a clash of wills the rift could not be mended. The final outcome? They agreed to disagree. As Scripture states, "They separated from one another."

The Permanent Separation

The fact is that the two men never ministered together again. They reached such a stalemate in their argument that one said, "I'm going this way," the other, "I'm going that way." If you take a map and study where each went, you will see they traveled in opposite directions—Barnabas and John Mark took to the sea and traveled to Cyprus; Paul and Silas (his new partner) stayed on the land and went northeast toward Syria, then swept over toward the west as they came to Cilicia and the other cities.

There was a loss of temper. There was an outburst of unrecorded, strong words. I am glad all the words are not recorded in the passage of Scripture, just as you and I are glad that our words in a violent outburst of a recent paroxysm were not recorded, right? I don't want to diminish the heat of their disagreement. There was a strong, highly charged debate between these two men of God.

One writer offers an imaginary dialogue that could have occurred that day between Paul and Barnabas.

PAUL   John Mark? We can't take him. He failed us last time.

BARNABAS   But that was last time.

PAUL   He's likely to fail us again. He's a deserter.

BARNABAS   He's had time to think it over. We've got to give him another chance. He's got the makings of a great missionary.

PAUL   Tell me, Barnabas, isn't it because he's your cousin that you want to take him again?

BARNABAS   That's not fair. You know I've tried to help many people who aren't related to me. I'm convinced this lad needs understanding and encouragement. He could be a great evangelist some day.

PAUL   We need someone who can stand up to persecution, an angry mob, beatings, perhaps jail. Our team has to be close-knit, thoroughly reliable. How can we trust a lad who failed like John Mark? No, Barnabas. Recall the word of the Master, "No man who puts his hand to the plow and looks back is fit for the kingdom of God."

BARNABAS   I've talked to him about his failure. I'm sure he won't defect again. To refuse him might do spiritual damage at the moment of his repentance. It'd be like breaking a bruised reed, like quenching smoking flax.

PAUL   It's too soon to trust him.

BARNABAS   Paul, remember how soon after your conversion I took a chance on you. The apostles were afraid of you, thinking you were faking your conversion in order to infiltrate the church at Jerusalem. I didn't make you prove yourself first. I'd rather not keep John Mark waiting. I vouch for him now.[5]

It could have been more passionate than that. Keep in mind that these are longtime friends. They had had significant years of ministry together. Their roots went way back. I have wondered if they might have been boyhood friends. Each of them owed the other a great deal. Barnabas had stood for Paul, and Paul had stood for Barnabas. In a burst of emotions mixed with conflicting convictions, their ministry together screeches to a halt, and they go in opposite directions.

If you have never had this happen, you cannot imagine the pain of it, especially if it happens between you and a coworker in ministry. Don't minimize the conflict. It's painful beyond description. All is not lost, however. I remind you, the upside of it is that this is how new churches or seminaries are sometimes started. This is sometimes how campus ministries are expanded. Disagreements prompt fresh starts, new works, broader visions. The event that caused it to happen isn't good. It is more like a rock hitting a placid lake, creating a sudden wake where there are hurt feelings, at least initially. But the ripples continue until people are greathearted enough to forget the pain and stop licking their wounds and proceed into new directions.

Who knows what ministries took place in Cyprus and regions beyond, thanks to the new missionary team, Barnabas and Mark? Furthermore, it was John Mark who wrote the Gospel of Mark. Even Paul stated at the end of his life, "Pick up Mark and bring him with you, for he is useful to me for service" (2 Tim. 4:11). And he later writes favorably of Barnabas as well. Paul was too much of a man of grace to spend the rest of his life nursing a wound.

A. T. Robertson is right: "No one can rightly blame Barnabas for giving his cousin John Mark a second chance nor Paul for fearing to risk him again. One's judgment may go with Paul, but one's heart goes with Barnabas. . . . Paul and Barnabas parted in anger and both in sorrow. Paul owed more to Barnabas than to any other man. Barnabas was leaving the greatest spirit of the time and of all times."[6]

I hope we never forget something that is recorded in the final verse of the Acts 15 account. After Barnabas took Mark and set sail for Cyprus, "Paul chose Silas and departed, being committed by the brethren to the grace of the Lord" (Acts 15:40).

One wonders if someone in the church didn't say, "Now, Paul, don't spend the rest of your life taking shots at Barnabas. You can handle this. Get over it and press on. Get on with it. It will take grace . . . the grace of the Lord."

It is interesting to me that the church does not commend Barnabas but commends Paul. I rather believe that they chose to side with Paul because they committed Paul to the new journey and not Barnabas. Maybe Barnabas left that night. Perhaps he chose not to stay around to negotiate his way through that minefield of opinions in the church at Antioch. The best part of all is that both of these strong-minded men got over the disagreement. That, too, takes enormous grace.

In too many cases the battle goes on and on and on, and the ministry becomes fractured because the opposing parties are not big enough to get over the initial hurt. Many people today emotionally are sitting in dark rooms, eaten up with bitterness because of an argument that they had with someone a long time ago. They feel they were humiliated, or they feel they weren't listened to. How many are living out their lives with their spiritual shades drawn, thinking to themselves, *I'll have nothing more to do with the church,* because of an argument they witnessed or maybe participated in? We need to be people who can disagree in grace and then press on, even if the disagreement leads to a separation.

Let me share a few things I have learned over the years that have to do with disagreements or with relating to those with whom I may not dot the same "i" or cross the same "t" theologically. To save time, I'll be specific and to the point. I'm not a hard-line, five-point Calvinist. However, I have no trouble calling those who do embrace this viewpoint my brothers and sisters in the faith. In fact, I continue to minister with them, and they with me. On more than one occasion I invited those who represent reformed theology to speak in our pulpit in Fullerton. I have no problem with that whatsoever. I love those folks! I don't see it as an issue worth breaking fellowship over. Grace covers the difference.

Here's another grace-binding example: I'm not a charismatic. However, I don't feel it is my calling to shoot great volleys of theological artillery at my charismatic brothers and sisters. Who knows how much good they have done and the magnificent ministries many of them have? The church I pastor is not a charismatic church. The doctrinal roots of our church are not in that camp—probably never will be. But that does not mean that we break fellowship with individuals who are of that persuasion or that we take potshots at them. There was a time in my life when I would have done that. Thankfully, I've grown up a little and learned that

God uses many of them, in song as well as in writing and in pulpits today. Grace helps to hold us close.

I do not embrace covenant theology, but I have a number of pastor friends who are covenant theologians. Some of them are in my circle of friends in the ministry. We disagree on certain points of doctrine, but we're on the same team. We're going to spend eternity together. We're going to meet the Lord in the air (whether they believe it or not!). So we might as well enjoy each other's company on earth.

I have a friend who jokingly says he is so premillennial he doesn't even eat Post Toasties in the morning. Well, God bless him . . . I'm just not that extreme. I happen to be premillennial and pretribulational in my theological position, but I don't see that as an issue worth breaking Christian fellowship over. The deity of Christ is certainly crucial. And the inerrancy of Scripture as well as a few other crucial issues. But most of the things we would name are not. Let's face it, there are far more things that draw us together than separate us.

The words of C. S. Lewis come to my mind. Following his conversion in 1929, he wrote to a friend: "When all is said (and truly said) about divisions of Christendom, there remains, by God's mercy, an enormous common ground."[7] In light of this, my encouragement for you today is that each one of us should pursue what unites us with others rather than the few things that separate us. The "common ground" is vast. It's high time we focus on that. It will take grace, I remind you.

I speak at a number of different schools, including Christian schools and colleges, seminaries, and secular universities. Even though I would not necessarily endorse or encourage someone to study at some of these schools, it does not mean that I should not speak there or minister there or ask God to use me as I minister there. Grace frees me to disagree with others and to speak openly of Christ even in places that disagree with me.

There was a time in my life when I had answers to questions no one was asking. I had a position that was so rigid I would fight for every jot and tittle. I mean, I couldn't list enough things that I'd die for. The older I get, the shorter that list gets, frankly.

As I mentioned at the beginning of this chapter, I am learning that growing old gracefully and graciously is an important assignment. If I lose an argument, I should lose it graciously. If I win an argument, I am to accept it humbly. The most important thing is to glorify God—win or lose.

MODELING GRACE THROUGH DISAGREEABLE TIMES

I close this chapter with several comments that may help you handle future disagreeable times in a gracious manner.

First, *always leave room for an opposing viewpoint.* If you don't have room for an opposing viewpoint, you're not going to do well when you have teenagers. Teens can be among our best teachers. I know ours have been. They haven't always been right, nor have I. However, I have learned in rearing teenagers that they are great at pointing out another point of view, if nothing else than just to make me think, just to challenge me, just to remind me that there is another way of viewing things. I can assure you, it has helped me in my ministry. It has certainly helped me in my relationship with those to whom I am personally accountable. Opposition is good for our humility.

Second, *if an argument must occur, don't assassinate.* An argument—even a strong clash—is one thing, but killing folks is another. I have seen individuals in an argument verbally hit below the belt and assault another's character. I've seen a lot of mudslinging happen in arguments related to the work of the church. I've seen brutal character assassinations occur in the name of religion—in public speaking as well as in writing—and they are all ugly memories. No need for that. If we must fight, let's fight fair.

Third, *if you don't get your way, get over it and get on with life.* If you don't get your way in a vote at a church, get over it. The vote was taken (if the church has integrity, the vote was handled with fairness); now get on with it. Just press on. And don't rehearse the fight or the vote year after year. The work of God slows down when we are not big enough to take it on the chin and say, "We lost!" Having been raised in the South, I didn't know the South lost the Civil War until I was in junior high school . . . and even then it was debatable among my teachers. Be big enough to say, "We lost." Grace will help.

Fourth, *sometimes the best solution is a separation.* There is good biblical support for this, remember. Paul and Barnabas simply couldn't go on together, so they separated. If I can't go on with the way things are in a particular ministry, I need to resign! But in doing so, I should not drag people through my unresolved conflicts because I didn't get my way. If separation is the best solution, doing it graciously is essential. If your disagreements are starting to outweigh your agreements, you ought to give strong consideration to pulling out. Who knows? This may be God's way of moving you to another dimension of ministry.

This chapter has been helpful for me personally. That may seem unusual, but occasionally an author needs to read his stuff with enough objectivity that it speaks directly to him. Through the years, disagreements voiced by various sources about matters of opinion have been intense. Some things especially have been hard to hear and painful to read. Cynthia and I have bitten our tongues on more than one occasion and refused to defend ourselves. In some cases we have been misrepresented, and though we've made a few attempts to correct the perception, misunderstanding persists. Erroneous statements and exaggerated rumors designed to discredit our ministry occasionally resurface. And it's painful. Things have been said against us that have caused some to question our credibility, which makes it difficult to stay silent and go on in grace. But we shall. Our confidence is that God will vindicate our integrity.

I now realize that the pain has been great because grace has been absent in so much of what others have thought, said, and written. But God gives grace for such times as these. What Cynthia and I must do is draw upon it, claim it, and give it in return . . . in abundance. I am convinced that God's grace will see us through those occasions, even when others disagree. It always has.

And so . . . graciously disagreeing, we press on. It's all part of practicing what one preaches, right?

10

Grace: Up Close and Personal

BESIDES THE BIBLE, perhaps the greatest book ever written was *The Pilgrim's Progress*. Those who are not familiar with this seventeenth-century classic would be surprised to know it was written by a man enduring his third term in jail. The first time, he was in for six long years, the second time, for another six. The reason for both of those times behind bars was the same: preaching the gospel of Jesus Christ. When he returned for a third sentence, John Bunyan, a tinker from Bedford, England, was led by God to write his immortal work. Like Handel when composing his musical magnum opus, *Messiah*, Bunyan's pen moved rapidly. As one man described it, "It moved, indeed, with the speed of a dream—and the dream became a book."[1]

The book, published over three hundred years ago, has touched lives literally around the globe. Who can imagine the multiple millions of copies, the numerous translations that have been released? Everywhere I turn, I find others who, like me, have worn out more than one copy and still find delight in returning to the volume for personal enrichment. I reserve this endorsement for very few books, but I would say without hesitation that it is a creative masterpiece where biblical truth is made relevant for any generation.

It is the fascinating story of a man called Christian whose pilgrimage from earth to heaven, from sin to salvation is full of all the struggles and pitfalls life could throw at him. Following his incredible journey, he reaches his long-awaited destination, the "paradise of God." From start to finish, Christian must deal with friend and foe alike, all of whom have descriptive names, like Evangelist, Help, Interpreter—who encourage him in his "progress"—and Pliable, Obstinate, Hypocrisy, Apollyon, a giant named Despair, and many others—who hinder him.

Of special trouble to Christian is Legality, whose dwelling, as you would imagine, was Mount Sinai. In the earlier part of his journey, Christian is traveling with a heavy pack on his back (sin), and none of those who worked against him could help relieve him of his burden . . . especially Legality, as one part states:

> This Legality . . . is not able to set thee free from the burden. No man was as yet ever rid of his burden by him; no, nor ever is like to be: ye cannot be justified by the works of the law.[2]

Shortly after encountering Legality, Christian is led by Interpreter into a large room full of dust. It had never been swept since the day it was built. Bunyan does a superb job describing how the room was swept and cleaned:

> Then he took him by the hand, and led him into a very large parlor that was full of dust, because never swept; the which after he had reviewed a little while, the *Interpreter* called for a man to sweep. Now, when he began to sweep, the dust began so abundantly to fly about, that Christian had almost therewith been choked. Then said the *Interpreter* to a damsel that stood by,

Bring hither the water, and sprinkle the room; the which, when she had done, it was swept and cleansed with pleasure.

Then said *Christian*, What means this?

The *Interpreter* answered, This parlor is the heart of a man that was never sanctified by the sweet grace of the gospel; the dust is his original sin and inward corruptions, that have defiled the whole man. He that began to sweep at first, is the *Law*; but she that brought water, and did sprinkle it, is the *Gospel*. Now, whereas thou sawest, that so soon as the first began to sweep, the dust did so fly about that the room by him could not be cleansed, but that thou wast almost choked therewith; this is to shew thee, that the law, instead of cleansing the heart (by its working) from sin, doth revive, put strength into, and increase it in the soul, even as it doth discover and forbid it, for it doth not give power to subdue.

Again, as thou sawest the damsel sprinkle the room with water, upon which it was cleansed with pleasure; this is to shew thee, that when the gospel comes in the sweet and precious influences thereof to the heart, then, I say, even as thou sawest the damsel lay the dust by sprinkling the floor with water, so is sin vanquished and subdued, and the soul made clean through the faith of it, and consequently fit for the King of glory to inhabit.[3]

It took *grace*, "the sweet grace of the gospel," to cleanse that room of all its defilements. It still does.

All those familiar with *The Pilgrim's Progress* have no trouble remembering that the pilgrim's name throughout the book is Christian. To my surprise, few remember his original name, even though it is plainly stated in the allegory. In the scene where it first appears, the pilgrim is conversing with a porter:

PORTER   What is your name?

PILGRIM   My name is now *Christian*, but my name at the first was Graceless.[4]

The same could be said for all of us today who claim the glorious name of Jesus Christ as our Lord and Savior. Our name is now Christian, but it has not always been so. That title was given to us the moment we believed, the day we took God at His word and accepted the gift of eternal life He offered us. Prior to the name change, we were Graceless, indeed.

My question is this: Now that Christ has come into our lives and ripped that heavy pack of sin off our backs, are we now full of grace? Having been Graceless for so many years, are we "grace conscious," are we "grace aware," are we experiencing a "grace awakening," are we truly becoming "grace-full"? Models of grace are needed now more than ever.

THE PROCESS THAT LEADS TO GRACE AWAKENING

Want a boost of encouragement? Our God is working toward that end in all of His children. It is His constant pursuit, His daily agenda, as He points us toward our final destination, "the Celestial City," as Bunyan calls it. Having cleansed our hearts of the debris of inward corruptions and the dust of sin's domination, God is now daily at work awakening grace within us, perfecting our character and bringing it to completion. Let me show you from four New Testament sources why I am so sure of that:

> And we know that God causes all things to work together for good to those who love God, to those who are called according to His purpose. For whom He foreknew, He also predestined to become conformed to the image of His Son, that He might be the first-born among many brethren. (Rom. 8:28–29)

> For I am confident of this very thing, that He who began a good work in you will perfect it until the day of Christ Jesus. (Phil. 1:6)

Who will transform the body of our humble state into conformity with the body of His glory, by the exertion of the power that He has even to subject all things to Himself. (Phil. 3:21)

Do not lie to one another, since you laid aside the old self with its evil practices, and have put on the new self who is being renewed to a true knowledge according to the image of the One who created him. (Col. 3:9–10)

Don't miss those key phrases: "become conformed," "He who began . . . will perfect" (bring to completion), "transform," and "being renewed." We are all engaged in the same process, our own "pilgrim's progress," under God's mighty hand and constant surveillance. He is working for us, not against us, and His plans are for good, not evil. His goal for us is clearly set forth: that we might become like His Son, "full of grace and truth."

As I think about our becoming people of awakening grace, I believe at least three things are involved in the process:

First, *it takes time.* Learning anything takes time. Becoming good models of grace takes years, it seems! Like wisdom, it comes slowly. God is in no hurry as He purges graceless characteristics from us. But we can count on this, for sure: He is persistent.

Second, *it requires pain.* The "dust" in our room doesn't settle easily. I know of no one who has adopted a "grace state of mind" painlessly. Hurt is part of the curriculum in God's schoolroom.

Third, *it means change.* Being "graceless" by nature, we find it difficult to be anything different. We lack it, we resist it, we fail to show it, but God never stops His relentless working. He is committed to our becoming more like His Son. Remember? "He who began a good work . . . *will* bring it to completion" (NIV, emphasis mine).

SOME EVERYDAY EXAMPLES OF CLAIMING GRACE

In *Mere Christianity* by C. S. Lewis we read:

> The real Son of God is at your side. He is beginning to turn you into the
> same kind of thing as Himself. He is beginning, so to speak, to "inject" His
> kind of life and thought . . . into you; beginning to turn the tin soldier into
> a live man. The part of you that does not like it is the part that is still tin.[5]

I am intrigued by the word picture painted by C. S. Lewis. While pon-
dering the thought of those areas that are "still tin" in my own life, I realized that *that* is where I must claim the grace of God. All of us could say
the same thing. And so I pulled my concordance off the shelf, located the
word *grace,* and began to study the places in the New Testament that
addressed or illustrated some common, everyday examples of "tin" where
most of us are still in need of claiming God's grace. I found five very tender spots where help is needed from our Lord: insecurity, weakness, abrasiveness, compromise, and pride. I realize these are all intensely personal
battles, but if grace doesn't come to our rescue up close and personal, who
needs it? And so, for the next few pages let's allow this soothing oil to
touch some of the "tin" in our lives. Maybe by bringing grace up this close
and making it personal, we'll be able to get rid of a few rusty spots that
have been a plague long enough. I hope it will help accelerate our own
pilgrim's progress toward an awakening of Christlike grace:

1. *Claiming the grace to be what I am* (the "tin" of insecurity)

> After that He appeared to more than five hundred brethren at one time,
> most of whom remain until now, but some have fallen asleep; then He
> appeared to James, then to all the apostles; and last of all, as it were to one
> untimely born, He appeared to me also. For I am the least of the apostles,
> who am not fit to be called an apostle, because I persecuted the church of

God. But by the grace of God I am what I am, and His grace toward me did not prove vain; but I labored even more than all of them, yet not I, but the grace of God with me. Whether then it was I or they, so we preach and so you believed. (1 Cor. 15:6–11)

In my years of ministry, during which I have rubbed shoulders with numerous Christians, I have observed that many of God's servants are afraid to be who they are. Granted, I find some who haven't a clue as to their own identity (since they are so busy pleasing people), but the majority are in another category: they know, but they are uncomfortable letting the truth be known. They are concerned about things such as their image, or what someone might think or say, or more often, "If they knew the *real* me, they wouldn't like me."

The scripture I just recorded is helpful. Paul writes candidly of his own poor track record. After listing the gallery of the "greats" to whom the risen Lord appeared (James and the apostles), he states "last of all . . . He appeared to me." This is not false humility; it's historical fact. But what speaks with vivid eloquence is how Paul refers to himself as "one untimely born." You may be shocked to know the Greek term refers to one born before the full period of gestation—one who was aborted—literally, "the dead fetus." It means one who was totally devoid of spiritual life.

If that isn't enough, Paul sees himself not simply as among the last but "least" of the apostles, having been one who persecuted the church. While those others he names were defending and building up the body, he was hard at work assaulting it, hoping to destroy it. That is Paul's estimation of himself when he stands alongside those men of God. That could have done a number on the man's self-esteem, but it didn't. While not denying the reality of his dark side, Paul refused to cringe and hide, crippled by feelings of insecurity. Why? The answer is clear: grace. God's awakening, invigorating grace changed his whole perspective. "But by the grace of God I am what I am, and His grace toward me did not prove vain; but I labored even more than all of them, yet not I, but the grace of God with me" (1 Cor. 15:10).

Grace made him what he was. Grace gave him courage to be who he was. Grace energized him to accomplish what he did. By realizing that he did not deserve and could never earn the privileges given him, Paul was freed to be exactly who he was and do precisely what he was called to do. Grace became his silent partner, his constant traveling companion, his invisible security, since he (in himself) was in no way deserving of the part he played in God's unfolding drama. I cannot help but mention that he refused to compare himself to and compete with his peers. Grace relieves us of all that. I love the way one commentary describes it: "In spite of his unfitness to bear the name, the grace of God has made him equal to it. The persecutor has been forgiven and the abortion adopted."[6]

If insecurity happens to be the "tin" in your life, I suggest large doses of grace applied daily. Bring it up close and personal. You will find that grace has healing power, bringing soothing relief. If it worked for Paul the persecutor, I can assure you it works for insecure pilgrims today.

2. *Claiming the grace to learn from what I suffer* (the "tin" of weakness)

And because of the surpassing greatness of the revelations, for this reason, to keep me from exalting myself, there was given me a thorn in the flesh, a messenger of Satan to buffet me—to keep me from exalting myself! Concerning this I entreated the Lord three times that it might depart from me. And He has said to me, "My grace is sufficient for you, for power is perfected in weakness." Most gladly, therefore, I will rather boast about my weaknesses, that the power of Christ may dwell in me. Therefore I am well content with weaknesses, with insults, with distresses, with persecutions, with difficulties, for Christ's sake; for when I am weak, then I am strong. (2 Cor. 12:7–10)

Another undeniable struggle all of us live with is our own human weaknesses, which crop up any number of ways again and again. We suffer. We hurt. We fail. We blow it. We feel bad. Medication won't relieve it. Prayer doesn't remove it. Complaining doesn't help it. Our problem? We are just human! Imperfection dogs our steps.

In Paul's case he lived with the "thorn," some form of excruciating pain that refused to leave except on rare occasions. When it returned, it never failed to leave him weak and feeling terribly human. How could he go on in spite of such suffering? The answer is the same as before: grace.

It was grace that made him "content with weaknesses." Once that contentment came, strength revived within him. Not even insults, distresses, or persecutions could sideline the apostle once grace gave him contentment in weakness.

It works not only for a first-century apostle-missionary; it works for us today. By not hiding or denying our weaknesses, others are made to feel closer to us. Vulnerability invites people in, helps them identify with and feel comfortable around us. Grace enables us to admit our struggles. When we find contentment even in our weaknesses, the anxiety that accompanies keeping up a good front vanishes, freeing us to be real. You don't have to rely any longer on power ties or a certain brand of wristwatch or alligator-skin shoes. How easy for those things to become unspoken grace killers.

I appreciate it when professional athletes don't hide their weaknesses, don't you? When we watch them perform with such dexterity and accuracy, we can easily believe that all parts of their lives are that slick and polished. When we lived in Boston back in the mid-1960s, Bill Russell was the star basketball center for the world-champion Celtics. It was fun watching him and his team play at the Boston Garden. He dominated the boards, and with effortless ease, he seemed to take charge of the whole court once the game got underway. The whole team revolved around his larger-than-life presence. Sports fans watched him from a distance, respecting his command of the sport. Then, in a radio interview, I heard a comment from Russell that immediately made me feel closer to him, though I have never met the man. The sports reporter asked the all-pro basketball star if he ever got nervous. Russell's answer was surprising. He said, in his inimitable style of blunt honesty, "Before every game, I vomit." Shocked, the sportscaster asked what he did if they played two games the same day. Unflappable Russell replied, "I vomit twice." All of a sudden the man no longer seemed like a specimen of athletic perfection . . . he had weaknesses too.

We have nothing to hide when it comes to the fragile and imperfect areas of our lives. Say it! Admit it! Grace will help you do so. It will get you safely through. Remember John Newton's lines:

> Through many dangers, toils, and snares
> I have already come;
> 'Tis grace hath brought me safe thus far,
> And grace will lead me home.[7]

Not self-effort, not perfectionism. (May God help you who are perfectionists and those who live with you. Both need tons of grace.) I heard the other day that a perfectionist is a person who takes pains and gives them to others. Grace will help you let the cracks of your life show. Let them show! No one can identify with those who give the impression of nothing but flawless performances and slick success. We can all identify with failure and imperfection. And God has ways of honoring those times.

I remember preaching a sermon during which I was struggling with a sore throat and laryngitis. I could not raise my voice above a whisper. So I thought, *I'll save my voice by whispering.* (I learned later that is the worst possible thing I could have done for my voice, but I didn't know it then.) When

I finished that sermon, I wanted to run. I felt my delivery was terrible. I thought it was the worst job I had ever done. Then something surprising happened. I don't know how many people contacted me later and said, "You'll never know how that ministered to me." There I was in obvious physical weakness and pain . . . hindered, restrained by something I could not control or stop. Yet it became encouragement to others, especially those who said they wondered if I ever struggled with weaknesses. Immediately they could identify with me rather than view me from a distance in some sort of unrealistic admiration. I think you see my point: grace in weakness enables us to become instruments of power in God's hands.

3. *Claiming the grace to respond to what I encounter* (the "tin" of abrasiveness)

> Conduct yourselves with wisdom toward outsiders, making the most of the opportunity. Let your speech always be with grace, seasoned, as it were, with salt, so that you may know how you should respond to each person. (Col. 4:5–6)

This "grace" has to do with our response to people. Have you noticed that life is really a series of responses? We spend our days responding to the lost who do not know the Savior, responding to those who are fellow members of the body, responding to children, to parents, to friends, to those in need, to colleagues at work, and to fellow students at school. In light of that, did you notice what Paul writes about the tendency toward abrasiveness, this "tin man" in all of us? He mentions the need for wisdom, talk seasoned with salt, the right kind of response to others. *Salt* here probably carries with it the idea of good taste, tactfulness, well-timed words. Grace will give us that and much more, like pleasantness. Let your speech always be attractive, charming, winsome, pleasant. When it comes to having words like that, grace is a master.

If I had the power in my hand to touch and heal one part of the body of Christ, I would touch the tongue, certainly including my own. It is the tongue that spreads more diseases in the body than any other organ—specifically, when it lacks grace, which gives needed tact. "Tact is like a girdle. It enables you to organize the awkward truth more attractively."[8] Truth alone can be a bit harsh and abrasive. Occasionally it is too sharp, sometimes brutal. There is nothing like a nice supply of grace to make the truth attractive. Grace helps us cushion our words so that the truth can be received without needless offense.

> Tactfulness is an approach to another human being which involves being sincere and open in communication while at the same time showing respect for the other person's feelings—and taking care not to hurt him unnecessarily. . . . It involves a trust or faith in the other person and communicates this message: I trust you will be able to handle what I'm going to tell you. I respect your feelings and will do my best to guard against my own destructive tendencies so that I don't hurt you unnecessarily.[9]

While I am on the subject of tact, an antidote for abrasiveness, this is a good time for me to mention the importance of a good sense of humor. If there is anything that will help strengthen the charming magnet of grace, it is the ability to laugh at oneself, to laugh at life, to find humor in everyday encounters with people. Talk about sprinkling salt to enhance the taste! Humor works like magic.

One of my long-term friends and mentors, Howard Hendricks, is a master at this. I have loved him and listened to him for over forty years! Time and again I've seen him warm up hundreds of people packed in the same room—very few of them knowing each other—by his winsome words, usually spiced with humor. What an ambassador of grace! If I have learned nothing else from the man, I have learned the importance of speaking the truth forcefully and clearly, yet in a nondestructive manner. Have you observed that some communicators virtually bludgeon people with the Bible? Never my friend Howard Hendricks. And it is amazing to see how people open up once they know we care about their feelings. Who was it? Mary Poppins, I think, who said, "A spoonful of sugar makes the medicine go down." If abrasiveness happens to be some of the "tin" you wrestle with, grace added to your speech will help you respond to whatever you encounter.

4.   *Claiming the grace to stand for what I believe* (the "tin" of compromise)

> Remember those who led you, who spoke the word of God to you; and considering the result of their conduct, imitate their faith. Jesus Christ is the same yesterday and today, yes and forever. Do not be carried away by varied and strange teachings; for it is good for the heart to be strengthened by grace, not by foods, through which those who were thus occupied were not benefited. (Heb. 13:7–9)

The writer is bringing his thoughts to a close. In doing so he addresses a concern on his heart, namely the tendency on the part of some to give up the faith because times are hard. Persecutions are abounding. Martyrdom is occurring. And some are wondering, *Have I really believed in vain? Should I continue this Christian walk?* Some, in fact, are recanting. And so the writer takes up his pen to encourage them to keep standing for what they believe. "Don't give up! Don't concede. Don't surrender." It is the tendency to compromise that concerns him.

That same tendency is present in every generation, certainly our own. While sitting snugly in church, surrounded by fellow Christians, we feel as strong and determined as a steer in a blizzard. We feel as if we would die for our faith. Yet twenty-four hours later, in the midst of our work, we're surrounded by those who hate the faith. It would be eye-opening to find out how many of these faith haters know we are Christians. In the workplace, there is the tendency to concede, to stay quiet when the subject of faith surfaces. Haven't you wondered why? The answer is here . . . we lack grace. Maybe you never realized it before, but grace strengthens us. It strengthens our hearts, awakens in us the courage to stand firm. How? What is it about grace that gives us strength to stand up for what we believe? Maybe it is because grace keeps us from being what we are not. Maybe it is the authenticity it prompts within us. Grace strips away the tin, rips off the masks, helps us to be ourselves so that when we speak of our faith it rings true. Could it be that you compromise your faith where you work or where you go to school because you've tried to appear to be something you're not? Grace is so relieving, so strengthening, it removes the phony.

So far we have uncovered four areas of "tin" commonly found in ourselves: insecurity, weakness, abrasiveness, and compromise. No one can argue that we need grace up close and personal to come to terms with each. But the list is incomplete without my including a final area that plagues us all.

5. *Claiming the grace to submit to what I need* (the "tin" of pride)

But He gives a greater grace. Therefore it says, "GOD IS OPPOSED TO THE PROUD, BUT GIVES GRACE TO THE HUMBLE." Submit therefore to God. Resist the devil and he will flee from you. (James 4:6–7)

You younger men, likewise, be subject to your elders; and all of you, clothe yourselves with humility toward one another, for GOD IS OPPOSED TO THE PROUD, BUT GIVES GRACE TO THE HUMBLE. (1 Pet. 5:5)

Both of those New Testament scriptures find their source in Proverbs 3:34: "Though He scoffs at the scoffers, / Yet He gives grace to the afflicted."

Charles Bridges, a fine nineteenth-century student of the Old Testament, writes: "On no point is the mind of God more fully declared than against pride. . . . A *lowly* spirit—a deep conviction of utter nothingness . . . is a most adorning grace. Nor is it an occasional or temporary feeling . . . but a habit, 'clothing' the man . . . 'from the sole of the foot to the head.' . . . He pours it [grace] out plentifully upon humble hearts."[10]

Few qualities are more stubbornly persistent within us than pride. It is ever present! I find it absolutely amazing that we who deserve to have been left as aborted fetuses and not given life (as Paul put it earlier) should have anything to feel proud about. Nevertheless, pride is always there, ever ready to defend itself. It is also clever. It has the ability to go underground and mask its ugliness in subtle, quiet ways. Because it doesn't fit the Christian life for anyone to be overtly proud, we find our pride in other ways: our work, our salaries, our prestige, our power and influence, our titles, our clothing, our approach to people, our tendency to manipulate. It is all so unattractive, so inappropriate. As powerful as any influence, pride is a classic grace killer.

But let it be understood that God will not bless what springs from pride. As Scripture repeatedly reminds us, He brings His mighty hand down over our lives and presses His sovereign fingers into areas where it hurts. We sigh, we squirm, we struggle, and (hopefully) we lay hold of grace and finally submit. What blessed submission! It is in those hurting areas where we cannot handle it on our own that God does His very best work.

George Matheson of Scotland echoes the discipline of his personal despair in his book *Thoughts for Life's Journey* when he writes:

My soul, reject not the place of thy prostration! It has ever been the robing room for royalty. Ask the great ones of the past what has been the spot of their prosperity; they will say, "It was the cold ground on which I once was laying." Ask Abraham; he will point you to the sacrifice of Moriah. Ask Joseph; he will direct you to his dungeon. Ask Moses; he will date his fortune from his danger in the Nile. Ask Ruth; she will bid you build her monument on the field of her toil. Ask David; he will tell you that his songs came from the night. Ask Job; he will remind you that God answered him out of the whirlwind. Ask Peter; he will extol his submission in the sea. Ask John; he will give the palm to Patmos. Ask Paul he will attribute his inspiration to the light that struck him blind. Ask one more—the Son of Man. Ask Him whence has come His rule over the world. He will answer, "From the cold ground on which I was lying—the Gethsemane ground; I received my sceptre there." Thou too, my soul, shalt be garlanded by Gethsemane. The cup thou fain wouldst pass from thee will be thy coronet in the sweet by-and-by. The hour of thy loneliness will crown thee. The day of thy depression will regale thee. It is the *desert* that will break forth into singing; it is the trees of thy silent *forest* that will clasp their hands.[11]

My fellow pilgrim, is the progress more painful than you expected? Thinking you were in for a Disneyland experience, have you been surprised to find yourself on cold, barren ground—lonely, depressed, and broken? Are you beginning to wonder if you are on the wrong road? Trust me, you are not. God is at work in you. His "mighty hand" is above you. His love is around you. His grace is available to you. Awake and claim it.

George Matheson and John Bunyan both would agree: you are in the "robing room for royalty."[12] The tailor's name is Grace . . . and when you are perfectly fitted, the process will end.

11

Are You Really A *Minister of Grace?*

THIS CHAPTER IS DEDICATED TO ALL WHO ARE IN MINISTRY.
I realize that statement prompts most of you to think, *Well, that leaves me out. I'm not a preacher, I'm not an evangelist or a missionary, I don't work for a church.* Let me clarify that my opening comment has to do with all who are in ministry, not just those in vocational Christian service. By "ministry" I am including anyone who serves some segment of the body of Christ on a consistent basis.

Perhaps you are a teacher of a class, an elected officer in a church, or maybe you're a counselor, a Christian speaker, a musician. Maybe you are involved in Christian education or camping . . . *whatever.* You may or may not earn your living from this source of activity, but you are deliberately and regularly engaged in some form of ministry-related involvement that influences others, most of whom are believers in Jesus Christ. You are the target of my thoughts throughout this eleventh chapter.

Now that I have your attention, I want to ask you a crucial question, which only you can answer: Are you really a minister of grace? This could be asked in a variety of other ways:

- When you do what you do, do you dispense grace?
- Are the people you serve given the freedom to be who they are, or do you force them to be who you expect them to be?
- Do you let others go, or do you smother them . . . control them?
- Would folks feel intimidated or relieved in your presence?
- Are you cultivating spontaneous, creative celebrants or fearful captives?
- Do you encourage, build up, and affirm those to whom you minister?

It's time to take off the gloves, rip off the masks, knock off the rationalizations, and face the truth head-on. Are you one who models and ministers grace or not? Is what you're doing the work of your own flesh energized by your own strength? Are you relying on your charisma to pull it off? Do you often have a hidden agenda? How about your motive? With a captive audience hanging on to your words and following your ministry with unquestioned loyalty, do you exploit them . . . do you use your power for your own purposes? Is the enhancement of your image of major importance to you, or can you honestly say that your work is directed and empowered by the Spirit of God? Is yours a grace-awakening ministry?

STRONG MESSAGE FROM A SPIRIT-DIRECTED PROPHET

To help you appreciate the value of being a minister of grace, I want to introduce you to one of the most obscure men in the Bible. He was a prophet who lived and wrote in the ancient days of the Old Testament. His name is Zechariah. His book is the next to last book of the Old Testament, just before Malachi. Most folks—even church folks—are not at all familiar with this powerful prophet. Therefore, a little background information is necessary before we can appreciate how he ties in to my earlier questions.

Historical Background

Jerusalem lay in ruins. Her wall of protection had been leveled, nothing more than piles of debris, rocks, and stones scattered across the landscape. The Hebrews' houses had been burned and destroyed years earlier, actually decades ago. Equally tragic, the temple of the Lord lay in ruins. The chosen people lived in captivity in the distant land of Babylon. After seventy years of this existence, some began to make their way back to the city of Jerusalem, back to their beloved Zion. Some returned under Nehemiah's leadership and rebuilt the wall. It proved to be quite a task because many of them who had returned earlier were more interested in constructing their own houses than they were in building a wall of defense around the city. But thanks to Nehemiah's persistence and the people's cooperation, that job finally got finished. In the meantime, the temple had only its foundation laid. There it sat in virtual neglect for fifteen or sixteen years; no one seemed to care. After completing the wall, the Jews went back to their own suburbs and returned to the rebuilding of their own houses. The wall was finished, but not the temple.

That need became a burden to a prophet named Haggai. No more single-minded prophet ever wrote in all the Bible than Haggai (his writings appear just before Zechariah). The man comes with strong, severe, and pungent admonitions. With sharp words and stinging rebukes, including a few sarcastic comments, Haggai communicated that the temple of God needed immediate attention. The late Kyle Yates said that Haggai "tips his arrows with scorn, wings them with sarcasm . . . then speeds them skillfully to the mark. . . . His duty was to take the scattered embers of national pride . . . and kindle the flame anew."[1]

That's an appropriate description of Haggai. But the fact is that folks can stand that kind of preaching only so long. After a while you become apathetic. The shouts and the admonitions, the commands, and even the sarcasm lose their bite among the indifferent as apathy returns. So the temple remained unfinished in spite of Haggai's persistent, albeit wearisome, harassment.

The governor through those tumultuous times was Zerubbabel, who lived with the task of getting the temple project completed. But he relied on the motivation of prophets to stir the citizens into action. Haggai did what he could, but it proved to be not enough. It took another prophet whom God brought on the scene as Haggai departed. That prophet's name was Zechariah; he had the same vision that Haggai had but a much different style of communicating it to the people. His predecessor had been severe and stinging in his reproofs. Not Zechariah. His approach was more colorful and gracious. As we would say today, Zechariah was easier to live with.

Kyle Yates wrote this of Zechariah:

A serious depression, with crop failures and apparent ruin, faced the Jewish people who had responded to the call of Haggai to build the house of God. Under the pressure of discouragement and want that faced them they found it easy to fall out. The blunt, prosaic hammering that Haggai did had its effect, but a new voice was needed to lift them into the kind of enthusiasm that would keep them working to the finish line. Zechariah came to the rescue to supply the needed help. . . .

He does not rebuke or condemn or berate the people. With striking colors and vivid imagination he paints glowing pictures of the presence of God to strengthen and help. Words of inspiration flow from his lips.[2]

Zechariah is a book of visions—striking, colorful, and at times mystical. There were occasions when not even the prophet himself understood what he saw, which is what we find in the fourth chapter of his book.

> Then the angel who was speaking with me returned, and roused me as a man who is awakened from his sleep. And he said to me, "What do you see?" And I said, "I see, and behold, a lampstand all of gold with its bowl on the top of it, and its seven lamps on it with seven spouts belonging to each of the lamps which are on the top of it." (Zech. 4:1–3)

As the chapter begins, an angel is speaking to him regarding the vision of a lampstand of gold. It has a bowl on the top and seven lamps on it with seven spouts. Then there are two olive trees, a tree on the right side and another on the left. By now Zechariah is wondering what this is all about. In fact, he asks, "What are these, my lord?" (v. 4). The angel answers, "Do you not know?" To which Zechariah honestly responds, "No, my lord." He had seen what God revealed, but he didn't know its meaning, its interpretation.

At this moment we come to a most interesting section of Scripture. We are not left at the mercy of an insightful expositor or some Hebrew scholar to tell us what it means. We get the answer directly from the mouth of the angel. The one who revealed the vision now interprets it for the prophet (and all who would later read this) to understand.

Timeless Reminder

The angel addresses Zerubbabel, the governor whose task it is to see the job to completion. Perhaps Zerubbabel has run low on hope in recent weeks. He has become weary as the building project has lingered unfinished. Maybe it seemed as though it would never be finished, hence the angel's words of hope to the governor:

This is the word of the Lord to Zerubbabel saying, "Not by might nor by power, but by My Spirit," says the LORD of hosts. "What are you, O great mountain? Before Zerubbabel you will become a plain; and he will bring forth the top stone with shouts of 'Grace, grace to it!'" (vv. 6–7)

Let's understand what he is saying. The mountain represents the enormous number of obstacles facing those who would take up the task. For example, there is apathy within the Jewish community in and around Jerusalem. There is opposition from outside the walls of Zion. There is weariness and a fair amount of indifference from those who had lived under the harsh, probing, and penetrating words of Haggai. In addition, the "mountain" would include a new generation of Jews who don't have a desire for building the temple, along with the tired, old generation who believes they've already paid their dues. The governor is caught in the middle of all this, along with an unfinished temple, and out of the blue comes a message from God that promises "the mountain will become as a plain." Good news! "The obstacles will be taken care of." In other words, "You don't have to shout louder or worry any longer. Trust in the Lord, Zerubbabel; God is at work! But before you exhibit all kinds of human ingenuity and creative skills from the flesh, remember, Zerubbabel, it is not by might nor by power." The primary responsibility for completing the temple is God's, not the governor's. It will be done by the Spirit of God as He moves among God's people.

Might and *power* (v. 6) intrigue me. They are words that describe human effort, another way of saying the energy of the flesh. They ring a familiar bell in the minds of all ministers, for every one of us has been guilty of occasionally doing the work of God in the energy of the flesh.

Theodore Laetsch, in his thorough work on *The Minor Prophets*, says:

The two Hebrew words *might* and *power* denote inner strength . . . inherent power, courageous bravery, fortitude, as well as manpower, large numbers of soldiers, riches, leaders, well-coordinated organizations, good financial systems, etc. The Lord's work, the building of His Temple, the inner growth, the expansion of His Church cannot be carried out by mere external means. Human strength and wisdom alone will fail. My Spirit must do it![3]

Talk about a relevant message for every minister today! It is this one: *Human wisdom and fleshly energy alone will fail.* God's best work is not going to be done by human might or by fleshly power. *The work of God, if done for His greater glory, must be accomplished through His gifted people.* When facing the mountain-like obstacles inherent in every ministry, we tend to rely on fleshly tactics to get a big job done: manipulations, guilt-giving methods, verbal force as well. Wrong! says this scripture. No! says the Spirit of God. Much of that is nothing more than a carnal display of human strength. It will backfire. As one hymn writer put it, "The arm of flesh will fail you, ye dare not trust your own."[4]

Our tendency to rely on our own strength is compounded by the very real fact that fleshly power gets results. Human ingenuity works. It raises funds. An excessive amount of energy and manipulation and scheming will cause a large number of people to do more and to work harder and to give money to get a project finished. Overnight results will occur. There is nothing that feeds our instant-gratification hunger like instant results. Only one major problem: in the final analysis the satisfaction will have a hollow ring to it. It will be empty, a study in futility. The work of the flesh will amount to zilch in light of eternity. *The glory will belong to the person who made it happen, and the rewards will stop there too.*

God has a better idea. In verse 7 the governor is promised a removal of the obstacles by God's power, and rather than his getting the glory, it will all go to God. And the final capstone of the whole project will be "Grace! Grace!" This temple will be completed . . . this building will be erected because of the grace of God. I appreciate the way Ken Taylor paraphrases this verse in *The Living Bible*:

> Therefore no mountain, however high, can stand before Zerubbabel! For it will flatten out before him! And Zerubbabel will finish building this Temple with mighty shouts of thanksgiving for God's mercy, declaring that all was done by grace alone. (v. 7)

In light of those immortal words from an ancient prophet, several questions emerge. Why are you relying on might and power rather than the Spirit of God? What is it that keeps you returning to human effort and manipulative schemes? What will it take to bring us back to a by-grace-alone style of ministry? How much longer will we continue in our hurry-worry leadership mode?

A Strong Warning

To all who are engaged in ministry, a warning is appropriate. Every project you undertake can be accomplished your way or God's way. The energy source of human strength is impressive and logical and effective. It works! Initially, folks cannot tell the difference. A ministry built by the energy of the flesh looks just like a ministry built by the energy of the Spirit. Externally, I warn you, it looks the same. But internally, spiritually, down deep in the level of motive, you know in your heart God didn't do it; you did it! There is no glory vertically. And equally tragic, there is no grace horizontally.

Let me put it to you straight. Restrain yourself from might and power if you are a minister. Deliberately give the Spirit time and room. Consciously hold yourself back from clever ingenuity and reliance on your own charisma. If you don't, you will live to regret it. You will become a "graceless" minister.

To my pleasant surprise, while reading again Spurgeon's *Lectures to My Students*, written over a hundred years ago, I came across a grand discourse on the "graceless pastor." Only Spurgeon could say it so well:

> A graceless pastor is a blind man elected to a professorship of optics, philosophizing upon light and vision, discoursing upon and distinguishing to others the nice shades and delicate blendings of the prismatic colours, while he himself is absolutely in the dark!
>
> He is a dumb man elevated to the chair of music; a deaf man fluent upon symphonies and harmonies! He is a mole professing to educate eaglets; a limpet elected to preside over angels. . . .
>
> Moreover, when a preacher is poor in grace, any lasting good which may be the result of his ministry, will usually be feeble and utterly out of proportion with what might have been expected.[5]

All this brings us back to my opening question: Are you *really* a minister of grace? Is yours a grace awakening ministry? Is your leadership characterized by grace? In almost thirty years of ministry, I have observed two very noticeable characteristics of those who lack grace and operate in the energy of the flesh. Both could be called grace killers. One has to do with projects and the other with people.

First, I notice that *those who operate in the flesh use human might in order to accomplish visible projects.* There are always telltale signs. Great emphasis is placed on "success." There is no hesitation to use strategies from the world, secular managerial styles are employed, impressive techniques are used, size and numbers mean too much, and manipulative methods are used for raising money. It is extremely important to make a good impression. Without exception, the importance is placed on impressing people, not glorifying God. Weaknesses are hidden. Vulnerability is out of the question. The great hope is to hear people exclaim, "Wow! Look at that." There is a gnawing hunger for a place in the headlines.

Second, I notice that *those with a might-and-power style rely on person-ality power to get their way with people.* Several ingredients go into this style of ministry: Charisma. Power plays. Pressure. Force. Threats. Control. Intimidation. Deceit, if necessary. Embarrassment, if essential. Rather than encouraging people to pray, to wait, to seek God's mind, and to rely on His Spirit for clear direction, this style of leadership (I have a hard time calling it "ministry") abuses people, uses them for unfair advantage, bullies them if they get in the way, and discards them once they are no longer "useful."

All who desire to be ministers of grace need the reminder that this counsel is not popular in a day of great emphasis on rapid church growth and highly efficient methods for making things happen. A prophet today who uses words like "not by might nor by power" is a lonely voice in the wilderness. You will not find it in newspapers or most magazines (secular or Christian), nor will you find it promoted in most churches. Sadly, it isn't overtly taught in most seminaries either. There, you may learn to handle the text of Scripture or a system for understanding theology, maybe a fairly good grasp of church history, but being a grace-oriented minister? Not likely.

My warning stands: *Anything that does not result in God's getting the glory ought to be enough to restrain our own might and power so His Spirit can do the job, which includes removing the obstacles.* It is easy to forget that not all the grace killers are "out there" trying to get people under the law. Some are "in here," within the ranks of leadership, trying to do God's will their way.

I once knew a very kind college president who framed a small sign and hung it on the wall leading to his office in the administration building on the campus. Only three words appeared, but they spoke with eloquence, inviting students and faculty in:

KINDNESS SPOKEN HERE.

Enough of the negatives and the warnings in this chapter. Let's turn our thoughts from those who are not examples of grace to how we might become better at modeling and promoting grace. Hopefully, the things we uncover from the New Testament will be so invigorating and inviting that some who are now grace killers will become grace givers. And speaking of that, what *are* some of the characteristics of a grace-awakening ministry? How would people know if there is grace to be found in your ministry? I've never seen anyone advertise it, at least not in printed form, but there are ways others can know that "Grace Is Shown Here." Five come to mind.

OBVIOUS MARKS OF A GRACE-AWAKENING MINISTER

The first of these characteristics is *generosity with personal possessions* (absence of selfishness). In the earliest days of the church, the generosity of God's people was notorious:

> And the congregation of those who believed were of one heart and soul; and not one of them claimed that anything belonging to him was his own; but all things were common property to them. And with great power the apostles were giving witness to the resurrection of the Lord Jesus, and abundant grace was upon them all. For there was not a needy person among them, for all who were owners of land or houses would sell them and bring the proceeds of the sales, and lay them at the apostles' feet; and they would be distributed to each, as any had need. (Acts 4:32–35)

There they were, a flock of sheep struggling for survival in a hostile world of Christ-hating citizens and politicians. They had every reason to live frightened, selfish lives of isolation and secrecy. Not so! Do you know why? We just read the answer: because "abundant grace was upon them all." That prompted a spirit of generosity, a genuine desire to meet needs. Can you believe the results? "There was not a needy person among them."

An atmosphere of grace creates an absence of selfishness. After all, it isn't your money; it's God's money. So you give it. It isn't your church; it's God's church, so you share it. They aren't your people, pastor; they're God's people, so you release them. It isn't your project; it's God's project, so you rely on Him. Going back to what we learned from Zechariah's vision, it is His work done His way for His glory. Even though you could raise twice the amount in the energy of the flesh, you refuse to do so. You won't do it! You will trust God to work in His way and in His time. Understand, you will present the need and invite a response, but you will refuse to strong-arm your own plan.

By the way, I've noticed that words like *mine* and *keep* and *ours* are not heard in ministries of grace. Neither does a suspicious kind of spirit pervade a place where there is grace. Instead, there is openhanded generosity.

I learned a lot about grace from the flock I served in Fullerton, California, from 1971 to 1994. What models of generosity! When a sister church in downtown Los Angeles was struggling for survival—the historic Church of the Open Door—we were moved with compassion. We kept hearing of their plight over television and reading about it in the paper. We began to pray for them. Our pastoral staff and boards unanimously agreed that we should do more than pray, however. One Sunday we announced that we were going to receive an after-church offering, all of which would be sent to that church to encourage them. I will never forget the enthusiasm. Everybody was thrilled to participate. I cannot remember the exact amount, but somewhere around eighteen thousand was contributed. In October 1989 the San Francisco earthquake took its toll on two of our sister churches in the Bay area. One was greatly damaged, and the other also needed a fair amount of repair. Again, we felt we should do more than pray and write. With only a brief announcement, an after-church offering was collected, allowing us to send over eight thousand to one church and more than four thousand to the other. Ours was not a wealthy church, but there was an abundance of grace, which brings generosity with personal possessions. Such unselfish joy is contagious.

Another characteristic of a grace-awakening ministry is *encouragement in unusual situations* (absence of predictability). Where grace abounds, you will not only find generosity with personal possessions, you will also find *encouragement in unusual settings.* Grace keeps us flexible, willing to adapt.

Some time after the Jerusalem church was established, God's desire was that they take the gospel to the Gentiles. We read in Acts 11 how it happened:

> So then those who were scattered because of the persecution that arose in connection with Stephen made their way to Phoenicia and Cyprus and Antioch, speaking the word to no one except to Jews alone. But there were some of them, men of Cyprus and Cyrene, who came to Antioch and began speaking to the Greeks also, preaching the Lord Jesus. (vv. 19–20)

They first went to Jews alone, but later they found themselves surrounded by Greeks, and so they went to the Greeks also. They didn't change their message. They were still preaching the Lord Jesus. But they were flexible with their method. The target changed from strictly Jews to Jews and Gentiles. That took grace.

When the church at Jerusalem heard of the large numbers of Gentiles who were turning to the Lord in Antioch, they sent Barnabas to check it out. Once in Antioch, he witnessed a new setting. Rather than an all-Jewish congregation, there were Greeks everywhere. He saw the grace of God at work, and he applauded it. He encouraged them. There was no legalism, no "you ought to be grateful" speeches. No place for shame or warnings. He modeled grace in a different setting. He adapted. Likewise, when you and I minister graciously, we have room for a different way of ministering.

Missionaries who do the best job are people of grace. If they minister cross-culturally, they don't try to change people into Western Christians. They don't try to make the American culture the standard for Christian living. When they are in Latin America, they minister to Latinos in a context of Latin America. When they are in Asia, they adapt to the Asian way of thinking because the mind of the Asian is so different from the Western mind. That is grace! There is a lack of predictability, true freedom, willing adaptability—a sense of comfort in other methods of expression. The absence of a narrow, rule-book mentality frees anyone for an open-hearted ministry. It is fun to be around those who minister like that. There is affirmation along with a lot of flexibility. Rather than requiring a predictable style of response, grace-awakening ministries encourage openness, acceptance, and a willingness to go with the cultural flow. Best of all, converts are given plenty of freedom to learn and to grow.

Years ago, when the Jesus-people ministry was meeting needs on the West Coast, some of the churches got pretty nervous with the results. Frankly, I admired the outreach of Calvary Chapel under Chuck Smith's competent and wise leadership; it became one of the dominant forces in that era. Interest in spiritual things remained strong, thanks to Chuck (and others, of course) who decided to reach out to those who were disillusioned on the bleak backwash of the Timothy Leary philosophy. Some of the churches flexed back then and as a result became harbors of hope for young men and women who had dropped out of society.

During that same era a young man stumbled into our church one Sunday evening. He was stunned to see a building full of folks, singing and having a great time together. There he stood, barefoot, in cutoffs, no shirt, full beard . . . all alone. I watched from the platform as he stared in amazement. We found out later it was the first time in his life he had ever been inside a church among a congregation. He wandered down a side aisle, looking at us like a calf staring at a new gate. One of our members invited him to sit next to him, shared his hymnal, and answered his questions. It was wonderful to see such grace in action. I loved it!

Following that particular evening meeting, the young man immediately came down front to talk. He had a dozen or more questions, all of them excellent. I noticed sand still sticking to the hairs on his legs. He was fresh off the beach. He was treated with kindness and respect. No one told him what he "should" wear or how he "should" act. A couple of fellows invited him to have a Coke and a hamburger with them. He was surprised and accepted. Not surprisingly, he was back the next Sunday. And the next. Within a matter of weeks he became a Christian. He spoke of how our love and acceptance won him. He publicly testified of his faith in Christ when he was baptized. The context of grace gave him room to grow, to think, to be himself, to ask questions. That young man later finished his university work, attended and graduated from seminary, and is now in ministry. I think he's even wearing shoes.

Now let me mention a third mark of grace: *life beyond the letter of Scripture.* When there is a grace-awakening ministry, there is an absence of dogmatism and Bible bashing. I love the way the apostle Paul writes these thoughts in 2 Corinthians 3:

> Not that we are adequate in ourselves to consider anything as coming from ourselves, but our adequacy is from God, who also made us adequate as servants of a new covenant, not of the letter, but of the Spirit; for the letter kills, but the Spirit gives life. (vv. 5–6)

I want to be careful here, lest you misunderstand. Paul's emphasis in this section of Scripture is on a new-covenant (as opposed to an old-covenant) ministry . . . a ministry of grace rather than law, a thought which he spends quite some time developing. Anyone who reads the second and third chapters of his second letter to the Corinthians with an open mind cannot help but observe a marked departure from what could be called a "traditional" type of ministry. Paul promotes:

- a lack of professional adequacy (2:16, 3:5)
- the presence of vulnerable authenticity (2:17)
- an emphasis on personal relationships (3:1–4)
- the importance of a servanthood mentality (3:6)

as he pleads for an attitude of grace, which leads to a teachable spirit rather than the hammerlike poundings of a dogmatic style of teaching.

Handling God's Word accurately is essential for those who minister. Only through its being correctly interpreted can it be correctly applied. The disciplines of good hermeneutics (correct method of biblical interpretation) and capable homiletics (clear communication of biblical truth) should be blended together by those who teach God's Book. Care must be taken, however, to interpret and communicate with grace. When grace is present, there is a spirit of openness, an attitude of compassion, which includes an absence of Bible bashing and dogmatism.

It is not uncommon for me to meet people who have come out of strict fundamentalist ministries where they were bruised and wounded by a grace killer who presented Scripture in such a rapid-fire, harsh manner that they felt beaten by the "letter of the law" rather than led and comforted by the Spirit of liberty. Having come out of such a climate many years ago, I understand whereof I write. "The letter kills," states Paul. But the Holy Spirit, ministering in a context of freedom mixed with the charm of grace, "gives life."

While we are here in 2 Corinthians 3, I find a fourth characteristic of a grace-awakening ministry: *liberty with creative expression.* When grace is present, there is plenty of freedom provided for creative expression. Paul writes of that this way: "Now the Lord is the Spirit; and where the Spirit of the Lord is, there is liberty" (v. 17). This means there is also an absence of expectations.

I really hope you will let these words seep in slowly and permanently guide your ministry: Where the Spirit of the Lord is, there is room—plenty of room—for liberty.

Commenting on the meaning of the liberty of the Spirit in verse 17, one New Testament authority writes:

> He means that so long as man's obedience to God is dominated and conditioned by obedience to a book and a code of laws he is in the position of an unwilling . . . slave. But when it comes from the operation of the Spirit . . . then the very centre of his being has no other desire than to serve and obey God, for then it is not law but love which binds him.[6]

I observe an interesting phenomenon among caring Christians. I notice that most of us are pretty good in evangelism when it comes to grace. Most of us don't require the lost person to clean up his life before he comes to the Savior. We flex, we bend, we forgive, we tolerate *whatever* among the unsaved. But we don't provide nearly as much liberty once folks come to the Savior. We don't care if they blow smoke in our faces while we witness to them. We don't even talk about it. We cough, we smile, and we continue to share Christ with them. "But they had better not blow smoke in my face as a Christian, not if they claim to be converted!"

Why not? What if that part of their life hasn't yet been dealt with by the Spirit of God? Why are we so intolerant of and impatient with our brothers and sisters? Where's the grace? Think of what others have to put up with when it comes to you and me. Think of the things in your life that are not yet cleaned up. Now maybe it isn't one of the "dirty dozen" or the "nasty nine" that is obvious to everyone, but think of the stuff you still have to work through—things I need to be gracious with you about . . . and you with me. I ask you, where is all this wonderful liberty of which Paul writes? Why do we lay such heavy expectations on each other? Furthermore, what makes us so afraid of creativity?

Do you encourage individuality? Do you find delight in a person on your discipleship team who is just the opposite in style from you? Do you live with that graciously? How about the kid in class who is bored? Let's say he is hyperactive . . . his mind is off somewhere else. I know he is a challenge. (Believe me, I understand. I was like that years ago and was a real task for my teachers.) But what an opportunity for us to demonstrate grace in finding creative expressions for those individuals, encouraging them to develop and become all they are meant to be. The creative minds today were quite likely the hyperactives of yesteryear, the ones who were bored stiff twenty years ago.

If the Spirit of the Lord provides liberty, I suggest that the saints of the Lord take their cues from Him and do the same. Rather than reminding people of all the things they are not, how great it would be—how full of grace, actually—to give them all the room they need to fail and recover, to learn and grow.

This reminds me of one more characteristic of a grace-awakening ministry: *release from past failures.* A ministry of grace doesn't keep bringing up the past for the purpose of holding it over people. There is an absence of shame. Paul addresses the sin in 1 Timothy 1:12–14:

> I thank Christ Jesus our Lord, who has strengthened me, because He considered me faithful, putting me into service; even though I was formerly a blasphemer and a persecutor and a violent aggressor. And yet I was shown mercy, because I acted ignorantly in unbelief; and the grace of our Lord

was more than abundant, with the faith and love which are found in Christ Jesus.

You may be surprised to know that the apostle Paul had every reason to feel ashamed. He was one whose past was dreadful: "formerly a blasphemer . . . persecutor . . . violent aggressor." Then how could the same man write, "I am not ashamed" (2 Tim. 1:12)? He gives us the answer here in 1 Timothy 1:14: grace was more than abundant. Blasphemy had abounded in his past, but grace superabounded. Violence and brutality had abounded, but grace superabounded.

What if it read "divorcée"? What if it read "homosexual"? What if it read "addict"? I realize it reads "blasphemer, persecutor, aggressor." But what if it read "prostitute" or "ex-con" or "financial failure" or "murderer"? In a grace-awakened ministry, none of those things in the past is allowed to hold those people in bondage. They are released, forgiven, and the believer is allowed to go on to a new life in Christ.

Grace releases people not only from sin but from shame. Do you do that in your ministry? Or do you make a note of those things and keep reminding yourself when that particular name comes up, "Well, you know, you'd better watch her" or "You've gotta watch him." Do you give people reasons to feel greater shame? Who knows what battles of shame most folks struggle with. It is enormous.

I have a couple of good friends who are Christian therapists, and they are excellent in their work. Interestingly, both have mentioned to me on separate occasions that one of the most frequent struggles they help people with is the inner struggle with shame. Since both counselors are believers in Christ, many of their clients are too; yet this does not free them from shame. To be completely candid about it, it usually intensifies the problem. Why? Because many in God's family are better at encouraging shame in others than they are at releasing it.

Before you question that, stop and think how often you have heard the five words "You ought to be ashamed" or how many times you have received a look that said the same. Shame is not only counterproductive, it is debilitating. It brings a thick, dark cloud of depression over an already hypersensitive conscience, severing what few threads of self-respect remain. It adds disgrace to what has already been done, leaving one to wallow in the mire of failure rather than claim the release that forgiveness can bring. It holds down rather than lifts up; it steals hope instead of offering encouragement. Shame is a classic grace killer.

Christians can be such shamers! We not only make people ashamed of their wrongs, we shame them for being different. I know a few Christians who have been made to feel ashamed because they never married. Others because they had made a lot of money, all of it honestly and through hard work. Some told me they felt ashamed because their sickness didn't go away, others because their depression didn't end quickly. I know one gentleman who is an absolute joy to be around. He told me it isn't uncommon for him to get looks as well as letters of rebuke because he has "too much fun in life." A fine Christian wife and mother told me that she was told she "should be ashamed" because she worked outside the home. She is in her mid-fifties, and all her children are married.

One of those therapists, Dr. Earl Henslin, often speaks on this subject. In doing so he distributes a small flier that includes the list of contrasts, on the facing page. Over the years, I have referred to this often and found it helpful. I think you will, too.

SHAME-BASED SPIRITUALITY	HEALTHY SPIRITUALITY
1. Having problems is sin.	Problems are a part of my human condition. I can bring them to God and my fellow Christians.
2. Emotions are sinful.	Emotions are neither good nor bad. It's what I do with them. "Be angry and sin not."
3. Compulsive disease is sinful.	There is a difference between disease and sinful behavior.
4. Having fun is sinful.	There are many different ways to delight in God's goodness.
5. Spirituality = Perfection.	Living within grace, not legalism.
6. Sexuality = Sin	Sexuality is a part of who we are as a people and is to be enjoyed.
7. Success (or its lack) is sinful.	Prosperity or poverty is not due to deficient spirituality.
8. Becoming a Christian fixes everything within me.	Accepting Christ in my life enables and empowers me to face issues.
9. If I am not healed, it is due to my lack of faith.	Having illness is not a sin. I can avail myself of the best treatment available.
10. Not being able to think of a clever 10th item may mean I'm not being led by God.	God probably likes the number 9 just as well.[7]

A QUICK REVIEW

We have covered a lot of ground in this chapter. Because it has been a bit lengthy, a quick recap might help.

Those who minister grace are essential in this day of graceless legalism and human might-and-power accomplishments. More than ever we need grace-awakening ministers who free rather than bind. These five characteristics are true of those who serve others in grace:

1. Generosity with personal possessions (absence of selfishness)
2. Encouragement in unusual settings (absence of predictability)
3. Life beyond the letter of Scripture (absence of dogmatic Bible-bashing)
4. Liberty for creative expression (absence of expectations)
5. Release from past failures (absence of shame)

Do you remember one of Paul's exhortations to Timothy? His words provide the marching orders for all who take these five characteristics seriously: "Be strong in the grace that is in Christ Jesus" (2 Tim. 2:1)! My fellow ministers, stand tall in it. Be firmly committed to it. Make grace your aim, your pursuit, your passion. Model it. Teach it. Demonstrate it.

Jefferson Starship is a singing group that rose to the top in the 1980s with a song that stayed on the popular hit parade for months: "We Built This City on Rock and Roll." Borrowing my idea from that title, I suggest that we do all we can to change whatever is necessary so that it won't be said, "We built this church on might and power," or, "We built this relationship on expectations and shame." Such things will not last. They will fade and ultimately fail. How much better to be able to say, "We built this ministry on truth and grace." Like a house built on rock, such a ministry will outlive us.

12

A Marriage Oiled by Grace

ACTRESS CELESTE HOLM spoke for all of us when she said, "We live by encouragement and we die without it; slowly, sadly, angrily."[1] There is no way to measure how many find themselves in that tragic situation, but we can be sure the number is astronomical.

The lack of encouragement and affirmation is all around us. It is for that reason so many hate to go to work every day. Or cannot wait to get out of school. Or dread facing the demands of a family. Or do not get more involved in community activities. Responsibilities become little more than a series of grinding, grim assignments without the relief provided by encouragement. This means that those who do affirm and encourage others are not only rare, they are remarkable. Almost invariably, I have found they are people of grace. They model the things I have been writing about in this book . . . and they do so in private just as consistently as they do in public. They value relationships even with the unknown and so-called unimportant.

My years in ministry have allowed me a great deal of exposure to the public, which has included a fair amount of travel. I am usually met at the airport by those whose job it is to transport me to a hotel or the place where I will be speaking. One of the things I enjoy about such encounters is the opportunity to spend several miles with these faithful folks who work behind the scenes, those whose faces and names are not generally known, yet they are vital links in the success of the meetings or the event that is about to transpire. Almost without exception I find these people to be gracious, servant-hearted givers who carry out their tasks with diligence and humility. Therefore, I deliberately do my best to treat them with grace — to express appreciation, to lift their spirits, to affirm the importance of their role in the particular ministry I have the privilege of being a part of.

I cannot tell you how many times such a person has expressed surprise that anyone has bothered to notice or taken the time to encourage. I recall one young man who, after we had gotten better acquainted and enjoyed a few laughs together, spoke candidly of how difficult it had been trying to please some of those he had assisted. He commented on one well-known public figure (whom he did not name) who was such a pain in private. "He griped 'cause I was a few minutes late," he said. "He was discourteous, demanding, and even rude to me. But when he spoke that night, you would think he was Dale Carnegie's twin!" My young friend admitted he had begun to get the impression that apparently that is the way it must be, even though his heart told him otherwise. The truth is, he found himself dying without encouragement — "slowly, sadly, angrily." What really threw him was that all his riders were Christians.

When will we ever learn? Those who make a lasting investment for good in our lives are not necessarily people with a name or people with reputations, but servant-hearted people with grace. These are people whose kindness is as consistent with a hardworking secretary as with the hand-clapping public. Not people who are guilty of polishing their public presence yet so uncaring about private relationships that they are tyrannical and insensitive. The words of Dag Hammarskjöld come to mind:

Around a man who has been pushed into the limelight, a legend begins to grow as it does around a dead man. But a dead man is in no danger of yielding to the temptation to nourish his legend, or accept its picture as reality. I pity the man who falls in love with his image as it is drawn by public opinion during the honeymoon of publicity.[2]

I pity someone else even more—his wife.

What does it take to make a person great . . . not just under the lights or before the camera but behind the scenes as well? What does it take to make one just as charming and thoughtful and encouraging with his or her mate as with those who sit in awe? I have the answer: *It takes grace*—the oil that lessens the friction in marriage, which is precisely what I want to address in this chapter.

We have thought about grace from God, grace that breaks sin's enslavement, grace in the church, grace between friends in times of disagreement, as well as grace among those in ministry. It is now time for us to think about the importance of grace between husbands and wives. In my opinion, it is here—in the privacy of one's home—that grace faces its major test, a test that begins not too many days after the honeymoon ends. As one wag put it, "Every marriage has three rings: engagement ring, wedding ring, and suffering." More times than I want to remember, I have found that it was easier to extend grace to a parishioner or one of the folks on our church staff than it was for me to treat Cynthia with grace. So as I write these things, understand that I write as an imperfect learner. We may have been married forty-eight years, but the oil of grace has not always flowed in abundance, certainly not from me. Like many married couples, we have had to admit that a "grace awakening" is just as needed in our home as it is in our church, perhaps more so.

While grazing through the New Testament over the past several years, I have found that marriage is addressed somewhat at length in three separate places, each time mentioning both husbands and wives. Those scriptures are 1 Corinthians 7, Ephesians 5, and 1 Peter 3. As I analyzed each section, I found that the Corinthians reference deals with marital realities that are tough to face, the Ephesians reference deals with marital responsibilities every couple must accept, and the Peter reference deals with the marital roles that need to be fulfilled. In each case, the secret of making it happen as God planned requires grace.

THE GRACE TO FACE MARITAL REALITIES

As I study the seventh chapter of 1 Corinthians, I find no fewer than three realities (of course, there may be more) to be faced by every married couple. I am so convinced of the significance of each one that I mention them to every couple I marry. I also have observed that among those I know whose marriages have not lasted, one or more of these realities was passively ignored or deliberately set aside.

First, *marriage requires mutual unselfishness.*

> Let the husband fulfill his duty to his wife, and likewise also the wife to her husband. The wife does not have authority over her own body, but the husband does; and likewise also the husband does not have authority over his own body, but the wife does. Stop depriving one another, except by agreement for a time that you may devote yourselves to prayer, and come together again lest Satan tempt you because of your lack of self-control. (1 Cor. 7:3–5)

Paul writes of "duty" and "authority" and "depriving"—all terms in this context having to do with sexual intimacy. The application is broader, however. What he is encouraging is unselfishness. What does it take to operate unselfishly? It takes grace. Grace to accept, to overlook, to understand. Grace to forgive. Grace to respect. Grace to yield one's own rights. Grace to affirm. Grace to restrain. Grace to give as well as grace to receive. Marriage requires mutual unselfishness. When I speak to those who are still single, I frequently address the issue of selfishness. I'll often say, "If you tend toward being selfish, if you're the type who clings to your own rights and has no interest sharing with others, please do the world (and certainly any potential mate) a favor and don't marry!" Why do I make such a strong statement? Because marriage, a good marriage, requires mutual unselfishness. It calls for grace to release rights and expect little in return.

There is a second reality: *Marriage means a lifelong commitment.*

> But to the married I give instructions, not I, but the Lord, that the wife should not leave her husband (but if she does leave, let her remain unmarried, or else be reconciled to her husband), and that the husband should not send his wife away. But to the rest I say, not the Lord, that if any brother has a wife who is an unbeliever, and she consents to live with him, let him not send her away. And a woman who has an unbelieving husband, and he consents to live with her, let her not send her husband away. (1 Cor. 7:10–13)

Unless you are ready for a commitment that lasts for life, again I say without hesitation, don't marry. If Paul is writing anything in this paragraph, he is writing this: "When you marry, you marry for life." He has permanence in mind. Did you observe his firm counsel along these lines?

- The wife should not leave her husband (v. 10).
- The husband should not leave his wife (v. 11).
- Let him not send her away (v. 12).
- Let her not send him away (v. 13).

To write it once would be sufficient. Twice would be extremely and unmistakably clear. Three times would be more than enough. But four times? The man means business!

Years ago Cynthia and I took the ugly word *divorce* out of our dialogues. We agreed we would not even store it in the arsenal of our argument vocabulary. No matter how heated our disagreements may be, we wouldn't threaten each other with that term. It does something to a marriage when you can count on your partner to stick around and hammer out your differences with each other instead of walking away from them.

What does it take to stick it out . . . to be permanently committed to each other? I repeat, it takes grace! There is not a divorcée reading these words who wouldn't agree with that. It takes an enormous amount of grace to negotiate through the minefield of disagreements. It takes grace to forgive and go on, grace to hang tough even though the same mistake is made over and over or the same sin committed again and again. A marriage well oiled by grace is durable, long-lasting—protected against the wear and tear of friction.

There's a third reality, just as important to remember as the first two: *Marriage includes times of trouble.*

> I think then that this is good in view of the present distress, that it is good for a man to remain as he is. Are you bound to a wife? Do not seek to be released. Are you released from a wife? Do not seek a wife. But if you should marry, you have not sinned; and if a virgin should marry, she has not sinned. Yet such will have trouble in this life, and I am trying to spare you. (1 Cor. 7:26–28)

Truer words regarding marriage were never written: "Such will have trouble." Every bride who thinks she has found the knight in shining armor who is going to save her from all her disappointments needs to remember, "such will have trouble." Every groom who thinks he has found Wonder Woman, the perfect blend of Mother Teresa, Betty Crocker, Annika Sorenstam, and Julia Roberts, needs to remember, "such will have trouble." I'll go one step further: Marriage and troubles are synonymous!

Without wanting to come across as the Ebenezer Scrooge of wedding bells and lovely ceremonies at the altar, I must say that *troubles are inevitable*. The list is endless. Trouble from calamities. Trouble from disease. Trouble from the old nature. Trouble from children. Trouble from family squabbles. Trouble from differing viewpoints about time, temperature, and trips. Trouble from neighbors. Trouble because of finances. Trouble due to pressure at work you can't turn off. Trouble, trouble, trouble! And it will require grace for the two of you to endure. Grace to accept, grace to forgive . . . grace to laugh much of it off, grace to keep going, grace to encourage the other in the midst of the periodic paths that lead through conflict and disagreement.

I don't know how many times Cynthia has taken my hand, looked me right in the eye, and said, "Honey, we'll make it through this." That took grace, and it lifted my spirit. On other occasions I have had the grace to help her. Without the grace to let each other be, our marriage would be stormy and full of struggles. We have very different temperaments. We also have tastes that don't always agree. Most noticeably, we also have opposite internal thermostats. She is perpetually cold in the winter . . . and often cool in the summer. I'm hot through both! This means that the place in our home that collects the most fingerprints is the thermostat. I regularly push it down; she continually pushes it up. It takes grace for me to live in a sweltering greenhouse . . . and grace for her to survive in a frosty igloo. I sweat; she freezes. I like it to be so cool you could hang meat in the kitchen; she likes it a couple of notches below the Arabian Desert.

But we've finally solved one temperature problem—the electric blanket battle: dual controls! I prefer my side Off or, if there's a blizzard outside (which is rare in Texas), maybe on one. She varies between seven and nine. Actually, I much prefer to sleep on top of the covers. She likes being buried beneath all those layers—it is unbelievable! But the best part comes when her side of the dual-control blanket finally burns out. We just flip that baby over—I take her side that no longer works and she gets mine, which seems like it's brand-new—and we get twice the life out of the sucker. Grace not only gives us tolerance, it saves us bucks.

THE GRACE TO ACCEPT PERSONAL RESPONSIBILITIES

So much for realities; let's focus next on the grace needed to accept responsibilities. That seems to be the emphasis in Ephesians 5:22–33.

I realize as we dig deeper into the subject of marriage that I am treading on delicate ground. To say it is controversial is to put it mildly. Some have taught the subjects of husband-wife responsibilities to such a severe extreme that little room is left to breathe on one's own or to think things through. On the other hand, these (and related verses) have been twisted and altered so much that their original impact has sometimes been neutralized. I want to guard against both extremes. My hope is to help you see two foundational facts: first, the wife's primary responsibility, and, second, the husband's primary responsibility. Neither is all that complicated, but for some strange reason, many marriages seem to consistently miss the mark.

The Wife's Primary Responsibility

As we determine the wife's basic responsibility, let's allow Scripture to speak first: "Wives, be subject to your own husbands, as to the Lord. For the husband is the head of the wife, as Christ also is the head of the church, He Himself being the Savior of the body. But as the church is subject to Christ, so also the wives ought to be to their husbands in everything" (Eph. 5:22–24).

These are familiar words to many Christians; therefore, they can easily lose their "punch." To guard against that, let's consider other versions and paraphrases of the same verses.

Wives, submit to your husbands as to the Lord. For the husband is the head of the wife as Christ is the head of the church, his body, of which he is the Savior. Now as the church submits to Christ, so also wives should submit to their husbands in everything. (NIV)

You wives must learn to adapt yourselves to your husbands, as you submit yourselves to the Lord, for the husband is the "head" of the wife in the same way that Christ is head of the Church and savior of the body. The willing subjection of the Church to Christ should be reproduced in the submission of wives to their husbands. (PHILLIPS).

Wives, submit yourselves to your husbands as to the Lord. For a husband has authority over his wife just as Christ has authority over the church; and Christ is himself the Savior of the church, his body. And so wives must submit themselves completely to their husbands just as the church submits itself to Christ. (TEV)

Wives, submit to your own husbands, as to the Lord. For the husband is head of the wife, as also Christ is head of the church; and He is the Savior of the body. Therefore, just as the church is subject to Christ, so let the wives be to their own husbands in everything. (NKJV)

As I examine these words, I find that *the wife's primary responsibility is to know herself so well and to respect herself so much, that she gives herself to her husband without hesitation.*

Let me suggest that you read the previous statement again, this time more slowly and preferably aloud.

In the context of this section of Scripture, there is an atmosphere of sweet harmony. If you take the time to read the verses (vv. 15–21) leading up to the three that are specifically addressed to wives, you will find that Paul emphasizes being wise (v. 15), being filled with the Spirit (v. 18), having a heart that is overflowing with joy (v. 19), giving thanks (v. 20), and possessing a submissive spirit to one another out of respect for Christ (v. 21). It is within that atmosphere of delightful harmony that a wife is best able to know and respect herself so much that she has little difficulty giving herself to her husband. In such a home there isn't a struggle for authority or rights. There is a willingness to release the controls. At the risk of repetition, it is a grace state of mind that prompts such attitudes.

I can hear some answering back, "If you only knew my husband, you would know how much grace it takes!" To which I'd probably agree, you are correct. But that is the challenge of it all. With the Lord Jesus Christ supremely in charge of your life, with the Spirit of God energizing your actions and softening your attitude, your words, and your responses, it is remarkable how powerful grace can be. It isn't called "amazing grace" for nothing! Just as God, in grace, stooped and loved you in an unlovely state, so, too, can His grace awaken within you the desire to stoop and give yourself to another who may be just as unlovely as we all once were.

The Husband's Primary Responsibility

Suddenly I am getting the feeling that a few husbands are beginning to feel a little smug as they are reading these pages. And so, for your sake we need to see what God's Word says to the man. Interestingly, He says a lot more to us men than He does to our wives. Take a look at verse 25 for starters: "Husbands, love your wives, just as Christ also loved the church and gave Himself up for her."

Here's a fresh thought: The wife is told to love her husband so much that she lives for him, but the husband is told to love his wife so much he would die for her.

The wife is given the analogy of the Savior's life. But the husband is given the analogy of His death. I call that love, men. Each husband is to love his wife enough to die for her.

I can't remember how often, following funerals, I have stood alongside men who have just buried a wife. Almost without exception I've had them fall on my shoulder in tears and say, "Oh, Chuck, why did it take this to stop me and to show me what I had in my wife?"

> Husbands, love your wives, just as Christ also loved the church and gave Himself up for her; that He might sanctify her, having cleansed her by the washing of water with the word, that He might present to Himself the church in all her glory, having no spot or wrinkle or any such thing; but that she should be holy and blameless. So husbands ought also to love their own wives as their own bodies. He who loves his own wife loves himself; for no one ever hated his own flesh, but nourishes and cherishes it, just as Christ also does the church, because we are members of His body. (vv. 25–30)

As I examine these words addressed to husbands, I find that *the primary responsibility of the husband is to love his Lord so deeply and to like himself so completely he gives himself to his wife without conditions.* As I asked you to do before, pause and read that again, more slowly and thoughtfully. Our love is to be without conditions. We need to take the word "if" out of our vocabulary. "If you will do . . . If you will say . . . If you will respond, then I will give myself." No, that is not the way our Savior loves us or loves the church. Notice verse 28 once again: "So husbands ought also to love their own wives as their own bodies. He who loves his own wife loves himself."

The next time you wonder if men really love their own bodies, stop by one of the physical fitness clubs. Incredible! There are mirrors everywhere but on the floor . . . and standing in front of them will be men admiring their muscles—really loving themselves. Knowing how true this self-love is for men, Paul uses it as an example of how men should love their wives—no conditions, no reservations. Again, grace is essential, so essential. It doesn't flow easily, however, when there is competition for authority or conditions placed on love. In a book titled *The Pleasers*, with the subtitle *Women Who Can't Say No—and the Men Who Control Them*, Dr. Kevin Leman makes some insightful observations:

> The cost of marriage is higher for wives than for husbands. If you are talking about good mental health and psychological well-being, the men have it better every time.
>
> Despite all of their complaints about marriage, more women than men find marriage a source of happiness. They cling to marriage regardless of the cost.
>
> Down through the centuries women have been the pleasers, men the controllers. Robert Karen, who conducts workshops for men and women on power and intimacy, refers to the "old" and "new" systems of male/female relationships. Our parents and grandparents knew a world that had stabler values and much more clearly defined roles for men and women. Power and responsibility were clearly assigned, and everyone knew where he or she stood. The system was often unfair to women, but it did offer them a certain amount of security. If a woman was willing to accept the ground rules and the limits that marriage imposed on her, she could be quite happy.
>
> A woman's job was to keep the home, raise the children, and be there for the whole family. The man's job was to go out and earn the living and "make contributions to society." Men were, in effect, put on a pedestal and wives were relegated to second-class citizenship.
>
> Enter women's liberation in the latter part of the twentieth century, and all this inequality is supposed to be dying out—but is it?

A Marriage Oiled by Grace

Women are finding that "having it all" is nothing that special. In fact, they are catching up with the men in having heart disease, ulcers, and other stress-related illnesses. Now they are allowed to get good jobs and earn excellent incomes, but the emotional balance of power at home is still much the same.

Most women still do the giving, while the men continue to take. The woman is the one who is more capable of compassion, support, and being there when needed. Men still aren't in touch with their feelings the way women are. They are less capable of reaching out to make emotional contact. But they are very capable of reaching out to take whatever a woman has to offer, and in so doing, they often take advantage.[3]

Dr. Leman uses a vivid word picture in this book. He calls "pleasers" the moths and "controllers" the flame. Men, be awfully careful in making strong statements regarding submission unless you have really done your homework. More often than not (especially in evangelical circles) such statements are a grand power play. When grace awakens in a husband's heart, he cares for the one God gave him, and he becomes increasingly aware of her value, her gifts, and her significance. The grace within him frees him to let her be.

I'm honest when I say, the better acquainted I become with the grace of God, the less I concern myself with authority in our home and the less threatened I feel. The more I become acquainted with the grace of God, the more I want to model servanthood, the more I desire to affirm and release my wife — the less I want to dominate and control her. Grace loves and serves; it gives and forgives. Grace doesn't keep a record of wrongs and then dangle them over our marriage partner's head. As we have learned in previous chapters, grace gives room — room to grow and to be, to discover and to create. When there is this kind of grace-awakened love, the man loves his wife as he loves himself, and the wife respects her husband, which is exactly as God planned it.

Nevertheless let each individual among you also love his own wife even as himself; and let the wife see to it that she respect her husband. (Eph. 5:33)

When that happens, there is no interest in being intimate with someone else. Jealousy and suspicion are also silenced.

Few grace killers are worse in a marriage than jealousy. I married a couple several years ago whom I shall long remember. During the premarital counseling sessions, I detected a strong jealous streak in the young man. I mentioned this to both of them, but they passed it off as not that important. He assured me he "used to struggle a little with it" but no more. Following their honeymoon and the first few months of marriage, they returned for some follow-up time—and what a change! Brimming with anger, she blurted out, "This man is so jealous of me that before he leaves for work in the morning he checks the odometer on my car . . . then when he comes home, sometimes even before he comes into the house, he checks it again. If I have driven a few extra miles, he quizzes me during supper. Suffering from a lack of trust and encouragement, she was dying "slowly, sadly, angrily."

I repeat, the more the grace of God is awakened in a marriage, the less husbands will attempt to control and restrict and the less wives will feel the need to "please no matter what." It makes marriage easier to manage.

- Grace releases and affirms. It doesn't smother.
- Grace values the dignity of individuals. It doesn't destroy.
- Grace supports and encourages. It isn't jealous or suspicious.

I know whereof I speak. For more years than I care to remember, I was consumed with jealousy. I was so insecure and fearful, it wasn't uncommon for me to drill Cynthia with questions—petty, probing questions that were little more than veiled accusations. It is amazing she endured it.

Finally we had one of those famous showdown confrontations every married couple has had. No need to repeat it, but she made it painfully clear that I was smothering her, that I was imagining things she never even thought of doing . . . and it had to stop. Her words hurt, but she did the right thing. I took her seriously.

I went to work on this ugly side of my life. I confessed my jealousy to Cynthia. I assured her I would never again treat her with such a lack of trust. I asked God for grace to help, for relief from the destructive habit I had formed, for the ability to love and give myself to this woman without all the choking conditions. I distinctly recall how much an understanding of grace helped. It was as if grace were finally "awake" in my life, and I could appropriate its power for the first time. It seemed to free me, first in small ways, and finally in major areas. I can honestly say today that I do not entertain a single jealous thought. Grace *literally* wiped the slate clean.

I have found that once Cynthia and I gave grace its proper place in our marriage, the struggles and arguments over submission ceased. It has been years (not an exaggeration) since either one of us has even mentioned the S word! I say again, once grace finds its place and brings the freedom only it can bring, a desire to control diminishes, and submission is no longer an issue.

Ephesians 5:33 sums up the responsibilities: "Nevertheless let each individual among you also love his own wife even as himself; and let the wife see to it that she respect her husband." The man who genuinely loves his wife finds that he must first have a healthy self-esteem, a strong and secure self-image. It is nothing short of incredible how that opens the gate to let grace flow through his life into his wife's life, which oils all the friction spots. Furthermore, the woman who truly respects her man must first see herself as valuable and significant. As she is given the freedom to grow and become what God meant her to be, her respect for her husband grows.

GRACE TO FULFILL DISTINCT ROLES

We live in a day where domestic roles have become blurred. The home reveals the consequences. Many children grow up not knowing the significance of female femininity or male masculinity. Bonding is short-circuited, thanks to the breakdown of marriages, and kids must opt for surrogate parents.

Traditional and dated though his words may seem, the apostle Peter goes to the heart of the issue and offers a couple of principles that still work . . . if we will only abide by them. He begins his section on the roles of wives and husbands by writing to those wives whose husbands couldn't care less about spiritual things:

> In the same way, you wives, be submissive to your own husbands so that even if any of them are disobedient to the word, they may be won without a word by the behavior of their wives, as they observe your chaste and respectful behavior. (1 Pet. 3:1–2)

Amazing! She wins her husband "without a word." How? She lives in such a convincing manner that he cannot help but notice. Peter selected a wonderful word that is translated "observe." It means "a keen looking into something," as you would watch a replay on a close call in sports. The husband takes careful notice of her winsome behavior, and it blows him away. Ultimately, she "wins" him with kindness.

Now, the tendency is to substitute external things for the right kind of attitude and behavior. Peter undoubtedly realized this because he goes on to say, "And let not your adornment be merely external—braiding the hair, and wearing gold jewelry, or putting on dresses" (3:3).

I have heard some use this verse as an opportunity to support their legalistic bias. They say the woman should not have her hair done and she should not wear cosmetics or any form of jewelry. Funny, I have never heard one of them say, "And neither should you put on a dress," even though that is also on the same list. No, this is not a list for legalists to camp on. The secret is in the word *merely*. Don't let your adornment be *merely* external. Don't limit your life to the externals; don't stop there. Don't yield to the tendency to substitute external adornment for internal character.

And that is why verse 4 is so important. It gives us the positive side: "But let it be the hidden person of the heart, with the imperishable quality of a gentle and quiet spirit, which is precious in the sight of God."

This doesn't mean that if you really fall in love with the Lord you can start looking like an unmade bed. I like to warn ladies about abusing this verse by taking it to an extreme. There's no need to look dowdy and plain because your interest is only on the inner person. That is not the idea. There needs to be a balance. There can be, in fact there need to be, external expressions of feminine beauty, but don't stop there. Guard against letting your external appearance take so much of your time and attention that you leave out the charm and loveliness of a beautiful interior. What holds a husband in the long haul is internal character. Externals finally fade. As age creeps in, much of the beauty you may have had as a young woman slips away.

This reminds me of a story I once heard. During a last-minute Christmas rush, a woman hurried up to a perfume saleswoman in a large department store and asked her, "Do you still have Elizabeth Taylor's *Passion?*" The hassled lady behind the counter responded with quick wit: "If I did, do you think I'd be working here?"

Long after external beauty fades, you will still have what really matters.

This brings me to the wife's role: *to model true femininity . . . character traits that are precious to God and impressive to her husband.* God will honor that. Furthermore, it will get results—lasting, satisfying, fulfilling results.

Verse 7 begins, "You husbands likewise . . ." Just as the wife has a role of submission to the Savior and to her husband, so the husband is to be in submission to Christ. Not nearly enough is said about this. We hammer on wives to submit to their husbands, yet we say all too little to husbands about bending their wills and yielding in full submission to their Lord. I've seldom seen an exception: when a husband lives his life in submission to Christ, he finds his wife cooperative and gracious in return.

> You husbands likewise, live with your wives in an understanding way, as with a weaker vessel, since she is a woman; and grant her honor as a fellow-heir of the grace of life, so that your prayers may not be hindered. (v. 7)

The phrase "live with" means to "be at home with." Not just come in the house after work, choke down supper, stare at a television, say nothing to his wife, and finally drop off to sleep (sound familiar?). To "live with" is to get to know, to be at home with, to make your mutual relationship a priority. In fact, Peter goes further. In this same verse he says, literally, "Live with your wife *according to knowledge*." Really get to know her. Find out what she is really like. What are her innermost thoughts? Discover her deepest hurts; find out her fears. Learn when and where she needs affirmation and encouragement, then give it. You may be surprised to find her dying "slowly, sadly, angrily" without your encouragement and affirmation. She's a weaker vessel physically. But that does not mean she is weaker emotionally, nor does it mean she is weaker in character. She's a woman, meaning she's not put together like a man. She has different needs, different feelings, entertains different wishes and dreams, sees life from a different perspective. Respect those differences; she will adore you for it. In other words, be a masculine model of grace in your home.

All this leads me to the husband's role: *to model genuine masculinity . . . unselfish and sensitive leadership that strengthens the home and gives dignity to the wife.* Remember what verse 7 says: "and grant her honor as a fellow-heir of the grace of life." If the husband provides genuine masculinity, unselfish and sensitive leadership, it is his way of granting honor to his wife. She will feel supported, affirmed, and treasured.

One of the by-products of a grace-filled marriage is that the kids will have little problem bonding. They will bond correctly. They will grow right. They will feel secure and confident. As they step into the real world as young adults, they will hit the road running. Your son will understand what it is like to be a man, and your daughter will have discovered what it means to be a woman. They will be well on their way to a healthy and happy maturity. And in this day, that is no small accomplishment.

We are also reminded in verse 7 that we are fellow-heirs together of the grace of life. We are mutual heirs of grace. Grace brings the husband and wife together . . . not one reigning over the other, not two separate people doing their own thing regardless of the other, but partners enveloped by grace, operating in grace, thinking with grace, releasing because of grace. Think of it as four enduring benefits:

- • Mutual equality (fellow)
- • Mutual dignity (heir)
- • Mutual humility (grace)
- • Mutual destiny (life)

And I can assure you, the magnet in a home like that is so strong you won't want to be anywhere else.

I've said for years that my favorite place on earth is just inside the door of my home. I absolutely love being home. It is there that I find maximum security and acceptance, fulfillment and accountability, responsibility and harmony, honesty and love. Why? Because we are committed to the same common denominator: grace.

A FITTING CONCLUSION

How do you bring a chapter like this to a close? I find it especially difficult since we have covered so much territory, all of it important. We have faced several marital realities. We have looked at the primary responsibilities of a husband and a wife. And we have also considered the distinct roles of both. All the way through we have returned to the essential importance of grace in order for these things to happen.

It is my firm conviction that there would not be nearly as many fractured relationships or dysfunctional families destroyed by affairs, abuse, disunity, or divorce if we simply met the needs within each others' lives. These needs are neither mysterious nor complicated, but when they remain unmet, they erode into grace killers, which lead to every form of unhappiness. What are those needs?

Allow me to let another person answer that question for me. Dr. Willard Harley wrote a fascinating book entitled *His Needs/Her Needs*. It is an in-depth study of extramarital affairs and how to avoid them. Dr. Harley invested more than twenty years of his career counseling married couples, many of whom were engaged in affairs. During those years, he gathered more than fifteen thousand questionnaires that deal with the sexual history and behavior of his clients. There are exceptions, of course, but generally speaking he has concluded that both women and men have five major needs. By identifying them, I find that it is easier to concentrate direct attention on them, applying the oil of grace where needed.

The table on the facing page offers a comparison of the major needs of men and women. Dr. Harley states that the key need for the woman is affection— feeling that she is truly prized, loved, and cherished. The key need for the man is sexual expression followed closely by respect.[4]

The words of actress Celeste Holm speak again, with relevance, to all married couples: "We live by encouragement and we die without it; slowly, sadly, angrily." My hope is that these few pages will make a difference first in your life and then in your home. As you apply the oil of grace to those major needs in your mate's life, may you be strengthened with the realization that you could not be engaged in any investment on earth that yields greater dividends. After all, what is more important than rescuing someone who is dying?

FIVE MAJOR NEEDS OF WOMEN	FIVE MAJOR NEEDS OF MEN
1. Affection	1. Sexual fulfillment
2. Conversation	2. Recreational companionship
3. Honesty and openness	3. An attractive spouse
4. Financial support	4. Domestic support
5. Family commitment	5. Admiration

13

The Charming Joy of Grace Giving

I HAVE A PERSONAL THEORY ABOUT CHRISTMAS. It explains, at least to my satisfaction, the mysterious magic of its magnetism. For years I have wondered what it was that annually draws people into the Yuletide season. Even though we get turned off in early October when we see all those fake trees being set up at department stores and in spite of the dreaded commercialism and crowds and "Jingle Bells" played three thousand times a week in the mall . . . somehow we cannot resist the spirit of the season once we find ourselves enveloped in the sights and smells unique to Christmas. Why?

As beautiful as the colorful lights and decorations may be, they are not the reason. As magnificent as the music and nostalgic memories may be, they aren't either. Neither is it the cakes and candy or the trip to Grandma's house or the parties with friends. My theory, I think, explains it best: Christmas scratches the itch of grace deep within us. It provides us an opportunity each year to deliberately get out of ourselves and do something tangible for someone else with no thought of or interest in being "paid back." It gives us a chance to counteract that selfish streak we all hate in ourselves. In simplest terms, Christmas (like no other annual celebration) prompts us to demonstrate true grace.

Would you like to put my personal theory to the test? Here's how. The next time December 25 rolls around and it is open-the-gifts time around the tree, force yourself to watch the *giver* rather than the one opening the gift. Some of the best photographs we have of the Swindoll family gathered around the tree are those taken of the giver of a certain gift at the time another family member is opening it. There is more than excitement; there is *sheer delight* written all over the face of the giver as he or she is totally absorbed in the charming joy of giving. I've finally figured it out—at that moment we are caught up in the full-on ecstasy of grace. When you stop to think about it, it isn't receiving gifts around the tree that makes Christmas so much fun; it's giving them. It's watching the other person's look of surprise or sensing that special surge of gratitude, which suddenly and without a word makes us feel close.

One year at Christmas my wife surprised all of us in the family by giving us matching bathrobes, each one with his or her name monogrammed on the front. She had the most fun of anyone! She brought in the gifts and set each one on the right lap. She told us not to open them until everyone was ready . . . then, "Go!" I deliberately watched Cynthia as one after another opened the package and shouted. She was dancing and laughing and clapping and jumping up and down—yes, *she* was! Then she had all of us put them on at the same time and "model" them, with hoods on and hands in pockets. By the time we finished, we looked like a roomful of monks from the order of St. Michael's, embracing each other and having the time of our lives. But nobody experienced more joy than the one who thought up the idea, pulled it off, then enjoyed the sheer pleasure of watching others take delight in her gift to each member of the family. Our Lord knew what He was talking about when He taught that it is more blessed to give than to receive.

I freely admit that I have racked my brain to find a way to reconstruct that same once-a-year delight throughout the year in this chapter on the joy of grace giving. If I could do that, we would all have our defenses down, and we would be on the edge of our seats anticipating what the Bible teaches about giving as God intended us to give. Unfortunately, many people, both within the church and without, honestly feel money is "filthy lucre" so we are better off not even mentioning it. I have actually heard laymen bragging that their minister has never once talked about money during the years he has been their pastor. While I have serious concerns about such silence, I understand how that could happen. I, too, tend to shy away from the subject.

WHAT MAKES US SO DREADFULLY DEFENSIVE

Having been engaged in ministry for about four decades, I can remember times when I could almost hear the groans and feel the sighs as I announced that I'd be speaking on giving that particular Sunday. Why do we feel that way? I think it is a lot like the groans and sighs we release in mid-October when the stores drag out the plastic trees and put Santa Claus in the window. Three specific analogies come to mind.

First, *it seems terribly repetitive.* The subject of giving is seldom approached creatively, and then when it is addressed, the comments are usually overstated and punctuated with guilt-giving remarks. Most often the congregation is not instructed as much as they are exhorted and exploited. Furthermore, there is neither subtlety nor much humor employed . . . only large helpings of hard-core facts mixed with a pinch of panic "because giving has dropped off." It doesn't take a Ph.D. from Yale to sense the objective during the first five minutes: give more! Same song, ninth verse. The repetitive cycle gets monotonous.

Second, *the whole thing has been commercialized.* Because grace has been separated from giving, greed has come in like the proverbial flood. Mr. and Mrs. Average Christian are punchy, suspicious, and resentful . . . sometimes for good reason. During the latter half of the twentieth century, all of us were embarrassed, weren't we? We saw shameful examples of greed employed in the name of religion. Unbelievable techniques were used to wrench money from the public's pocket, and we've gotten fed up with the gimmicks. Everybody wants more, not just religious folks. Enough is never enough.

I heard about a guy who gave his girlfriend his lottery ticket . . . and to their surprise, it won three million dollars! But the government taxed *him* for the cash. And then, if that weren't bad enough, when his ex-wife heard that he was now worth a lot of money, she upped the ante on the alimony payments.

Third, *there always seems to be a hidden agenda.* Just as merchants don't go to a lot of extra expense and trouble getting their stores ready for Christmas simply for the fun of it, neither do most ministers speak on financial stewardship because it is a fun subject. The bottom line is usually uppermost. The emphasis is seldom on the charming joy of grace-oriented giving but rather on the obligation and responsibility to give "whether you like it or not."

This is an appropriate time for me to mention a couple of things, just to set the record straight. How and why we give is of far greater significance to God than what we give. Attitude and motive are always more important than amount. Furthermore, once a person cultivates a taste for grace in giving, the amount becomes virtually immaterial. When those age-old grace killers, guilt and manipulation, are not used as leverage, the heart responds in generosity. Giving at that point becomes wonderfully addictive.

Late one year I challenged someone who means a lot to me to be more generous throughout the new year than she had ever been in her life. Because she is not wealthy and because she is unmarried and therefore has only a single source of income, this lady lived under the fear of running out of money if she followed the lead of her heart. Being a true model of grace and having a heart of compassion, she had often been prompted within to be more generous, but her fear restrained her. All she needed was a little encouragement to replace her fear with faith . . . which she did throughout the new year. She told me at the end of that year that she had never given more in one year in all her life, nor had she ever been so full of joy. In addition, she said the Lord had abundantly met every one of her financial needs, which motivated her to do a repeat performance in the year to come. That lady who has discovered this new dimension of grace is my sister, Luci. I am exceedingly proud of her for taking a giant step of faith as she has trusted God to honor her generosity. Today she is addicted to giving. The Lord is mightily using her presence as a significant part of the Women of Faith ministry.

WHAT MAKES GIVING SO WONDERFULLY ADDICTIVE?

It is not my intention to make a saint out of Luci. Neither do I wish to leave the impression that only a few who have some kind of "gift of giving" can know the joy of generosity. That is simply not the case. It is true, God does lead some to be unique examples of extreme generosity, but my thoughts in this chapter are not limited to them. My hope is to help you and others like you to see how grace can liberate you to become a model of unusual and consistent generosity, all the while filling you with inexpressible joy. No, this is not some ideal reserved for a chosen few; this is reality for all of God's people to claim.

Now is the right moment to step into the time tunnel and return to the first century. The original church in Jerusalem had fallen on hard times. Unable to pull itself out of a financial slump, thanks to the depressed economy in Judea and other Palestinian regions, those early believers were facing a bleak and barren future.

As is often the case in our own times, while one part of the world was suffering great need, another was flourishing. The Greeks in Corinth were doing quite well, which prompted Paul to urge them to give financial assistance to their fellow Christians in Jerusalem. His words to the Corinthian believers regarding this need are recorded in 2 Corinthians 8 and 9, two of the finest chapters in all the Bible on grace giving.

At the beginning of his charge he mentions the generosity of the struggling churches in Macedonia who gave during days of affliiction. In spite of their own poverty, and with great joy, they took delight in giving to those in need. On the basis of their example, Paul urges the Corinthians to follow the example they set. Those words of background information will help you understand the apostle's opening remarks:

> Now, brethren, we wish to make known to you the grace of God which has been given in the churches of Macedonia, that in a great ordeal of affliiction their abundance of joy and their deep poverty overflowed in the wealth of their liberality. For I testify that according to their ability, and beyond their ability they gave of their own accord, begging us with much entreaty for the favor of participation in the support of the saints, and this, not as we had expected, but they first gave themselves to the Lord and to us by the will of God. (2 Cor. 8:1–5)

Paul admits that he was surprised. He states that what the Macedonians gave was "not as we had expected." Of greater importance, their gifts did not originate in their purses and wallets. No, "they first gave *themselves* to the Lord" (emphasis mine), and then they gave their money. Grace giving begins in the heart. Grace-oriented generosity is the overflow of a liberated heart. This assures us that it has nothing to do with one's investment portfolio or monthly salary. Whether Macedonian or Corinthian, American or Canadian, Asian or Australian, the challenge is the same: First and foremost, we are to give ourselves to the Lord. When we do, our treasure will follow the leading of our heart.

Returning to my earlier question, What is it that makes all this so addictive?

First, *it helps us keep a healthy balance.* "But just as you abound in everything, in faith and utterance and knowledge and in all earnestness and in the love we inspired in you, see that you abound in this gracious work also" (2 Cor. 8:7).

In many a church there is faith; there is good teaching ("utterance"), a working knowledge of the Christian life; there is zeal, spiritual passion, and a great deal of love . . . but generosity? A superabundant willingness to give? Often that is the one ingredient conspicuous by its absence. How easy to take, to be blessed, instructed, encouraged, exhorted, affirmed, and strengthened—all those things received in abundance—yet fail to balance the receiving with our giving.

Did you notice how Paul refers to financial support? He calls it "this gracious work," and he exhorts us to "abound" in it. The Christian life takes on a healthy balance when our taking in and giving out stay in step. You and I feel closer to the Savior because that is what He did . . . He gave. "For you know the grace of our Lord Jesus Christ, that though He was rich, yet for your sake He became poor, that you through His poverty might become rich" (2 Cor. 8:9).

Study those words for a moment. Here was someone who was rich, eminently rich. At his disposal was the wealth of heaven, so mind-boggling it is beyond description. Yet He left it all as He came to give Himself for us. Why? That we, in turn, might pick up the riches of His life and follow His model.

The second reason that giving is addictive is that *in giving we model the same grace of Jesus Christ*. I am impressed that the verse of Scripture doesn't say, "for you know the obligation of the Lord Jesus Christ," or "You know the sense of duty," though that is true. It was a duty that He come to earth. But Paul doesn't write, "You know the requirement" or "You know the sacrifice." No, he mentions only the grace. When our Lord Jesus left heaven, He didn't leave gritting His teeth and clenching His fists, shouting, "Okay . . . Okay!" It wasn't obligation . . . it was grace that motivated Him to come. It was grace within Him that brought Him to Bethlehem as a little baby. It was grace within Him that allowed His hands and feet to be pierced with nails and grace within Him to say, "Father, forgive them. They do not know what they are doing." When you give knowing there will be no gift in return, you have modeled the purest form of the grace of the Lord Jesus Christ. It will help if you think about giving in that way.

Third, giving by grace is addictive because in doing so *we counteract selfishness and covetousness*. Read slowly and carefully the first five verses of 2 Corinthians 9:

> For it is superfluous for me to write to you about this ministry to the saints; for I know your readiness, of which I boast about you to the Macedonians, namely, that Achaia has been prepared since last year, and your zeal has stirred up most of them. But I have sent the brethren, that our boasting about you may not be made empty in this case, that, as I was saying, you may be prepared; lest if any Macedonians come with me and find you unprepared, we (not to speak of you) should be put to shame by this confidence. So I thought it necessary to urge the brethren that they would

go on ahead to you and arrange beforehand your previously promised bountiful gift, that the same might be ready as a bountiful gift, and not affected by covetousness.

Sometime in the past the Corinthians had promised that they would participate in an offering to answer needs in Jerusalem. But for some reason, they had left their promise. Their pledge had begun to wear thin. So Paul writes, in effect, "I just want to prod you a little and say you need to finish what you said you were going to do. I don't want your covetousness to get the best of you."

It can, can't it? Have you gotten a raise within the last twelve months? Isn't it easy, when that happens, for covetousness to take charge? Something we had wished we could own is now within reach. We come into a little money, whether it is a nice income-tax refund check or from some unexpected source, and it is easy for greed to cause a pledge to wear thin or a previous promise ("Lord, if I made more, I'd give more!") to be forgotten. And, by the way, this is a good time to insert: It is better to emphasize someone's giving rather than someone's income. I think Americans are enamored of how much people make. Frankly, that's the wrong thing to talk about. If I read the Scriptures correctly, I don't find the Lord's concern resting on what one makes nearly so much as on what one gives.

In an article entitled "Planned Giving—Legalism or Love?" which appeared in *Moody Monthly* magazine, May 1986, Sylvia and John Ronsvalle stated that "the average church member gives only 2.5 percent of his income to the church."[1] I've also heard my longtime friend and financial counselor Ron Blue frequently mention in his seminars:

If all Christians were reduced to a welfare income and they tithed on that amount, the church would double its receipts.

In working with our clients, it has been our experience that, with planning, their giving goes up, on an average, about four times what they were giving prior to doing planning.

The problem is not a lack of desire to give, but more so confusion because of the tremendous uncertainty and conflicting advice we live with on a day-to-day basis.[2]

Wise words from a trustworthy source.

In his book, *Human Options,* Norman Cousins mentions a fact that surprised me:

The cash lost each year in the United States amounts to about seventy-five dollars per capita—money that has fallen out of pockets, is misplaced, and so forth. The total average income for most of the human occupants on this planet comes to about sixty-nine dollars per person annually. The average American thus loses more money each year than almost anyone else earns. . . .

The essential problem in a computerized age remains the same as it has always been. That problem is not solely how to be more productive, more comfortable, more content, but how to be more sensitive, more sensible, more proportionate, more alive.[3]

When I lived in Orange County, adjacent to Los Angeles County in Southern California, one of our local newspapers reported some disappointing statistics. (Note: 1980s data)

Orange County residents are making more money but sharing less of it with charities, the Orange County Annual Survey found.

Compared with charitable giving elsewhere in the country, the average Orange County resident could pass for Ebenezer Scrooge.

The 1987 survey found the average annual donation in Orange County was $262—"unduly low" for the then-median income of $42,000, according to the survey.

But giving was even less in 1988. The average annual contribution plummeted 30 percent to $182, even though median annual income grew by 5 percent, to $44,000. . . .

The rate of donation declined from 0.6 percent of income in 1987 to 0.4 percent in 1988. A Gallup Poll released in October found that even the least-generous people nationally contributed an average of 1.5 percent of their annual income.[4]

The secret is not *making* more money. No one ever changed his or her giving pattern strictly because of increased income. I repeat, the focus should not be on the amount of money someone makes. Our Lord rarely emphasized that. Rather, His concern is on what one gives and the importance of releasing it in grace. What a wonderful way to counteract selfishness and covetousness. You will find that when grace awakens within you, selfishness will no longer win the day! It will be defeated and finally eclipsed by generosity.

Let me mention a fourth reason generosity based on grace is so addictive: *You can't help but be generous when grace consumes you.* "Now this I say, he who sows sparingly shall also reap sparingly; and he who sows bountifully shall also reap bountifully" (2 Cor. 9:6).

Here is an encouraging verse for anyone who fears that giving more will result in "running out." If I read these words correctly, the bountiful sower becomes that kind of reaper. I cannot explain the magic, the beauty, and the wonder of it all, but this much I know for sure: we cannot outgive our God.

The Grace *Awakening*

WHAT MAKES GRACE SO ATTRACTIVE?

Beginning in 2 Corinthians 9, verse 6, through the end of the chapter, I discover four things that make grace so attractive, not just at the Christmas season but all through the year. In verse 7 we are told: "Let each one do just as he has purposed in his heart."

Here is the first reason grace is so attractive: *Grace individualizes the gift.* When you give by grace, you give individually. You give proportionately to your own income. You have needs, and you have an income to meet those needs. That combination is unlike anyone else's on earth. You are an individual. When you give on that basis, your gift is an individual kind of gift. We are not all shoved into a tank, blended together, then "required" to give exactly 10 percent. (Though if everyone gave 10 percent, we would have such an enormous surplus in God's work we would not know what to do with the extra . . . but I'm sure we'd quickly find out.) It is much more individualized than that. Grace, remember, brings variety and spontaneity.

If you are married, how about regularly discussing your giving plans with your mate? Or if you are single and you have a job where your salary is increasing and you respect your parents and their giving habits, how about talking over with them a game plan for giving during this next year? By discussing it, you can discover ways to individualize your style of giving. Paul puts it this way: "Each *one* do *just* as he purposed in his heart" (emphasis mine).

You know our problem? Most folks don't "purpose." They don't plan; they impulsively react. But God says, "Let each one do just as he purposed in his heart." Think of how carefully you would plan a room addition. You leave nothing to chance, making certain not to miss one detail, one electrical socket in your planning, one window placement, or one place where you will or will not use carpet. You purpose and plan exactly how you want to add on to the house. I challenge you to do the same with your giving. Give grace a chance! Start with planning, praying, and thinking it through. Determine the amount and where your gift will go and when, and then release it with joy.

The second reason grace is so attractive is that *grace makes the action joyfully spontaneous:* "not grudgingly or under compulsion; for God loves a cheerful giver" (v. 7).

I never have been able to understand why everyone in the church looks so serious during the offering. Wouldn't it be great if when the offering plates are passed in church next Sunday, instead of grim looks, stoic silence, and soft organ music you hear laughter? I can just imagine: "Can you believe we're doing this?" "Put it in the plate, honey. Isn't this great? Put it in!" . . . followed by little ripples of laughter and applause across the place of worship. Wonderful! Why not? Deep within the heart there is an absence of any compulsion, only spontaneous laughter. The word *cheerful* is literally a Greek term from which we get the word *hilarious.* "God loves a *hilarious* giver."

I have said all through my ministry, and I repeat it again: If your giving isn't done with hilarity, don't bother. Giving is not for the unbeliever or for those who are grim and resentful. Such giving will not be blessed. The best kind of giving has no strings attached.

In an excellent and creative article titled "The Gift of Giving," author Calvin Miller addresses what I'm getting at:

> The wise men started it all, some say. Still, I like the way the Magi gave their gifts, for they presumably returned "to the East" without expecting Mary and Joseph to give them anything in return.
>
> Their gifts were meant for the baby Jesus, but there seemed to be no . . . obligation in their giving. . . .
>
> Often at Christmas, gifts become a subtle power play, resulting in obligation. Such gifts may subtly say, "While my gift appears free, repay me in kind," or "Enjoy this, Joe, but you owe me one now. . . ."

Let me suggest two ways to give a grace gift.

First, be sure it's impossible to measure the cost of your gift. My daughter's Italian mother-in-law has taught her to cook authentic Italian foods. So when my daughter wants to please me most, she fills a bowl with meatballs swimming in her marvelous marinara sauce, and I am content through long winters. . . .

Second, realize that non-material gifts are the best way to say, "Don't try to pay me back." . . .

One friend promised to pray for me all through the Christmas season. Another friend who knows I am fond of Shakespeare gave me a book of Shakespearean quotes from his personal library.[5]

You see, as I write about giving in this chapter, I am not limiting my remarks to money. Don't worry; monetary generosity will fall into place when grace is in place. Money will take care of itself.

Now for a third reason grace is so attractive: *Grace enables us to link up with God's supply line.* Look at verse 8: "And God is able to make all grace abound to you, that always having all sufficiency in everything, you may have an abundance for every good deed." When we possess an attitude of grace, we give. We give ourselves. We give from what we earn. And He, in turn, gives back in various ways, not matching gift for gift, but in an abundance of ways, He goes beyond.

A fourth reason grace is so attractive: *Grace leads to incomparable results.*

Because of the proof given by this ministry they will glorify God for your obedience to your confession of the gospel of Christ, and for the liberality of your contribution to them and to all, while they also, by prayer on your behalf, yearn for you because of the surpassing grace of God in you. (2 Cor. 9:13–14)

As I read these verses, I find at least three results I would call "incomparable":

1. Others give God the glory.
2. They learn, by example, to be generous.
3. The relationship transcends any gift we give.

Allow me one final bit of counsel: Once you begin to give on the basis of grace, do so *confidentially*. In plain English, keep your mouth closed. Keep the extent of your giving to yourself. Ideally, do so anonymously. And He who rewards in secret will fulfill His part of the bargain.

The "apostle of grace" concludes this lengthy section on giving by announcing, "Thanks be to God for His indescribable gift!" (v. 15). Paul had a pretty good vocabulary, but when he attempted to describe God's gift of Christ, he ran out of Greek words. He simply couldn't find a word for it, so he admits it is *indescribable*.

GOD'S ALL-TIME CHRISTMAS GIFT

Once again I am reminded of Christmas . . . God's "indescribable" Gift to us, the greatest example of grace giving in the history of time. Holding nothing back, He cared enough to send the best gift of all. When you stop and think about it, He chose the Gift we needed most.

One particular Christmas I received a boost of encouragement through numerous cards, colorful greetings, and meaningful letters. Among them was a simple white sheet of paper—no name, no address, not even a postmark on the envelope in which it came. Printed in beautiful calligraphy on the center of the sheet was a message that captures the essence of God's grace in sending us His Son.

> If our greatest need had been information,
>   *God would have sent us an educator.*

If our greatest need had been technology,
   God would have sent us a scientist.
If our greatest need had been money,
   God would have sent us an economist.
If our greatest need had been pleasure,
   God would have sent us an entertainer.
But our greatest need was forgiveness,
   so God sent us a Saviour! [6]

On that first Christmas morning, when Mary first unwrapped God's "indescribable" Gift, grace awakened.

14

Grace: It's Really *Accepting!*

WHEN I BEGAN THIS BOOK, I stated in the opening chapter
that grace is *really* amazing. As I write the closing chapter, I want to emphasize that grace is *really* accepting as well. It not only gives with joyful generosity, it receives with grateful humility. When a person truly experiences a
"grace awakening" and begins to understand and demonstrate the kind of
love I have been describing, there is not only the amazing desire to extend
encouragement, affirmation, support, and reassurance to others, there is also
an accepting attitude that allows others to reciprocate in like manner. As easy
and simple as that may sound, it is neither. In fact, it cuts cross-grain against
our natural tendency to be self-sufficient and invulnerable. Before you reject
that thought, think realistically. Just how open and accepting are you when
others extend unexpected and undeserved grace in your direction?

THE FLIP SIDE OF SEVERAL STRENGTHS

We who believe so firmly in the pursuit of strong character often forget that
such pursuits have a downside. I can think of four off the top of my head.

First, *with a commitment to excellence there comes an attitude of intolerance.* There is absolutely nothing wrong with pursuing excellence. Those who do are on a warpath against mediocrity, laziness, and incompetence. But the flip side of excellence cannot be denied: the tendency to be intolerant. If you work for an individual whose goal is the pursuit of excellence, you need no convincing. You have found there is little margin for error. To ignore a mistake is out of the question. No flaw is considered too small to correct. No accomplishment is so well done it cannot be improved.

One of the best-selling books of the 1980s was *In Search of Excellence,* in which the authors hailed companies who modeled standards of excellence in eight primary areas. The implication was clear: You wish to be excellent? Do not tolerate anything less. It's the same motto we heard from a professional football coach back in the 1970s: "Winning isn't everything; it's the only thing." The downside of such an intolerant philosophy is that it can be interpreted as rejection by anyone who fails to measure up.

Second, *with a lifestyle of discipline there come impatience and the tendency to judge.* Unfortunately, both come in the same package. A person who works hard to stay fit by eating better and less, plus maintaining a consistent, rigorous exercise program, tends to be impatient with those who eat too much and refuse to exercise even a little. The overeaters may view themselves as pleasingly plump. But Mr. Atlas and his iron-pumping wife, Wonder Woman, see them as slobs, plain and simple. Such a contrast reminds me of some amazing statistics I came across in a couple of similar sources that paint a statistical portrait of America (Note: 1980s data.). Among the things that happen each day in our country:[1,2]

- Americans purchase 45,000 new automobiles and trucks, and smash up 87,000.
- We eat 75 acres of pizza, 53 million hot dogs, 167 million eggs, 3 million gallons of ice cream, and 3,000 tons of candy.

- We also jog 17 million miles and burn 1.7 billion calories while we're at it.
- $2,021,918 is spent on exercise equipment, $3,561,644 on tortilla chips, and $10,410,959 on potato chips.
- Americans drink 524 million servings of Coca-Cola and are served 2,739,726 Dunkin' Donuts.
- 101,280,321 adults are on diets.

My point is this: If you're a jogger who burns off hundreds of calories while clicking off six or seven miles a day, you may have no patience with the fella who eats half an acre of pizza and washes it down with a couple of quarts of his favorite cola. Discipline and impatience tend to occupy the same body.

Third, *with a broad education and a love for culture and the arts, there is usually the flip side of exclusive sophistication.* Cultural buffs stick together. Art lovers are in their own world, and God help any poor soul who prefers country-western and foot-stompin' bluegrass music but finds himself among those who prefer Brahms or Chopin or Tchaikovsky! Because I happen to enjoy most any kind of music other than opera, I smiled when I read Haddon Robinson's admission: "I do not appreciate opera; what is worse, I have several friends who do."[3] As wonderful, delightful, and satisfying as the cultural world may be, none can deny the air of exclusive sophistication that accompanies it.

There is also a fourth flip side that comes to my mind: *With an emphasis on independence and high production, there is the presence of pride.* If you are an independent worker, an independent thinker, or if you have become independently wealthy by nothing other than sacrifice and hard work from ground zero up, chances are good that you have a great deal of pride. You have struggled for every dime you've made. You took no handouts, got no breaks, and refused all shortcuts to success. Whatever you got, you earned it the "old-fashioned way." Whatever you needed, you dug down deep and refused to quit until you got it. And as a result, you made it to the top, and it is no secret that you're proud of it. Then one day, along comes somebody who wants to do something for you, someone who desires to extend to you a little undeserved, unearned grace. Lots of luck.

Right now, do you know whom I'm thinking of? A lovely young woman who was very coordinated, athletic, strong, healthy, capable, independent of spirit, and talented. She loved to ride horseback; in fact, she loved everything about life. She was popular and fulfilled. Her name is Joni Eareckson Tada. But, as a result of a fateful dive into the Chesapeake Bay in 1967, her world was suddenly reduced to a wheelchair. Joni, still a delightful and beautiful person, is now a quadriplegic. Once independent, she is now forced to depend on others for survival. Can you imagine the difficulty of such a challenge? What a battle I would have with pride! And let's face it, it would be a struggle for any strong-willed, independent, highly productive person to be forced into a reversal of roles, from independence and achiever to dependence and acceptance.

How difficult it is for those of us who are able to produce a great deal to be accepting and receiving of the grace of others. We are not only determined, we are driven. We set a goal and we achieve it. We meet deadlines because we apply the necessary discipline, and we produce. Accompanying all that is an ironlike mind-set and spirit that is so involved in giving, giving, giving that when someone graciously comes to give to us, we are quasi-embarrassed. We may hide it, but we are uneasy, reluctant. To use words we can now understand, we resist grace. Capable and frequent givers find it the next thing to impossible to be grateful and willing receivers.

This especially reveals itself in the individual who has lived a great deal of his or her adult life without Jesus Christ. If you are independent and proud, successful and strong, productive and competent, you are fairly sufficient on your own. Then along comes someone who tells you about the Savior, Jesus Christ, offering you something you don't deserve and cannot earn. The normal response is, "No thanks. No help wanted. I've made it this far; I'll make it the rest of the way." It is possible you may cope fairly well with life, but I must remind you that you will not make it beyond death. As Jesus Himself taught, "For what is a man profited if he gains the whole world, and loses or forfeits himself?" (Luke 9:25).

EXAMPLES OF RESISTING AND ACCEPTING GRACE

While reading through the Bible in preparing for this book, I made a note of several lives that illustrate both resisting grace and accepting grace. Though the people we'll be looking at lived centuries ago, their circumstances, surroundings, and attitudes pulsate with relevance, making it easy for us to identify with each one.

Two Old Testament Examples: Moses and Samson

Exodus 3 records the account of a man who resisted grace when it was offered to him. His name was Moses. As we step into his life in the third chapter of Exodus, he is eighty years old. His life is a study in contrasts between his first forty years and his second forty years.

During his first forty years he was remarkable. His résumé was nothing short of impressive. He was the adopted son of Pharaoh's daughter. Raised in elegance. Educated at the Temple of the Sun. Experienced as a warrior. Capable as a speaker. Respected and confident. Josephus, the Jewish historian, suggests that he was what we would call the "Pharaoh-elect." He was being primed to take the throne as the next Egyptian pharaoh. He had won battles fighting Ethiopia and other countries. Perhaps he had a chest full of medals for bravery. He had a polished chariot and servants available at the snap of his fingers. When he rode through the fields, surely the people shouted, "Bow the knee. Bow the knee!" He was the epitome of nobility, the pride of ancient Egypt.

While in the court of Pharaoh, he was apparently spoken to by his God and was told that he was to deliver the Hebrews from bondage. He determined to obey. One day he happened upon an Egyptian assaulting a Hebrew. Without hesitation, he acted in the Hebrew's defense and murdered the Egyptian. To borrow from the words of the prophet Zechariah, Moses attempted to free the Hebrews by "might and power," rather than doing the deliverance God's way and in God's time. Tragically, he thought he could lead the exodus in the energy of the flesh.

God (as always) put thumbs down on the process. There Moses was, forty years old, no longer the darling of the nation. Everything for him changed . . . almost overnight. Pharaoh had no more use for him. He was instantly humiliated as he ran for his life. His guilt must have been unbelievable. His whole life went "down the tubes." It would be like building, building, building, building all through your adult life and, shortly after you reach the pinnacle of success, doing something stupid financially or ethically or perhaps morally. It destroys your family. It destroys your reputation. It ultimately destroys your business, even ends your career. And you wind up behind bars. (Scripture calls that sowing the wind and reaping the whirlwind—see Hosea 8:7.)

The bars on Moses' jail happened to be the Midian Desert, a sudden and unexpected career change. And for the next forty years, Moses' God remained silent. There is no record here or anywhere in Scripture that God spoke to Moses while he was a shepherd working for his father-in-law. Here Moses is on the stinging sands of the Midian Desert with a flock of sheep—the same man who had the leadership of a nation in his grip and had blown it! Disqualified, he had escaped to the desert. Guilt and remorse consumed him, leaving him with no other thought than this: *It's all over.* Keep in mind, all of that is the background to Exodus 3.

Grace: It's Really Accepting!

One morning Moses awakens and leads the flock of sheep to the backside of the desert. He may have been there hundreds of times before, but today is different. Today the silence of God will be broken, much to Moses' surprise.

> Now Moses was pasturing the flock of Jethro his father-in-law, the priest of Midian; and he led the flock to the west side of the wilderness, and came to Horeb, the mountain of God. And the angel of the Lord appeared to him in a blazing fire from the midst of a bush; and he looked, and behold, the bush was burning with fire, yet the bush was not consumed. (Exod. 3:1–2)

If you have traveled much in the desert, you know that a bush may suddenly, on its own, burst into flames. But of course they always burn up. This one didn't. The flame persisted, but the bush was not consumed. Moses was puzzled. The longer he stood and studied the bush, the more it burned and burned and burned. Abruptly out of the midst of the bush came a voice he hadn't heard for decades: "Moses! Moses!" Incredible moment! He knew that voice. He remembered it from forty years before. There was no other voice like that one. He thought his life was finished. He had made such a mess of things that he had been convinced he would never hear that voice again. How wrong he was!

Do you know what is in that voice? Grace. Have you heard it? Sitting in a bar some night trying to drown your fears and loneliness, did you hear the voice? Sitting in jail, having ruined your reputation, have you heard that voice? Leaving a divorce court with horrendous memories of what might have been, as you returned all alone to your apartment, did you hear the voice? Having messed up your life through a series of events too shameful to rehearse, did you convince yourself you were through forever? Or have you forgotten the voice? Listen again! That voice comes from God's heart of grace, and it is calling your name. You may have been saying for a long time now, "It is over. It is finished. I am through. There is no chance." Grace knows no such restrictions. Let grace awaken! Like the bush that kept burning, grace keeps reaching.

F. B. Meyer writes eloquently of this moment.

There are days in all lives which come unannounced, unheralded; no angel faces look out of heaven; no angel voices put us on our guard: but as we look back on them in afteryears, we realize that they were the turning points of existence. Perhaps we look longingly back on the uneventful routine of the life that lies beyond them; but the angel, with drawn sword, forbids our return, and compels us forward. It was so with Moses. . . .

. . . Then, all suddenly, a common bush began to shine with the emblem of Deity; and from its heart of fire the voice of God broke the silence of the ages in words that fell on the shepherd's ear like a double-knock: "Moses, Moses."

And from that moment all his life was altered. The door which had been so long in repairing was suddenly put on its hinges again and opened.[4]

Moses thought he was finished forever. Do you know why? *Guilt. Shame.* Don't think for a moment that because of those twin grace killers, Moses jumped at the chance to lead the Exodus. Remember, he was finished as far as his mind was concerned. But not God's. What we have in the balance of chapter 3 and into chapter 4 is a dialogue, better defined as an argument. God is saying "Go," and Moses is answering "No." God initiates the invitation: "Come now, and I will send you to Pharaoh, so that you may bring My people, the sons of Israel, out of Egypt" (Exod. 3:10).

Had he heard that before? For sure. That was four decades ago, back in Egypt, before he impulsively killed the Egyptian, remember? Maybe his mind was playing tricks on him. *It can't be real . . . or is it? God is saying the same thing he said forty years ago—but it can't be God! No way would He give me another chance!*

Examine the argument. Moses answers, "Who am I?" If God had interrupted, He would have said, "You're nothing. But you don't have to be somebody to be used by Me." Grace means God uses nobodies. Grace also means He makes nobodies into somebodies. The problem is this: Our shame screams so loudly and our guilt is so huge, we convince ourselves we're not useful, and we think we cannot measure up. After all, you may think, *I have to be somebody special to be useful or important to God.* But the fact is He does great things through nobodies. He does some of His best work with those who think they are finished and, humanly speaking, should be. Moses' words reveal his inability to accept grace. "Who am I, that I should go to Pharaoh, and that I should bring the sons of Israel out of Egypt?"(v. 11).

I love God's answer! "Certainly I will be with you, and this shall be the sign to you that it is I who have sent you: *when* you have brought the people out of Egypt, you shall worship God at this mountain" (v. 12, emphasis mine). Notice God said *when*, not *if*. God will get His way. You will look back and say, "I really cannot explain how, but God did it." That is the way it is with grace.

Moses' fear begins to surface.

> Then Moses said to God, "Behold, I am going to the sons of Israel, and I shall say to them, 'The God of your fathers has sent me to you.' Now they may say to me, 'What is His name?' What shall I say to them?" (v. 13)

Dear, anxious Moses! He's already got a worry list started. Listen to him rehearse his "they may say" concerns. Don't miss his use of the scare word, *may*. It is typical of all who are afraid of acting on grace. The worry hasn't happened yet. But, you know, "Lord, they may say, 'What is His name?' and I won't have all the answers." God's answer is designed to bring comfort: "You will have all of Me." But the man is still unconvinced. He simply cannot accept God's grace.

The argument continues into Exodus 4. Moses' guilt is enormous! His shame has him pinned to the mat. God hasn't yet convinced him that neither guilt nor shame is appropriate. Moses' answer begins with "What if?" (That is another missile from his arsenal of worry.)

> Then Moses answered and said, "What if they will not believe me, or listen to what I say? For they may say, 'The Lord has not appeared to you.'" (Exod. 4:1)

Moses is saying, in effect, "Lord, I won't have their respect. Some of them may even remember I'm the man who killed the Egyptian. They may say, 'You've got a record. You're a killer!'" God reassures him, "You'll have all of My power. You will have all the power you need." And after God performs a miracle in front of him, using Moses' own hands, He adds, "If I can do that with a staff and with a serpent, believe Me, I can take your power, as little as it is, and I can use it." Moses is still hesitant. "Please, Lord, I have never been eloquent, neither recently nor in time past, nor since Thou hast spoken to Thy servant; for I am slow of speech and slow of tongue" (Exod. 4:10).

Too many years in the hot desert had blurred Moses' memory. When he was younger, "he was a man of power in words and in deeds" (see Acts 7:22). He was once eloquent. But for the last forty years, he had just been talking to those woolies in the wilderness. And you don't cultivate your public-speaking skills in the wilderness with the sand stinging your face and the sun turning your skin to leather. It is survival city out there, nothing more. So he whines, "Lord, I'm not qualified. Those Egyptians are well trained and well educated." And he jumps to the conclusion, "I'm not eloquent." In no uncertain terms, the Lord tells him, "You'll have all that is needed." What God wants is an obedient heart and availability.

God commands, "Go, and I'll be with your mouth." Isn't that beautiful? I've claimed that verse on a number of occasions, especially when I have had to stand before audiences I didn't know. I just said, "Lord, You promised Moses You'd be with his mouth, so I ask You to be with mine. I'm satisfied to be Your mouthpiece. My heart's prepared, so please speak through my vocal cords." Time and again, He has "been with my mouth."

In verse 13 Moses is still arguing: "Please, Lord, now send the message by whomever Thou wilt." That may sound humble, but the man is really trying to get out of the assignment. "Send somebody else." One paraphrase reads, "Send anybody else," which, being interpreted, certainly meant, "Send anybody but me." And the Lord says, "Okay, you have a brother. His name is Aaron. I'll send him." Remember Aaron? He is the one who will encourage the people only weeks later, to build and worship the golden calf. One of the heartaches of Moses' life was his brother. Yet God graciously allowed Moses to have him as his spokesman.

When it comes to accepting grace, the first thing to remember is this: *We resist grace when our guilt and shame have not been adequately dealt with.* Most folks, it seems, are better acquainted with their guilt and shame than with their God. Grace nullifies guilt. It renders shame powerless. Many of you who are reading these lines are better students of what you have done wrong than you are of what God wants to do with you now that you have made things right. And you are using your guilt and shame as a way to stay away from God's best.

One more thought on this. You know the last person on earth we forgive? Ourselves. We will forgive an enemy more easily and quickly than we will forgive ourselves. But not until we have fully accepted the forgiveness of the Lord God will we be ready to let His grace awaken in us.

Alexander Whyte writes beautifully of Moses' life and ours:

> Some of you will know what forty years in the wilderness, and at the back of the Mount of God, have done for yourselves. You know how those years have reduced and subdued your too-high temper, and weaned you off from

the shams and the sweetnesses of this world, and given you some eyes and some heart to suffer the loss of all things. . . . And if forty years have wrought such a change in such a slow-hearted scholar of God as you are, you will not wonder at the man Moses as he came back from the land of Midian. Any use you are, or are ever likely to be, or have now any hope or any ambition to be — it all has its roots in the great grace of God to you.[5]

I hope you will never forget the following: any person being greatly used of God is a recipient of God's great grace. Not one deserves it. Not one is adequate for the blessings that he or she is receiving. But God in His sovereign mercy has chosen to give great grace to an imperfect, ill-deserving individual . . . in spite of and in greater measure than his or her guilt and shame.

Judges 16 is our next stop. We have considered Moses. Let's look next at Samson. Those who have been raised in the church know the story of Samson fairly well. I remember as a little boy having a Bible that included colorful pictures. I remember often looking at the picture of how some artist thought Samson looked and trying to imagine what it was like to be that strong. And I didn't understand as a little boy that he was not strong because of something external . . . not because he looked fit or kept himself in shape. He was strong because of the grace of God.

Before the man was even born, his parents asked the Lord to guide them in the rearing of this little boy they would soon have in their arms. He had a godly set of parents who prayed for God's grace to be upon their son. And sure enough, before he was born, God promised, "He will be a Nazirite from birth. He will be set apart unto Me. He will begin to deliver Israel from the hand of the Philistines."

So when the boy was born, Samson's parents set him apart to God as a Nazirite. That means he was never to drink strong drink, he was never to touch a dead animal carcass or a human corpse, and he was never to cut his hair. His hair became long and flowing, a symbol of his strength. And sure enough, exactly as God predicted, he began to deliver Israel from the Philistines. The problem with Samson, as you may already know, is that he refused to control his lust, resulting in the collapse of his world.

We read in Judges 15:20: "He judged Israel twenty years in the days of the Philistines."

For two continuous decades Samson was in the process of delivering Israel from the hand of the enemy. For twenty years he did his work. For twenty years he carried out his divine calling. And yet, immediately on the heels of that verse we read that he went in to a harlot (16:1), and shortly thereafter we find him in the valley of Sorek, which is Philistine country, playfully lusting in the lap of Delilah. And the rest is a study in tragedy. The man toys with his relationship with God as he tells Delilah the secret of his strength. And after he falls asleep on her lap, she calls for help from her conspirators-in-hiding, who come and shave his head. When Samson awakens, he doesn't even realize both the Lord and his strength have departed from him. Bald, vulnerable, insensitive, he doesn't know how helpless he is. Soon, however, he is at their mercy. One verse tells it all: "Then the Philistines seized him and gouged out his eyes; and they brought him down to Gaza and bound him with bronze chains, and he was a grinder in the prison" (Judg. 16:21).

What a tragic set of affairs! A victim of his lust, Samson became a prisoner of hated enemies. After being brutally blinded, he was led away to live in the excrement and filth of a Philistine dungeon and to labor as a grinder. Here is the once-strong judge of Israel in a place he deserved, humanly speaking. He played with fire and couldn't escape getting burned. In the words of Proverbs 5:22, he was "held with the cords of his sin." And if you and I were to vote as judges on the bench, we would say, "Guilty! Let him live there the rest of his life." Justice had her due. The man got what he deserved, no question.

But God never runs out of grace. Read the next verse in case you doubt that. "However, the hair of his head began to grow again after it was shaved off" (Judg. 16:22).

To borrow from the apostle Paul's words, "Where sin abounded, grace superabounded." If men and women had had their way in that day, they would have said, "May he be bald the rest of his life." But God doesn't operate like that. You think Samson wasn't thrilled the morning he awoke and felt a little fuzz? Talk about grace awakening! You think he didn't check his head *every morning* from then on? With more hair came additional strength. And as his strength returned, so did his determination to fulfill the mandate given by God at his birth: to deliver Israel from the Philistines.

Here's the rest of the story.

> Now the lords of the Philistines assembled to offer a great sacrifice to Dagon their god, and to rejoice, for they said, "Our god has given Samson our enemy into our hands." When the people saw him, they praised their god, for they said, "Our god has given our enemy into our hands, Even the destroyer of our country, Who has slain many of us." It so happened when they were in high spirits, that they said, "Call for Samson, that he may amuse us." (Judg. 16:23–25)

In other words, they're saying, "We need that Israelite clown in here. Bring him in to make us laugh!"

> So they called for Samson from the prison, and he entertained them. And they made him stand between the pillars. Then Samson said to the boy who was holding his hand, "Let me feel the pillars on which the house rests, that I may lean against them." Now the house was full of men and women, and all the lords of the Philistines were there. And about 3,000 men and women were on the roof looking on while Samson was amusing them. (Judg. 16:25–27)

I love what follows! "Then Samson called to the Lord and said, 'O Lord God, please remember me and please strengthen me just this time, O God'" (Judg. 16:28). Here is a man who certainly does not deserve the attention of God . . a man who should have forfeited all rights to prayer, but he humbly calls on the name of his God. How could he? Grace. Maybe you have read this story dozens of times, but you may have never focused on what was happening in the last part of verse 28: "just this time, O God, that I may at once be avenged of the Philistines for my two eyes."

Here is a second principle about receiving grace: *We accept grace when we release all our expectations.* When we no longer feel we deserve special favors, grace awakens deep within us. It flows to and through those who have no expectations.

When I was in Fullerton, every Christmas season I had the pleasure of speaking to the single parents' fellowship in our church. Great folks. The room was always packed. Hundreds of teachable, open, and, yes, broken, humble folks. The thing I loved the most about speaking to our single parents was that they had no expectations of me. Do you realize how seldom that happens to me? Can you imagine how wonderful and freeing it is to stand in front of a group and know that you can blow it and have hundreds of people who understand and even enjoy it! Those folks knew what it meant to be rejected, shoved aside, forgotten. The remainder of their adult life was being spent, they felt, recovering from failure. Therefore, they had no great expectations of life in general or of me in particular. When I stepped up to the plate, I didn't have to knock a homer. They appreciated it if I just bunted. No big expectations. Actually, they appreciated my just suiting up and showing up.

That word picture gives me an idea. Let's say we're at the World Series, and it is the bottom of the ninth. The Texas Rangers are playing the Houston Astros. It is a game the Rangers really need to win, and the score is tied. The batter steps up to the plate, and he prays for a homer. The next thing we know . . . *boom!* He smashes one over the wall. We all scream, jump up and down, and shout.

But let's go further for the sake of illustration. Let's just imagine the manager of the Rangers ran out of players (everybody was hurt or something), and he had to use the bat boy in the bottom of the ninth. (I know, I know. You realists won't like this, but go along with me, okay?) Here's this inexperienced bat boy, stepping up to the plate at the Ballpark in Arlington, and he prays for a homer. Nobody has any expectations . . . least of all the bat boy. Then, *boom!* He smashes one into the second deck. Now if Butch the bat boy knocks one out, that is grace. If the bat boy saves the game, that is superabounding grace. Our problem is that most of us see ourselves as the slugger, not as Butch the bat boy. Sluggers expect a homer. Bat boys live their lives surprised.

Samson did not deserve new strength! But *without expectations*, he prayed, "Just this once, Lord, I claim Your grace." He was a washout, a failure, a man with a bad record. No expectations. And God, in grace, granted him his request. There are few grace killers more effective than expectations. Only when we release them are we ready to accept the grace God offers.

Two New Testament Examples: Peter and Paul

John 13 records a third story. The scene portrayed in this chapter took place at the Last Supper, an intimate setting. Jesus is with His men for the last time before His arrest and trial. Actually, it is just a few hours before the crucifixion. Do you know what the disciples were doing before Jesus washed their feet? I am sure that many would think they were praying. On the contrary, according to Luke 22:24–26, they began arguing over who was the greatest. Can you imagine?

"I'm going to sit on Jesus' right."

"No, that's my position. I am confident He will have me sit there."

"Well, I'm at least going to sit on the left."

"You don't deserve the left hand. You don't deserve the end of the table!"

They were arguing back and forth over who would be at the top of the heap in the kingdom.

What most folks don't realize is that all twelve had come into the room for the meal, and nobody had washed anybody's feet. If you've ever lived in or visited a home in the Orient, you understand how inappropriate their negligence was. To enter with dirty feet was as improper as coming into the room with your shoes on. In those days, a house servant was normally stationed at the door. And if there was not an appointed servant, it was a self-appointed servant-heart who waited at the door with a towel and a basin and washed feet as people arrived. Not these twelve! They were so busy worrying and arguing over who would be considered top dog that they forgot about taking care of their dirty feet.

But Jesus remembered:

[He] rose from supper, and laid aside His garments; and taking a towel, He girded Himself about. Then He poured water into the basin, and began to wash the disciples' feet, and to wipe them with the towel with which He was girded. And so He came to Simon Peter. He [Peter] said to Him, "Lord, do You wash my feet?" (John 13:4–6)

The Amplified Bible renders John's account of Peter's emphatic resistance this way: "Lord, are my feet to be washed by You?" I mean, the audacity! As Peter said that, I would imagine he also pulled his feet up under him. Can't you feel the resistance?

Anyone who has made a study of Peter can understand his reluctance. He was the spokesman for the group, clearly the leader among the Twelve. He normally operated in a rather confident and proud manner.

But let's not be too critical. The man was passionately loyal, fervently committed to the mission of Christ. However, being strong and capable, he could not tolerate the thought of admitting need or weakness.

Even when Jesus had told him earlier, "Peter, Satan would sift you as wheat!" the disciple had responded by saying, in effect, "Lord, all the other disciples may turn away, but I will *never* turn my back on You." And yet within a matter of a few hours he lied three times straight: "I don't even know Him. I swear, I don't know Him!"

We should not be surprised at Peter's strong reluctance: "Never shall You wash my feet!" (v. 8). Our Lord had stooped and reached out in grace, but Peter dogmatically refused. In rather emphatic Greek, John records Peter's statement of independence: "By no means will You wash my feet unto the age." Today we'd say, "No way, Lord . . . never!"

Here we find a third principle about receiving grace: *We resist grace when our pride is still paramount.* Of all the internal killers ready to pounce on grace, none is more assaulting than pride. Each time grace reaches, pride resists. Each time grace offers, pride refuses. Yes, each and every time, pride leaves no room for grace. Awakening grace and a proud heart cannot coexist.

Are you still impressed with your title, your public image, what people think of you? Is your position more important to you than your salvation? Are you still overly impressed with what you're doing? Do you look for subtle ways to pay back when someone gives to you? Or can you simply and graciously say, "Thank you"? If your pride is under proper restraint, you could even be vulnerable enough to say, "You know, I really needed what you gave me. Thank you."

That is hard to do when you are proud, like our friend Peter. Pride holds us back and conveys a false image that says, "I am without need." Haven't you ever looked at someone you really respected and wondered, *Does that person ever have a need? Can that individual imagine what it is like to live in the kind of world I live in?* The truth is that all of us are needy people; it's just that some of us hide it better than others.

If you really want to be a model of grace, get hold of that killer within you named pride. Force it to the mat. Make it surrender. If your feet are dirty and grace offers to wash them, don't listen to pride for two seconds. Be grateful for cleansing grace.

So far we have looked at three lives. First, Moses resisted grace because his guilt was not sufficiently dealt with. Second, Samson accepted grace because his expectations had been done away with. Third, Peter resisted grace because his pride was still paramount. We're ready now for a fourth and final example—Paul. What a magnificent model! He accepted grace because *he no longer put confidence in the flesh.*

What was his flesh like? What was it like to be in the skin of Saul of Tarsus, a.k.a. the apostle Paul? Read and try to imagine . . . He was "circumcised the eighth day, of the nation of Israel, of the tribe of Benjamin, a Hebrew of Hebrews; as to the Law, a Pharisee" (Phil. 3:5). The consummate Pharisee, to the letter of the Law! You could not find a flaw, not even in his zeal. Continuing his pedigree—"as to zeal, a persecutor of the church; as to the righteousness which is in the Law, found blameless" (v. 6).

Paul says, "That's my record." But God cut him down to size. In the eyes of the world, he was impressive. But before the eyes of God, he was lost and in great need. Look at how he states that fact: "But whatever things were gain to me, those things I have counted as loss for the sake of Christ" (v. 7). A few lines later he admits:

> Not that I have already obtained it, or have already become perfect, but I press on in order that I may lay hold of that for which also I was laid hold of by Christ Jesus. Brethren, I do not regard myself as having laid hold of it yet; but one thing I do: forgetting what lies behind and reaching forward

to what lies ahead, I press on toward the goal for the prize of the upward call of God in Christ Jesus. (vv. 12–14)

Paul says, in effect, "For too many years I went full speed ahead in the wrong direction. Now I realize how off target I really was. Christ alone is worth my zeal and passion! There is no other course worthy of pursuing. There I was on the wrong road earlier in life, but no longer."

You know what I read here? I read the testimony of a humble man who has lost all confidence in his own track record. He has gotten beyond his pedigree and his press clippings. He is now a man who has decided to "put no confidence in the flesh, although I myself might have confidence even in the flesh" (vv. 3–4). Finally he got his priorities straight. When that happened, everything fell into place.

I repeat, *we accept grace when we no longer put confidence in the flesh.* By "flesh" I mean what we can achieve in our own strength or what we have done or might do for our own glory. The flesh, as I have mentioned several times in this book, is an all-powerful destructive force.

Those who master that inner struggle are wonderful recipients of grace. Do you know what God has for people like that? A future that is magnificent beyond belief, relaxed, full of contentment and relief.

WHAT IT TAKES TO LET GRACE IN

What I have been writing about is letting grace into our lives—being open to it, allowing it to occur, permitting it to permeate us so completely that we awaken others to its glorious freedoms. Rather than resisting it as Moses and Peter did, my plea is that we accept it, like Samson (the undeserving) and Paul (the supercapable).

But how? First, it takes *an admission of humanity.* In other words, an attitude that says in authentic honesty, "I am only human—I'm no prima donna, I can't walk on water, and I won't try to impress you." Grace awakens within folks like that.

Second, it takes *an attitude of humility*. Nothing is so welcomed by grace as true humility, which is nothing more than a realization of one's standing before God (He is tops, number one, preeminent) and a willingness to be cut down to size in order for Him to be exalted and glorified. Humility has learned the hard way that no person can operate in the flesh and produce any good thing, so it prevents us from trying.

What a wonderful future God has for people who accept grace. It is almost too good to be true. When George MacDonald, the great Scottish preacher, was talking with his son about the glories of the future, his little boy interrupted and said, "It seems too good to be true, Daddy." A smile spread across MacDonald's whiskered face as he answered back, "Nay, laddie, it is just so good it must be true!"[6]

It is in accepting grace that we can begin to model amazing grace. Only then do we realize how good grace really is.

Conclusion

BACK WHEN I FIRST WROTE THIS BOOK ON GRACE, I had no idea what would transpire between my starting and my finishing the volume.

I stated at the outset that this is essentially a book about freedom . . . claiming it for ourselves and extending it to others. By now you understand what I meant by that statement. I had no idea that before I arrived at the conclusion of the book the entire world would have witnessed the most powerful example of freedom one could imagine: the fall of the Berlin Wall.

While I was writing on the importance of letting grace awaken— which necessitates our pursuing freedom at any and all cost—the daily newspaper, the magazines, and the television screen were pulsating with the same message. One remarkable scene followed another . . . story after story, all of them representing one of the greatest of all words: freedom. I watched, and I wept and sang as they did. I shouted as one section after another of the infamous wall tumbled to the ground, giving renewed hope

277

to people who often wondered if they would ever know the thrill of being liberated from social, economic, and religious bondage. Now they do. Now they are free indeed.

The stones and the steel, the barbed wire, and the guards that once separated East from West and dream from reality are now, for all practical purposes, gone. The people of East Berlin no longer awaken each dawn to face another grim and bleak day of colorless existence due to enforced restrictions. *Now free at last*, they awaken to the new dawn of liberty.

One of the most moving scenes I watched on television was a group of men taking turns with a sledge, pounding away on one section of the wall. One would grab the massive sledgehammer and strike the stone with all his might. After ten or fifteen blows, another would step in and do the same. While one blasted with the sledge, the others stood near, singing, cheering, and occasionally dancing in circles. Although I was half a world removed, I felt a knot in my throat as I smiled along with those men I have never met. All were deliriously happy. Finally, at long last, the stones loosened, and they could see daylight through the hole.

Interestingly, as I revised the book for its second release in 1996, the news was full of our fighting for the freedom of the people of Iraq. The wall of tyranny in that country was being shattered and people were dancing in those ancient streets!

There is another wall that is now being torn down. Because it is invisible, it is all the more insidious. Because it has been standing for centuries instead of decades, it is far more overpowering and stubborn. The stones that comprise the wall are formidable, intimidating, and thick. They would hold us back from all the things that God intended His people to enjoy. They still keep untold millions in bondage. I have identified many of them from without and from within throughout these pages — from without: legalism, expectations, traditionalism, manipulation, demands, negativism, control, comparison, perfectionism, competition, criticism, pettiness, and a host of others; and from within: pride, fear, resentment, bitterness, an unforgiving spirit, insecurity, fleshly effort, guilt, shame, gossip, hypocrisy, and so many more . . . grace killers, all!

My hope has been to create an appetite for grace that is so strong nothing will restrain us from pursuing the freedom and spontaneity it can bring—a longing so deep that a new spiritual dawn, a "grace awakening," if you will, cannot help but burst through the wall of legalism. Since I am a Christian minister, much of my involvement and exposure is in the realm of the church and Christian organizations. It has been my observation that even here most folks are not free; they have not learned to accept and enjoy the grace that has come to us in Jesus Christ. Though He came to set us free, it saddens me to say that many still live behind the wall of bondage. Regrettably, the stones of constraint are everywhere to be found. Instead of being places of enthusiastic, spontaneous worship, many churches and Christian ministries have become institutions that maintain a system of religion with hired officials to guard the gates and to enforce the rules.

In vain I have searched the Bible for examples of early Christians whose lives were marked by rigidity, predictability, inhibition, dullness, and caution. Fortunately, grim, frowning, joyless saints in Scripture are conspicuous by their absence. Instead, the examples I find are of adventurous, risk-taking, enthusiastic, and authentic believers whose joy was contagious even in times of painful trial. Their vision was broad even when death drew near. Rules were few, and changes were welcome. The contrast between then and now is staggering.

The difference, I am convinced, is grace. Grace scales the wall and refuses to be restricted. It lives above the demands of human opinion and breaks free from legalistic regulations. Grace dares us to take hold of the sledgehammer of courage and break through longstanding stones. Grace invites us to chart new courses and explore ever-expanding regions, all the while delighting in the unexpected. While others care more about maintaining the wall and fearing those who guard it, grace is constantly looking for ways to freedom. Grace wants faith to fly, regardless of what grim-faced officials may say or think or do.

Thank you for walking with me through the pages of this journey. It has been a stimulating challenge to write these thoughts. In many ways, I feel as though I have been plowing new ground, blazing new trails. Not much has been written on personal, liberating grace from an evangelical perspective . . . at least I have not found much along these lines. Perhaps this book is enough to encourage you to join the movement and get you started on your own venture. I hope so. But as you strike out on your own, beware. As surely as Bunyan's hero encountered every test and temptation en route to the Celestial City, you will come up against one legalistic stone after another, each existing for the same purpose: to keep you from the freedom you have in Christ.

Whatever you do, don't quit! Press on. It is worth all the effort. The good news is that you are not alone.

There is a "grace awakening" loose in the land. The ranks are swelling. Will you become a part of them? While you take your turn with the sledgehammer and pound away, a host of us are standing near, and some of us may be half a world away, cheering you on. Don't think of it as a lonesome, isolated task. You are breaking through to freedom, and no one is more delighted than the Lord Jesus Christ, who has promised you His grace. Never forget His words: "If therefore the Son shall make you free, you shall be free indeed." Stay at it. By the grace of Almighty God, the new movement will someday sweep across every continent, and the long-standing wall that has kept people in bondage for centuries will come tumbling down. And we shall all be free. Free in Christ, free indeed. Free at last.

Notes

ACKNOWLEDGMENTS
1. John Newton, "Amazing Grace" (1779).

CHAPTER 1   GRACE: IT'S *Really* AMAZING!
1. Dr. Karl Menninger, M.D., with Martin Mayman, Ph.D., and Paul Pruyser, Ph.D., *The Vital Balance* (New York: Viking Press, 1963), 204–205.
2. Ibid., 22.
3. Donald Grey Barnhouse, *Romans, Man's Ruin*, vol. 1 (Grand Rapids, Mich.: Wm. B. Eerdmans Publishing Company, 1952), 72.
4. Benjamin Warfield, in *Great Quotes and Illustrations*, compiled by George Sweeting (Waco, Tex.: Word, 1985), 133.
5. Sir Edward C. Burne-Jones, in *Let Me Illustrate* by Donald Grey Barnhouse (Westwood, N.J.: Fleming H. Revell Company, 1967), 145–146.

CHAPTER 2   THE FREE GIFT
1. William Ernest Henley, "Invictus," in *The Best Loved Poems of the American People*, selected by Hazel Felleman (Garden City, N.Y.: Garden City Books, 1936), 73.
2. James Russell Lowell, "The Present Crisis" (1844). Taken from 15th ed. of *John Bartlett's Familiar Quotations*, 567.
3. Donald Grey Barnhouse, *Romans, God's Remedy*, vol. 3 (Grand Rapids: MI: Wm. B. Eerdmans Publishing Company, 1954), 208.
4. Augustus Toplady, as cited in *Romans: The New Man, An Exposition of Chapter 6* by Martyn Lloyd-Jones (Grand Rapids, Mich.: Zondervan Publishing House, 1973), 19.
5. Augustus Toplady, "Rock of Ages" (1776).
6. Dorothea Day, "My Captain," in *The Best Loved Poems of the American People*, selected by Hazel Felleman (Garden City, N.Y.: Garden City Books, 1936), 73–74.

CHAPTER 3   ISN'T GRACE RISKY?
1. Martyn Lloyd-Jones, *Romans: The New Man, An Exposition of Chapter 6* (Grand Rapids, Mich.: Zondervan Publishing House, 1973), 8–9.
2. Reprinted from *What Luther Says*, vol. 2 (St. Louis, Mo.: Concordia Publishing House, 1959), 614.

CHAPTER 4   UNDESERVING, YET UNCONDITIONALLY LOVED
1. John Newton, "Amazing Grace" (1779).
2. Jackie Hudson, "People Grow Better in Grace," *Worldwide Challenge*, April 1988, 11–13, an adaptation from her book *Doubt: A Road to Growth*.
3. Elisabeth Elliot, *The Liberty of Obedience* (Waco, Tex.: Word, 1968), 32.
4. Ibid., 33.
5. John Newton, "Amazing Grace" (1779).
6. Ibid.
7. John Bunyan, cited in *The Grace of God* by William MacDonald (Kansas City, Kans.: Walterick Publishers, 1960), 30.

CHAPTER 5   SQUARING OFF AGAINST LEGALISM
1. Patrick Henry, in a speech in Virginia Convention, Richmond [March 23, 1779]. Taken from 15th ed. of *John Bartlett's Familiar Quotations*, 383.
2. Charles Sumner, "Slavery and the Rebellion"; speech at Cooper Institute [November 5, 1864]. Taken from 15th ed. of *John Bartlett's Familiar Quotations*, 539.
3. S. Lewis Johnson, "The Paralysis of Legalism," *Bibliotheca Sacra*, 120, no. 478 (April–June 1963): 109.
4. Daniel Taylor, *The Myth of Certainty* (Waco, Tex.: Word, 1986), 34–36.
5. Eugene H. Peterson, *Traveling Light* (Colorado Springs: Helmers & Howard Publishers, Inc., 1988), 57–58.
6. A. T. Robertson, *Word Pictures in the New Testament*, vol. 4 (Nashville: Broadman Press, 1931), 284.
7. Eugene H. Peterson, *Traveling Light*, 67.
8. Mike Yaconelli in *The Wittenburg Door* (Dec. 1984/Jan. 1985), issue 82.
9. Ralph Keiper, cited in *When the Saints Come Storming In* by Leslie B. Flynn (Wheaton, Ill.: Victor Books, a Division of Scripture Press Publications, Inc., 1988), 42.
10. Paul Tournier, *Guilt and Grace* (New York: Harper & Row Publishers, 1962), 98.

CHAPTER 6   EMANCIPATED? THEN LIVE LIKE IT!
1. Abraham Lincoln, in his second inaugural address, March 4, 1865, cited in *Abraham Lincoln: The Prairie Years and the War Years* by Carl Sandburg (New York: Harcourt, Brace & World, 1954), 664.

2. Ibid.
3. Shelby Foote, *The Civil War, A Narrative*, vol. 3 (New York: Vantage Books, 1986), 1045.
4. Gordon S. Seagrave, cited in *Quote Unquote* compiled by Lloyd Cory (Wheaton, Ill.: Victor Books, a division of Scripture Press Publications, Inc., 1977), 123. World rights reserved.
5. Donald Grey Barnhouse, *Romans, God's Freedom*, vol. 6 (Grand Rapids, Mich.: Wm. B. Eerdmans Publishing Company, 1961), 34. All rights reserved under International and Pan-American and Universal Copyright Conventions.
6. Abraham Lincoln in Washington, D.C., Aug. 26, 1863, as cited in *The Life, Public Service and State Papers of Abraham Lincoln* by Henry Raymond (New York: Darby and Miller, 1865), 753.

CHAPTER 7   GUIDING OTHERS TO FREEDOM
1. William Barclay, *The Daily Study Bible, The Letter to the Romans* (Edinburgh: The Saint Andrews Press, 1957), 92. Used by permission.
2. Jay Adams, *Competent to Counsel* (Nutley, N.J.: Presbyterian and Reformed Publishing Company, 1970), 145.
3. John Henry Jowett, *The Epistles of St. Peter*, 2nd ed. (London: Hodder and Stoughton, 1906), 93.

CHAPTER 8   THE GRACE TO LET OTHERS BE
1. Viktor Frankl, *Man's Search for Meaning* (New York: Pocket Books, 1980), 104–105.
2. William Barclay, *The Daily Study Bible, The Letter to the Romans* (Edinburgh: The Saint Andrews Press, 1957), 200. Used by permission.
3. Gladys M. Hunt, "That's No Generation Gap!" *Eternity*, October 1969, 15.
4. Reprinted with permission from Leslie Flynn, *When the Saints Come Storming In* (Wheaton, Ill.: Victor Books, a division of Scripture Press Publications, Inc., 1988), 37.
5. Ibid., 44.
6. Wyatt Prunty, "Learning the Bicycle" (for Heather), *The American Scholar* 58, no. 1 (Winter 1989): 122. Used by permission of the author.

CHAPTER 9   GRACIOUSLY DISAGREEING AND PRESSING ON
1. G. Campbell Morgan, *Acts of the Apostles* (Old Tappan, N.J.: Fleming H. Revell, 1924), 369.
2. William Barclay, *The Acts of the Apostles* (Edinburgh: The Saint Andrew Press, 1964), 107. Used by permission.
3. Chrysostom, cited in *The Acts of the Apostles* by William Barclay, 108.
4. Franz Delitzsch, *Commentaries on the Old Testament, Proverbs of Solomon*, vol. 2 (Grand Rapids, Mich.: Wm. B. Eerdmans Publishing Company, n.d.), 165.

Notes

5. Leslie Flynn, *When the Saints Come Storming In* (Wheaton, Ill.: Victor Books, a division of Scripture Press Publications, Inc., 1988), 64–65.
6. A. T. Robertson, *Word Pictures in the New Testament, The Acts of the Apostles*, vol. 3 (Nashville: Broadman Press, 1930), 241.
7. C. S. Lewis, in the preface to *Christian Reflections* and cited in *A Mind Awake: An Anthology of C. S. Lewis*, ed. Clyde S. Kilby (New York: Harcourt Brace Jovanovich, 1980), 128.

CHAPTER 10   GRACE: UP CLOSE AND PERSONAL
1. William MacDonald, *The Grace of God* (Kansas City, Kans.: Walterick Publishers, 1960), 54.
2. John Bunyan, *The Pilgrim's Progress* (New York: The Heritage Press, 1942), 28.
3. Ibid., 35–36.
4. Ibid., 54.
5. C. S. Lewis, *Mere Christianity* (New York: Macmillan Publishing Co., 1964), 162.
6. Archibald Robertson and Alfred Plummer, *The International Critical Commentary, A Critical and Exegetical Commentary on the First Epistle of St. Paul to the Corinthians* (Edinburgh: T. & T. Clark, 1961), 341.
7. John Newton, "Amazing Grace" (1779).
8. Taken from *Quote Unquote*, compiled by Lloyd Cory (Wheaton, Ill.: Victor Books, a division of Scripture Press Publications, Inc., 1977), 319.
9. Sven Wahlroos, *Family Communication* (New York: New American Library, Inc., a subsidiary of Pearson, Inc., 1983), 159.
10. Charles Bridges, *A Commentary on Proverbs* (Carlisle, Penn.: The Banner of Truth Trust, 1846), 41–42.
11. George Matheson, *Thoughts for Life's Journey* (London: James Clarke & Co, 1907), 266–267.
12. Ibid., 266.

CHAPTER 11   ARE YOU REALLY A MINISTER OF GRACE?
1. Kyle Yates, *Preaching from the Prophets* (Nashville, TN: Broadman Press, 1942), 201.
2. Ibid., 205–206.
3. Theodore Laetsch, *Bible Commentary, The Minor Prophets* (St. Louis, MO: Concordia Publishing House, 1956), 428.
4. George Duffield, "Stand Up, Stand Up for Jesus" (1858).
5. Charles Haddon Spurgeon, *Lectures to My Students* (Grand Rapids, Mich.: Zondervan Publishing House, 1954), 98.
6. William Barclay, *The Daily Study Bible, The Letter to the Corinthians* (Edinburgh: The Saint Andrews Press, 1963), 216–17.
7. Earl Henslin, Psy.D., "Shame-based and Healthy Spirituality," an unpublished chart. All rights reserved. Used by permission.

Notes

CHAPTER 12   A MARRIAGE OILED BY GRACE

1. Celeste Holm, *Reader's Digest Treasury of Modern Quotations*. Taken from *Reader's Digest*, February 1974 (New York: Reader's Digest Press, 1985), 484.
2. Dag Hammarskjöld, *Markings* (New York: Alfred A. Knopf, 1964), 66.
3. Kevin Leman, *The Pleasers: Women Who Can't Say No—and the Men Who Control Them* (Old Tappan, N.J.: Fleming H. Revell, 1987), 287–88.
4. Willard F. Harley, Jr., *His Needs/Her Needs* (Old Tappan, N.J.: Fleming H. Revell, 1986), 10.

CHAPTER 13   THE CHARMING JOY OF GRACE GIVING

1. Sylvia and John Ronsvalle, "Opinion," *Moody Monthly* (May 1986): 12.
2. From a lecture by Ronald W. Blue, president of Ronald Blue & Co, 1100 Johnson Ferry Road, Suite 600, Atlanta, Georgia 30347.
3. Norman Cousins, *Human Options* (Berkeley, Calif.: Berkeley Publications, 1983), 103.
4. Carroll Lachnit, "OC residents make more but give away less," *The Orange County Register*, 6 December 1988, A6.
5. Calvin Miller, "The Gift of Giving," *Moody Monthly* (December 1988): 23–25. Used by permission of the author.
6. Source unknown.

CHAPTER 14   GRACE: IT'S REALLY ACCEPTING!

1. Thomas N. Heymann, *On an Average Day* (New York: Ballantine Books, 1988).
2. Tom Parker, *In One Day: The Things Americans Do in a Day* (Boston: Houghton Mifflin Co., 1984).
3. Haddon Robinson, *Biblical Preaching, The Development and Delivery of Expository Messages* (Grand Rapids, Mich.: Baker Book House, 1980), 31.
4. F. B. Meyer, *Moses, the Servant of God* (Grand Rapids, Mich.: Zondervan Publishing House, 1953), 33–34.
5. Taken from *Whyte's Bible Characters from the Old Testament and the New Testament* by Alexander Whyte. Copyright © 1952, 1967 by Zondervan Publishing House. Used by permission. Alexander Whyte, Bible Characters, vol. 1, The Old Testament (London: Oliphants Ltd., 1952), 139–140.
6. Greenville MacDonald, *George MacDonald and His Wife* (a reprint of a 1924 ed.) (New York: Johnson Reproductions, a subdivision of Harcourt, Brace Jovanovich, n.d.), 172.

The Grace *Awakening* Devotional

A Thirty-Day Walk in the Freedom of Grace

CONTENTS

Introduction   291

DAY 1
Claiming the Package   292

DAY 2
The Power of Grace   295

DAY 3
Understanding Grace   298

DAY 4
Grace: A Many Splendored Thing   301

DAY 5
Grace Unlimited   304

DAY 6
Bonus   307

DAY 7
Grace for the Sinful   310

DAY 8
The Risk in Grace   313

DAY 9
Alternatives to Grace   317

DAY 10
The Inescapable Tension   321

DAY 11
Practical Suggestions for Guarding Against Extremes   325

DAY 12
Undeserving, Yet Unconditionally Loved   328

DAY 13
Defining Liberty   331

DAY 14
Defining Legalism   336

DAY 15
Four Antilegalistic Strategies   340

DAY 16
Claiming Our Freedom from Sin's Control   344

DAY 17
Grace and Freedom   347

DAY 18
Free to Eat, or Not   350

DAY 19
When God Says Do or Don't   353

DAY 20
Free to Choose Freedom   356

DAY 21
Careful Warning to All Who Are Free   360

DAY 22
Two-Dimensional Grace   363

DAY 23
Guiding Grace   366

DAY 24
A Few Actions That Signify Grace   370

DAY 25
Agreeing about Disagreements   373

DAY 26
Modeling Grace through Disagreeable Times   378

DAY 27
Awakening Grace   382

DAY 28
Grace That Releases   385

DAY 29
Marital Grace   388

DAY 30
The Attraction of Gracious Giving   391

CONCLUDING DAY
Free Indeed   394

*A*new movement is on the horizon. It is a movement of freedom, a joyful release from the things that have bound us far too long. More and more Christians are realizing that the man-made restrictions and legalistic regulations under which they have been living have not come from the God of grace but have been enforced by people who do not want others to be free. It is not an overstatement to describe this movement as an awakening that is beginning to sweep across the country. Nothing could please me more. This awakening to freedom is long overdue. It fits the times in which we are living.

When the sixteenth-century European Reformers brandished the torch of freedom and stood against the religious legalists of their era, grace was the battle cry: salvation by grace alone, a walk of faith without fear of eternal damnation. The church hated them and called them heretics. When the eighteenth- and early nineteenth-century revival, preached fervently by John Wesley, Jonathan Edwards, George Whitefield, and a handful of other risk-taking spokesmen for God, spread across Great Britain and into America, it was again grace that led the way. And there was again strong resistance from those who frowned upon the message of freedom in Christ. Interestingly, that sweeping movement came to be known as "The Great Awakening." What I am sensing these days is yet another awakening in the genre of those history-making movements. Perhaps it is best defined as "The Grace Awakening," a message whose time has come.

For the next thirty days, I trust you will experience a liberating dose of God's grace. I also trust it will leave you hungry to know and experience more, for grace keeps us fully engaged with God, who is the inexhaustible source of grace. Once you've experienced a grace awakening, you will be awake in new ways to all God wants to do in your life.

—CHARLES SWINDOLL

DAY 1

Dear brothers and sisters, if another Christian is over-come by some sin, you who are godly should gently and humbly help that person back onto the right path. And be careful not to fall into the same tempta-tion yourself.

Galatians 6:1 NLT

CLAIMING THE PACKAGE

*T*his day—this very moment—millions are living their lives in shame, fear, and intimidation who should be free, productive individuals. The tragedy is they think it is the way they should be. They have never known the truth that could set them free. They are victimized, existing as if living on death row instead of enjoying the beauty and fresh air of the abundant life Christ modeled and made possible for all of His followers to claim. Unfortunately, most don't have a clue as to what they are missing.

That whole package, in a word, is *grace*. That's what is being assaulted so continually, so violently. Those who aren't comfortable denying it have decided to debate it. Similar to the days of the Protestant Reformation, grace has again become a theological football kicked from one end of the field to the other as theologians and preachers, scholars and students argue over terms like frustrated coaches on opposite sides trying to gain advantage over each other. It is a classic no-win debate that trivializes the issue and leaves the masses who watch the fight from the stands confused, polarized, or worst of all, bored. Grace was meant to be received and lived out to the fullest, not dissected and analyzed by those who would rather argue than eat. Enough of this! It's time for grace to be awakened and released, not denied . . . to be enjoyed and freely given, not debated.

Grace received but unexpressed is dead grace. To spend one's time debating how grace is received or how much commitment is necessary for salvation, without getting into what it means to live by grace and enjoy the magnificent freedom it provides, quickly leads to a counterproductive argument. It becomes little more than another tedious trivial pursuit where the majority of God's people spend days looking back and asking, "How did we receive it?" instead of looking ahead and announcing, "Grace is ours . . . let's live it!" Deny it or debate it and we kill it. My plea is that we claim it and allow it to set us free. When we do, grace will become what it was meant to be—*really* amazing! When that happens, our whole countenance changes.

REFLECTING ON GRACE

If you know any believers (even yourself) who are "living their lives in shame, fear, and intimidation," describe what you think has caused those feelings.

How would you define God's grace?

In what ways has your life been most deeply affected by God's grace?

AWAKENING TO GRACE

John 8:3–11

The scribes and the Pharisees brought a woman caught in adultery, and having set her in the center of the court, they said to Him, "Teacher, this woman has been caught in adultery, in the very act. Now in the Law Moses commanded us to stone such women; what then do You say?" And they were saying this, testing Him, so that they might have grounds for accusing Him. But Jesus stooped down and with His finger wrote on the ground. But when they persisted in asking Him, He straightened up, and said to them, "He who is without sin among you, let him be the first to throw a stone at her." And again He stooped down and wrote on the ground. When they heard it, they began to go out one by one, beginning with the older ones, and He was left alone, and the woman, where she was, in the center of the court. Straightening up, Jesus said to her, "Woman, where are they? Did no one condemn you?" She said, "No one, Lord." And Jesus said, "Neither do I condemn you. Go. From now on sin no more."

According to John, the gospel writer, what was the real issue for the scribes and Pharisees when they asked Jesus to determine the fate of this woman?

How did Jesus express grace toward the woman, without letting her off the hook for her behavior or condoning her sin?

How did Jesus express grace toward the woman's accusers?

WALKING IN GRACE

What does it mean to you to be able to enjoy "the beauty and fresh air of the abundant life" Christ has given you?

"Grace is ours . . . let's live it!" How will you live God's grace today?

Is this approach to grace different from the way you were raised? If so, how?

*In Him we have redemption through His blood, the
forgiveness of our trespasses, according to the riches of
His grace.*

Ephesians 1:7

THE POWER OF GRACE

Candidly, I know of nothing that has the power to change us from within like the freedom that comes through grace. It's so amazing that it will change not only our hearts but also our faces. And goodness knows, some of us are overdue for a face change! Were you reared by parents whose faces said "No"? Or are you married to someone with a "No" face? If that is true, you may envy those who had "Yes"-face parents or are married to "Yes"-face mates. All of us are drawn to those whose faces invite us in and urge us on.

During his days as president, Thomas Jefferson and a group of companions were traveling across the country on horseback. They came to a river which had left its banks because of a recent downpour. The swollen river had washed the bridge away. Each rider was forced to ford the river on horseback, fighting for his life against the rapid currents. The very real possibility of death threatened each rider, which caused a traveler who was not part of their group to step aside and watch. After several had plunged in and made it to the other side, the stranger asked President Jefferson if he would ferry him across the river. The president agreed without hesitation. The man climbed on, and shortly thereafter the two of them made it safely to the other side. As the stranger slid off the back of the saddle onto dry ground, one in the group asked him, "Tell me, why did you select the president to ask this favor of?" The man was shocked, admitting he had no idea it was the president who had helped him. "All I know," he said, "is that on some of your faces was written the answer 'No,' and on some of them was the answer 'yes.' His was a 'Yes' face."

Freedom gives people a "Yes" face. I am confident Jesus had a "Yes" face. I have never seen Him, but I've determined from what I've read about Him that this was true. What a contrast He must have been! He was surrounded by lettered men, religious, robed, *righteous*, law-quoting, professional men whose very demeanor announced "No!" Pious without, killers within . . . yet none of their poison seeped into His life. On the contrary, He revolutionized the entire direction of religion because He announced "Yes" while all His professional peers were frowning "No." That has intrigued me for years. How could it be? What was it that kept Him from getting caught in their grip? In one word, it was grace. He was so full of truth and grace, He left no inner space for their legalistic poison.

REFLECTING ON GRACE

What do you think would be the most obvious characteristics of a "Yes" face?

Do you know someone who has a "Yes" face? How does being around that person make you feel?

The author pictures Jesus with a "Yes" face. Do you? Explain.

AWAKENING TO GRACE

2 Corinthians 1:18–22

But as God is faithful, our word to you is not yes and no. For the Son of God, Christ Jesus, who was preached among you by us—by me and Silvanus and Timothy—was not yes and no, but is yes in Him. For as many as may be the promises of God, in Him they are yes; wherefore also through Him is our Amen to the glory of God through us. Now He who establishes us with you in Christ and anointed us is God, who also sealed us and gave us the Spirit in our hearts as a pledge.

In this passage, to what specific areas does "yes" apply?

Consider what each of the following results of God's "yes" means to you:

- You are established in Christ.

- You are anointed.

- You are sealed.

- You have been given the Spirit in your heart as a pledge.

WALKING IN GRACE

Considering the four areas listed above, in which ones do you need to accept God's "yes" toward you?

Do you think you have a "Yes" face? Why or why not?

How can you begin to develop a "Yes" face?

DAY 3

And the Word became flesh, and dwelt among us,
and we saw His glory, glory as of the only begotten
from the Father, full of grace and truth.

John 1:14

UNDERSTANDING GRACE

What exactly is grace? And is it limited to Jesus' life and ministry? You may be surprised to know that Jesus never used the word itself. He just taught it and, equally important, He lived it. Furthermore, the Bible never gives us a one-statement definition, though grace appears throughout its pages . . . not only the word itself but numerous demonstrations of it. Understanding what grace means requires our going back to an old Hebrew term that meant "to bend, to stoop." By and by, it came to include the idea of "condescending favor."

If you have traveled to London, you have perhaps seen royalty. If so, you may have noticed sophistication, aloofness, distance. On occasion, royalty in England will make the news because someone in the ranks of nobility will stop, kneel down, and touch or bless a commoner. That is grace. There is nothing in the commoner that deserves being noticed or touched or blessed by the royal family. But because of grace in the heart of the queen, there is the desire at that moment to pause, to stoop, to touch, even to bless.

The late pastor and Bible scholar Donald Barnhouse perhaps said it best: "Love that goes upward is worship; love that goes outward is affection; love that stoops is grace."

To show grace is to extend favor or kindness to one who doesn't deserve it and can never earn it. Receiving God's acceptance by grace always stands in sharp contrast to earning it on the basis of works. Every time the thought of grace appears, there is the idea of its being undeserved. In no way is the recipient getting what he or she deserves. Favor is being extended simply out of the goodness of the heart of the giver.

Understanding Grace

REFLECTING ON GRACE

Describe an instance in your life when you received someone's unexpected act of grace.

Describe a time when you demonstrated God's grace by "bending down" for someone else.

As a way of understanding what Donald Barnhouse said (in the previous excerpt), narrow the scope of love to marital love, parental love, or Christian love. Then paraphrase his statement.

AWAKENING TO GRACE

John 1:14–17

And the Word became flesh, and dwelt among us, and we beheld His glory, glory as of the only begotten from the Father, full of grace and truth. John testified about Him and cried out, saying, "This was He of whom I said, 'He who comes after me has a higher rank than I, for He existed before me.'" For of His fullness we have all received, and grace upon grace. For the Law was given through Moses; grace and truth were realized through Jesus Christ.

"Love that goes upward is worship; love that goes outward is affection; love that stoops is grace." How did Jesus illustrate the kind of love that John called "grace" in this passage?

How would you describe the difference between law and grace?

Write a brief explanation for each of these phrases:

"We have all received . . . grace upon grace."

"Grace and truth were realized through Jesus Christ."

🖎 WALKING IN GRACE

When you recognize God's grace toward you—His unearned favor—how do you feel?

Identify at least one conflict or difficult relationship that you believe would benefit from a gracious gesture on your part.

Pray for someone you know who struggles to accept or understand God's grace. What other ways can you help that person to encounter grace?

DAY 4

*For the LORD God is a sun and shield; The LORD
gives grace and glory; No good thing does He with-
hold from those who walk uprightly.*

Psalm 84:11

GRACE: A MANY SPLENDORED THING

W̶e use grace to describe many things in life:

- a well-coordinated athlete or dancer
- good manners and being considerate of others
- beautiful, well-chosen words
- consideration and care for other people
- various expressions of kindness and mercy

Those statements remind me of Christ. What a perfect illustration of grace! Think of several examples with me. He stood alongside a woman caught in adultery. The Law clearly stated, "Stone her." The grace killers who set her up demanded the same. Yet He said to those self-righteous Pharisees, "He who is without sin, let him cast the first stone." What grace! Under the Law they had every legal right to bury her beneath the rocks in their hands . . . and they were ready. There they stood with self-righteous fire in their eyes, but He intervened in grace.

When His friend Lazarus died, Martha met Him on the road and Mary later faced Him in the house. Both blamed Him for not coming earlier: "If You had been here, my brother would not have died!" There is strong accusation in those words. He took them in grace. With the turn of His hand, He could have sent them to eternity, but He refused to answer them in argument. That is grace.

When He told stories, grace was a favorite theme. He employed a gracious style in handling children. He spoke of the prodigal son in grace. As He told stories of people who were caught in helpless situations, grace

301

abounded . . . as with the good Samaritan. And instead of extolling the religious official who spoke of how proud God must be to have him in His family, Christ smiled with favor on the unnamed sinner who said, "God, be merciful to me, a sinner." Even from the cross, He refused to be angry toward His enemies. Remember His prayer? "Father, forgive them . . ." No resentment, no bitterness. Amazing, this grace! Remarkable, the freedom and release it brought. And it came in full force from the only One on earth who had unlimited power, the Son of God.

REFLECTING ON GRACE

Which of the descriptions of grace in the list on page 16 comes closest to your own understanding of the term? Why?

Choose one of the biblical examples given and explain how you see Jesus exercise grace in that instance.

What recurring failure or struggle in your life reminds you most painfully of your need for God's grace?

AWAKENING TO GRACE

Luke 7:41–48 NLT

Then Jesus told him this story: "A man loaned money to two people—five hundred pieces of silver to one and fifty pieces to the other. But neither of them could repay him, so he kindly forgave them both, canceling their debts. Who do you suppose loved him more after that?"

Simon answered, "I suppose the one for whom he canceled the larger debt."

"That's right," Jesus said. Then he turned to the woman and said to Simon, "Look at this woman kneeling here. When I entered your home, you didn't offer me water to wash the dust

from my feet, but she has washed them with her tears and wiped them with her hair. You didn't give me a kiss of greeting, but she has kissed my feet again and again from the time I first came in. You neglected the courtesy of olive oil to anoint my head, but she has anointed my feet with rare perfume. I tell you, her sins—and they are many—have been forgiven, so she has shown me much love. But a person who is forgiven little shows only little love." Then Jesus said to the woman, "Your sins are forgiven."

Although Jesus never used the word *grace*, it permeated His actions and words. How does this story of the woman illustrate the way grace affects people?

What were the three comparisons Jesus made between the way Simon treated Him and the way the woman treated Him?

Jesus left a fourth comparison incomplete, allowing Simon to fill in the gap. What was Jesus' final point?

WALKING IN GRACE

Grace is not grace unless it costs something. In Jesus' parable, it cost the money lender 550 pieces of silver. Describe a time when expressing grace turned out to be a costly gesture for you. Would you do it again?

Which of your attitudes or actions might be hindering your capacity to recognize grace in your relationship with God?

Make this last answer a subject of prayer today.

Day 5

Surely He scorns the scornful, but gives grace to the humble.

Proverbs 3:34 NKJV

GRACE UNLIMITED

*M*y plea is that we not limit grace to Christ. We, too, can learn to be just as gracious as He. And since we can, we must—not only in our words and in great acts of compassion and understanding but in small ways as well. Let me describe four practical expectations you can anticipate as you get a firm grasp on grace.

First, *you can expect to gain a greater appreciation for God's gifts to you and others.* What gifts? Several come to mind. The free gift of salvation. The gift of life. The gift of laughter, of music, of beauty, of friendship, of forgiveness. Those who claim the freedom God offers gain an appreciation for the gifts that come with life.

Second, *you can expect to spend less time and energy critical of and concerned about others' choices.* Wouldn't that be a refreshing relief? When you get a grasp on grace—when you begin to operate in a context of freedom—you become increasingly less petty. You will allow others room to make their own decisions in life, even though you may choose otherwise.

Third, *you can expect to become more tolerant and less judgmental.* Externals will not mean as much to you. You'll begin to cultivate a desire for authentic faith rather than endure a religion based on superficial performance. You will find yourself so involved in your own pursuit of grace, you'll no longer lay guilt trips on those with whom you disagree.

Fourth, *you can expect to take a giant step toward maturity.* As your world expands, thanks to an awakening of your understanding of grace, your maturity will enlarge. Before your very eyes, new vistas will open. It will be so transforming, you will never be the same.

🌺 REFLECTING ON GRACE

Which of the four results to the practice of grace listed above do you most long to see in the way you relate to others?

Why do you think it is so important to speak about the action of grace as "gifts"?

How does a deeper understanding of grace help people grow more spiritually mature?

🌺 AWAKENING TO GRACE

Colossians 1:3–6 NKJV

We give thanks to the God and Father of our Lord Jesus Christ, praying always for you, since we heard of your faith in Christ Jesus and of your love for all the saints; because of the hope which is laid up for you in heaven, of which you heard before in the word of the truth of the gospel, which has come to you, as it has also in all the world, and is bringing forth fruit, as it is also among you since the day you heard and knew the grace of God in truth.

How does Paul explain the results of grace to the believers in Colosse?

To what does this passage point as the source for hearing and understanding grace?

Looking at the way Paul begins his letter to fellow believers, what does this passage reveal to you about his gracious attitude?

⚬ WALKING IN GRACE

Rewrite into your own words each of the four results of exercising grace from today's reading.

1.

2.

3.

4.

Would a person spending time with you yesterday have known you live under God's grace? Why or why not?

In what ways can you aim for more grace-worthy attitudes today?

Write a note to a Christian friend expressing your gratitude for his or her faith and your joy in knowing that he or she understands God's grace.

DAY 6

It is God who saved us and chose us to live a holy life.
He did this not because we deserved it, but because
that was his plan long before the world began—to
show his love and kindness to us through Christ Jesus.

2 Timothy 1:9 NLT

BONUS

*M*ost people I know look forward to payday. You do too, right? For a week, or perhaps a two-week period, you give time and effort to your job. When payday arrives, you receive a hard-earned, well-deserved paycheck. I have never met anyone who bows and scrapes before his boss, saying, "Thank you. Oh, thank you for this wonderful, undeserved gift. How can I possibly thank you enough for my paycheck?" If we did, he would probably faint. Certainly, he would think, *What is wrong with this guy?* Why? Because your paycheck is not a gift. You've earned it. You deserve it. Cash it! Spend it! Save it! Invest it! Give it! After all, you had it coming. In the workplace, where wages are negotiated and agreed upon, there is no such thing as grace. We earn what we receive; we work for it. The wage "is not reckoned as a favor but as what is due."

But with God the economy is altogether different. There is no wage relationship with God. Spiritually speaking, you and I haven't earned anything but death. Like it or not, we are absolutely bankrupt, without eternal hope, without spiritual merit; we have nothing in ourselves that gives us favor in the eyes of our holy and righteous heavenly Father. So there's nothing we can earn that would cause Him to raise His eyebrows and say, "Now maybe you deserve eternal life with Me." No way. In fact, the individual whose track record is morally pure has no better chance at earning God's favor than the individual who has made a wreck and waste of his life and is currently living in unrestrained disobedience. Everyone who hopes to be eternally justified must come to God the same way: on the basis of grace; it is a gift. And that gift comes to us absolutely free. Any other view of salvation is heresy, plain and simple.

✎ REFLECTING ON GRACE

Looking back on your own track record, in what ways have you tried to *earn* God's grace?

What does it mean to you that grace cannot be earned—that your salvation is a *free gift?*

What type of behavior by other people might make you raise your eyebrows and discount them from God's grace?

✎ AWAKENING TO GRACE

Matthew 20:1–16

For the kingdom of heaven is like a landowner who went out early in the morning to hire laborers for his vineyard. When he had agreed with the laborers for a denarius for the day, he sent them into his vineyard. And he went out about the third hour and saw others standing idle in the market place; and to those he said, "You also go into the vineyard, and whatever is right I will give you." And so they went. Again he went out about the sixth and the ninth hour, and did the same thing. And about the eleventh hour he went out, and found others standing around; and he said to them, "Why have you been standing here idle all day long?" They said to him, "Because no one hired us." He said to them, "You go into the vineyard too."

When evening came, the owner of the vineyard said to his foreman, "Call the laborers and pay them their wages, beginning with the last group to the first." When those hired about the eleventh hour came, each one received a denarius. When those hired first came, they thought that they would receive more; but each of them also received a denarius. When they received it, they grumbled at the landowner, saying, "These last men have worked only one hour, and you have made them equal to us who have borne the burden and the scorching heat of the day." But he answered and said to one of them, "Friend, I am doing you no wrong; did you not agree with me for a denarius? Take what is yours and go your way, but I wish to give to this last man the same as to you. Is it not lawful for me to do what I wish with what is my own? Or is your eye envious because I am generous?" So thus the last shall be first, and the first last.

Fairness is still an important issue today. How much of your spiritual life is focused on whether God has been fair to you?

In this passage, what is the relationship between grace and fairness? Do you think they are opposing concepts?

With which group of workers in this passage do you most identify? Why?

WALKING IN GRACE

Think of a time when you saw a friend bestow grace upon someone. How did you react? If you felt bitterness, how could you have reacted differently?

For which of your actions do you expect to receive a reward from God?

In what specific ways has God been gracious to you today?

Day 7

Can we boast, then, that we have done anything to be accepted by God? No, because our acquittal is not based on our good deeds. It is based on our faith.

Romans 3:27 NLT

Grace for the Sinful

*F*or the next few moments, graze slowly over this paragraph of truth recorded by Paul in the letter to the Ephesians. Take your time. Don't hurry.

> And you were dead in your trespasses and sins, in which you formerly walked according to the course of this world, according to the prince of the power of the air, of the spirit that is now working in the sons of disobedience. Among them we too all formerly lived in the lusts of our flesh, indulging the desires of the flesh and of the mind, and were by nature children of wrath, even as the rest. But God, being rich in mercy, because of His great love with which He loved us, even when we were dead in our transgressions, made us alive together with Christ (by grace you have been saved), and raised us up with Him, and seated us with Him in the heavenly places, in Christ Jesus, in order that in the ages to come He might show the surpassing riches of His grace in kindness toward us in Christ Jesus. For by grace you have been saved through faith; and that not of yourselves, it is the gift of God; not as a result of works, that no one may boast. (Ephesians 2:1–9)

Pay close attention to ten single-syllable words, "by grace . . . through faith . . . it is the gift of God."

One of my greatest anticipations is some glorious day being in a place where there will be no boasting, no namedropping, no selfishness. Guess where it will be? Heaven. There will be no spiritual-sounding testimonies that call attention to somebody's super-colossal achievements. None of that! Everybody will have written across his or her life the word "Grace."

"How did you get up here?"

"Grace!"

"What made it possible?"

"Grace."

"What's your name?"

"Grace."

REFLECTING ON GRACE

When you share your spiritual autobiography with others, how much of it is based on what you've done and how much on what God's done?

In what ways has God's grace given you courage to honestly tell others about your life experiences?

Think of several common "spiritual-sounding" phrases (for example: "God changed my life" or "I'm blessed"). Choose two or three of your favorite phrases and ask yourself, "What would I say if someone asked me what I mean when I say this?"

AWAKENING TO GRACE

Jeremiah 9:23–26

Thus says the LORD, "Let not a wise man boast of his wisdom, and let not the mighty man boast of his might, let not a rich man boast of his riches; but let him who boasts boast of this, that he understands and knows Me, that I am the LORD who exercises lovingkindness, justice and righteousness on earth; for I delight in these things," declares the LORD.

> *"Behold, the days are coming," declares the LORD, "that I will punish all who are circumcised and yet uncircumcised— Egypt and Judah, and Edom and the sons of Ammon, and Moab, and all those inhabiting the desert who clip the hair on their temples; for all the nations are uncircumcised, and all the house of Israel are uncircumcised of heart."*

According to the passage, what are the three most likely topics people boast about? Which one do you struggle with the most?

Even the people of Judah, who were called God's people, still were "uncircumcised of heart." How does the second paragraph above indicate that external symbols and rituals are not the same as knowing God?

If these verses were written today, what modern religious rituals or identifying symbols might be mentioned as merely external forms of "circumcision"?

WALKING IN GRACE

Describe an event in your life that taught you a memorable lesson about God's character. What did you learn?

What do you regard as your greatest accomplishment in life? How would you react if someone else received all the recognition for that achievement?

What happens to God's grace when you begin to show off or take credit for changes that God's grace has produced in you? In what ways could you boast about His grace in the presence of others?

DAY 8

You may say, "I am allowed to do anything." But I reply, "Not everything is good for you." And even though "I am allowed to do anything," I must not become a slave to anything.

1 Corinthians 6:12 NLT

THE RISK IN GRACE

*I*s grace risky? You bet your life it is. I am well aware that this issue of grace is indeed controversial; especially when I am calling for a new awakening to the freedom Christians have in Christ. A few will take what I write about grace and go crazy with it. Others will misread what I write, and misquote me, misunderstand me, and charge me with caring little about the holiness of God because (they will say) I give people the freedom to sin. On the other hand, some in the camp of carnality will thank me for relieving their guilt, because in their misunderstanding they now think it is okay for them to continue in their loose and carefree lifestyle. I wish these things would not occur, but that is the chance I'm willing to take by holding nothing back in order that the full message of grace be set forth. Yes, grace that is presented in all its charm and beauty is risky. It brings grace abusers as well as grace killers out from under the rocks!

Let's return to a key verse of Scripture, Romans 5:1: "Therefore, having been justified by faith, we have peace with God through our Lord Jesus Christ."

In order for anyone to stand securely and be at peace before a holy and just God, that person must be righteous. Hence, our need for justification. Remember the definition of justification? It is the sovereign act of God whereby He declares righteous the believing sinner while still in his sinning state. It doesn't mean that the believing sinner stops sinning. It doesn't even mean that the believing sinner is *made* righteous in the sense of suddenly becoming perpetually perfect. The sinner is *declared* righteous. God sovereignly bestows the gift of eternal life on

the sinner at the moment he believes and thereby declares him righteous while the sinner still lives a life marked by periodic sinfulness. He
hasn't joined a church. He hasn't started paying tithes. He hasn't given
up all to follow Christ. He hasn't been baptized. He hasn't promised to
live a sacrificial, spotlessly pure life. He has simply taken the gift of
eternal life. He has changed his mind toward Christ (repentance) and
accepted the free gift of God apart from works. Period. Transaction
completed. By grace, through faith alone, God declares the sinner
righteous (justification), and from that moment on the justified sinner
begins a process of growth toward maturity (sanctification). Day by day,
bit by bit, he learns what it means to live a life that honors Christ. But
immediately? No way.

Please understand, to be justified does not mean "just as if I'd never
sinned." I hear that often and it always troubles me. In fact, it weakens the
full impact of justification. Justification really means this: Even though I
still sin periodically and have found myself unable to stop sinning on a
permanent basis—God declared me righteous when I believed. And
because I will continue to sin from time to time, I find all the more reason
to be grateful for grace. As a sinner I deserve vengeance. As a sinner I'm
afraid of justice. And so, as a sinner, my only hope for survival is grace. In
its purest form, it makes no earthly sense!

◌ REFLECTING ON GRACE

Why is grace risky?

Describe how grace killers and grace abusers react to the concept of grace.
Do you know anyone like this?

How would you explain the concepts of justification and sanctification to
a new believer?

The Risk in Grace

Romans 6:15–18

❧ AWAKENING TO GRACE

What then? Shall we sin because we are not under law but under grace? May it never be! Do you not know that when you present yourselves to someone as slaves for obedience, you are slaves of the one whom you obey, either of sin resulting in death, or of obedience resulting in righteousness? But thanks be to God that though you were slaves of sin, you became obedient from the heart to that form of teaching to which you were committed, and having been freed from sin, you became slaves of righteousness.

Which kind of grace abuser is Paul cautioning against in this passage?

Explain what it means to be a slave of righteousness.

Describe your vision of total freedom. How does your picture mesh with this passage?

❧ WALKING IN GRACE

What prerequisites do you expect of others before you acknowledge or believe they have been saved? After what you've read so far, do you need to change your thinking? Why or why not?

When it comes to God's grace, how can you reach a balance between killing it and abusing it?

Think of your own process of spiritual growth toward maturity. What are two major lessons God has taught you on your path to sanctification?

1.

2.

I have swept away your sins like the morning mists. I have scattered your offenses like the clouds. Oh, return to me, for I have paid the price to set you free.

Isaiah 44:22 NLT

Alternatives to Grace

*I*f I choose not to risk, if I go the "safe" route and determine not to promote either salvation by grace or a lifestyle of grace, what are the alternatives? Four come to my mind, all of which are popular these days.

1. *I can emphasize works over grace.* I can tell you that as a sinner you need to have a stronger commitment to Christ, demonstrated by the work you do in His behalf, before you can say that you truly believe. My problem in doing so is this: A sinner cannot commit to anything. He or she is spiritually dead, *remember?* There is no capacity for commitment in an unregenerate heart. Becoming an obedient, submissive disciple of Christ follows believing in Christ. Works *follow* faith. Behavior *follows* belief. Fruit comes *after* the tree is well rooted. Martin Luther's words come to mind:

> No one can be good and do good unless God's grace first makes him good; and no one becomes good by works, but good works are done only by him who is good. Just so the fruits do not make the tree, but the tree bears the fruit. . . . Therefore all works, no matter how good they are and how pretty they look, are in vain if they do not flow from grace.

2. *I can opt for giving you a list of dos and don'ts.* The list comes from my personal and/or traditional preferences. It becomes my responsibility to tell you what to do or not to do and why. I then set up the conditions by which you begin to earn God's acceptance through me. You do what I tell you to do or you don't do what I tell you not to do, and you're "in." You fail to keep the list, you're "out." This legalistic style of strong-arm teaching is

one of the most prevalent methods employed in evangelical circles. Grace is strangled in such a context. To make matters worse, those in authority are so intimidating, their authority is unquestioned. Rare are those with sufficient strength to confront the list-makers.

3. *I can leave no room for any gray areas.* Everything is either black or white, right or wrong. And as a result, the leader maintains strict control over the followers. Fellowship is based on whether there is full agreement. Herein lies the tragedy. This self-righteous, rigid standard becomes more important than relationships with individuals. We first check out where people stand on the issues, and then we determine whether we will spend much time with them. The bottom line is this: We want to be *right* (as we see it, of course) more than we want to love our neighbors as ourselves. At that point our personal preferences eclipse any evidence of love. I am of the firm conviction that where grace exists, so must various areas of gray.

4. *I can cultivate a judgmental attitude toward those who may not agree or cooperate with my plan.* Grace killers are notorious for a judgmental attitude. It is perhaps the single most un-Christlike characteristic in evangelical circles today.

A quick glance back through the time tunnel will prove beneficial. Jesus found Himself standing before the brain trust of legalism, the Pharisees. Listening to Him were also many who believed in Him. He had been presenting His message to the crowd; it was a message of hope, of forgiveness, of freedom.

> "As He spoke these things, many came to believe in Him. So Jesus was saying to those Jews who had believed Him, 'If you continue in My word, then you are truly disciples of Mine; and you will know the truth, and the truth will make you free'" (John 8:30–32).

He spoke of the liberating power of the truth. Even though the official grace killers rejected His message, He assured them it could make them free. All who embrace grace become "free indeed."

Free from what? Free from oneself. Free from guilt and shame. Free from the damnable impulses I couldn't stop when I was in bondage to sin. Free from the tyranny of others' opinions, expectations, demands. And free to what? Free to obey. Free to love. Free to forgive others as well as myself. Free to allow others to be who they are—different from me! Free to live beyond the limitations of human effort. Free to serve and glorify Christ. In no uncertain terms, Jesus Christ assured His own that His truth was able to liberate them from every needless restriction: "So if the Son makes you free, you will be free indeed" (John 8:36). I love that. The possibilities are unlimited.

❧ REFLECTING ON GRACE

Which of the four alternatives to grace described above have you experienced in the past? What spirit was cultivated by such approaches?

What is the danger inherent in each of these alternatives?

Picture yourself completely unhampered by these four alternatives to grace. What would this freedom feel like to you? How would it transform your daily life?

❧ AWAKENING TO GRACE

Galatians 5:1–9

It was for freedom that Christ set us free; therefore keep standing firm and do not be subject again to a yoke of slavery.

Behold I, Paul, say to you that if you receive circumcision, Christ will be of no benefit to you. And I testify again to every man who receives circumcision, that he is under obligation to keep the whole Law. You have been severed from Christ, you who are seeking to be justified by law; you have fallen from grace. For

> *we through the Spirit, by faith, are waiting for the hope of right-*
> *eousness. For in Christ Jesus neither circumcision nor uncircum-*
> *cision means anything, but faith working through love.*
>
> *You were running well; who hindered you from obeying the*
> *truth? This persuasion did not come from Him who calls you. A*
> *little leaven leavens the whole lump of dough.*

What alternative to grace was being pushed on the Galatians by certain grace killers?

According to Paul's warning, what would happen to God's grace if the people followed the grace killers' advice?

Consider the actions and appearance you expect of other Christians. How do your requirements interfere with God's grace?

WALKING IN GRACE

List the aspects of freedom mentioned in the last paragraph of Day 9.
I am free from:

I am free to:

Which aspect of freedom you listed resonates with you the most? Why?

As someone who is "free to live beyond the limitations of human effort," how will you allow your life to demonstrate that grace today?

DAY 10

It's like this: When I was a child, I spoke and thought and reasoned as a child does. But when I grew up, I put away childish things.

1 Corinthians 13:11 NLT

THE INESCAPABLE TENSION

*B*ecause of grace we have been freed from sin, from its slavery, its bondage in our attitude, in our urges, and in our actions. But having been freed and now living by grace, we can actually go too far, set aside all self-control, and take our liberty to such an extreme that we again serve sin. But that isn't liberty at all, that's license. And knowing of that possibility, many opt for legalism lest they be tempted to live irresponsibly. Bad choice. How much better to have such an awesome respect for the Lord we voluntarily hold back as we apply self-control.

I remember when I first earned my license to drive. I was about sixteen, as I recall. I'd been driving off and on for three years (scary thought, isn't it?). My father had been with me most of the time during my learning experiences, calmly sitting alongside me in the front seat, giving me tips, helping me know what to do. My mother usually wasn't in on those excursions because she spent more of her time biting her nails (and screaming) than she did advising. My father was a little more easygoing. Loud noises and screeching brakes didn't bother him nearly as much. My grandfather was the best of all. When I would drive his car, I would hit things . . . *Boom!* He'd say stuff like, "Just keep on going, Bud. I can buy more fenders, but I can't buy more grandsons. You're learning." What a great old gentleman. After three years, I finally earned my license.

I'll never forget the day I came in, flashed my newly acquired permit, and said, "Dad, look!" He goes, "Whoa! Look at this. You got your license. Good for you!" Holding the keys to his car, he tossed them in my direction and smiled, "Tell you what, son . . . you can have the car for two hours, all on your own." Only four words, but how wonderful: "All on your own."

321

I thanked him, danced out to the garage, opened the car door, and shoved the key into the ignition. My pulse rate must have shot up to 180 as I backed out of the driveway and roared off. While cruising along "all on my own," I began to think wild stuff—like, *This car can probably do 100 miles an hour. I could go to Galveston and back twice in two hours if I averaged 100 miles an hour. I can fly down the Gulf Freeway and even run a few lights. After all, nobody's here to say, "Don't!"* We're talking dangerous, crazy thoughts! But you know what? I didn't do any of them. I don't believe I drove above the speed limit. In fact, I distinctly remember turning into the driveway early . . . didn't even stay away the full two hours. Amazing, huh? I had my dad's car all to myself with a full gas tank in a context of total privacy and freedom, but I didn't go crazy. Why? My relationship with my dad and my granddad was so strong that I couldn't, even though I had a license and nobody was in the car to restrain me. Over a period of time there had developed a sense of trust, a deep love relationship that held me in restraint.

After tossing me the keys, my dad didn't rush out and tape a sign on the dashboard of the car, "Don't you dare drive beyond the speed limit" or "Cops are all around the city, and they'll catch you, boy, so don't even think about taking a risk." He simply smiled and said, "Here are the keys, son, enjoy it." What a demonstration of grace. And did *I* ever enjoy *it!* Looking back, now that I'm a father who has relived the same scene on four different occasions with my own children, I realize what a risk my father had taken.

✣ REFLECTING ON GRACE

How do you distinguish between liberty, license, and legalism?

Why do you think many believers opt for legalism? Why does the author say this is a bad choice?

Think of a time that someone's demonstration of grace and love "held you in restraint."

The Inescapable Tension

☙ AWAKENING TO GRACE

1 Corinthians 3:1–4 NLT

Dear brothers and sisters, when I was with you I couldn't talk to you as I would to mature Christians. I had to talk as though you belonged to this world or as though you were infants in the Christian life. I had to feed you with milk and not with solid food, because you couldn't handle anything stronger. And you still aren't ready, for you are still controlled by your own sinful desires. You are jealous of one another and quarrel with each other. Doesn't that prove you are controlled by your own desires? You are acting like people who don't belong to the Lord. When one of you says, "I am a follower of Paul," and another says, "I prefer Apollos," aren't you acting like those who are not Christians?

In the above passage, what specific things were the Corinthians doing that told Paul they were being controlled by their sinful desires?

Replace the names "Paul" and "Apollos" with current Christian denominations (including your own). How often are you involved in these kinds of arguments?

Paul describes immature believers. How would he describe mature Christians?

☙ WALKING IN GRACE

What person has been most influential in shaping your beliefs? To what degree have you put that person's teachings through an honest evaluation?

How willing are you to question your most basic beliefs and let God's truth unfold?

Give yourself permission today to do something freeing—purely out of love for God, regardless of what other people think.

Describe something your past legalistic attitude prevented you from doing but which your new attitude of grace gives you the freedom to do.

Blessed are those who do not condemn themselves by doing something they know is all right.

Romans 14:22 NLT

PRACTICAL SUGGESTIONS FOR GUARDING AGAINST EXTREMES

*T*hree suggestions come to mind as I think about living with the risks of grace and putting all this into balanced living.

First, *guard against extremes if you want to enjoy the freedom grace provides.* Try your best to keep balanced, then enjoy it. No reason to feel guilty. No reason to be afraid. Try this first: Simply give yourself permission to be free. Don't go crazy . . . but neither should you spend time looking over your shoulder worrying about those who "spy out your liberty," and wondering what they will think and say.

Second, *treat grace as an undeserved privilege rather than an exclusive right.* This will also help you keep a balance. Live gratefully, not arrogantly. Have fun, but don't flaunt. It is all in one's attitude, isn't it? It has nothing to do with financial status or where you live or what clothes you prefer or which car you drive. It has everything to do with attitude.

Third, *remember that while grace came to you freely, it cost the Savior His life.* It may seem free, but it was terribly expensive when He purchased it for us. And who wouldn't want to be free, since we have been purchased from the horrors of bondage?

Grace is God's universal good news of salvation. The tragedy is that some continue to live lives in a deathlike bog because they have been so turned off by a message that is full of restrictions, demands, negativism, and legalism. You may have been one of those held in bondage, victimized by a system that has stolen your joy and snuffed out your hope. If so, I have some wonderful news. You've gotten very close to the border. There's a flag flying. And on that flag is a cross. And if you come into this camp of grace beneath the cross, you'll never have to be in that awful bog again.

You will be free . . . *free at last.*

✍ REFLECTING ON GRACE

What are some habits or actions that help you lead a balanced life?

Take time to monitor your attitude this week. How often do you drift to extremes? When are you most balanced?

If you have been in "a deathlike bog" because of restrictions placed on you by legalism, what steps will you take to move out of the bog and into the "camp of grace beneath the cross"?

✍ AWAKENING TO GRACE

Philippians 2:1–11

Therefore if there is any encouragement in Christ, if there is any consolation of love, if there is any fellowship of the Spirit, if any affection and compassion, make my joy complete by being of the same mind, maintaining the same love, united in spirit, intent on one purpose. Do nothing from selfishness or empty conceit, but with humility of mind regard one another as more important than yourselves; do not merely look out for your own personal interests, but also for the interests of others. Have this attitude in yourselves which was also in Christ Jesus, who, although He existed in the form of God, did not regard equality with God a thing to be grasped, but emptied Himself, taking the form of a bond-servant, and being made in the likeness of men. Being found in appearance as a man, He humbled Himself by becoming obedient to the point of death, even death on a cross. For this reason also, God highly exalted Him, and bestowed on Him the name which is above every name, that at the name of Jesus EVERY KNEE SHOULD BOW, of those who are in heaven and on earth and under the earth, and that every tongue will confess that Jesus Christ is Lord, to the glory of God the Father.

Considering how Christians have so many varied opinions, what do you think Paul meant when he told believers to be of "the same mind"? What is our "one purpose"?

What practical instructions are given to those who desire to live a gracious life?

In this passage, what does Paul reveal about Christ's attitude? How did this attitude affect His actions?

WALKING IN GRACE

Into what kind of extremes are you most likely to fall? Are there certain steps you can take now to avoid turning away from God's grace?

Grace should be enjoyed! Describe how you last truly enjoyed this gift from God.

Identify at least one person who would benefit from hearing about the freedom of God's grace. How can you share His grace with that person today?

But by the grace of God I am what I am, and His grace toward me did not prove vain.

1 Corinthians 15:10

UNDESERVING, YET UNCONDITIONALLY LOVED

Whatever he became, according to his own statement, Paul owed it all to "the grace of God." When I ponder the words from that grand apostle, I come up with what we might call his credo. We can reduce it to three single-syllable statements, the first consisting of only eight words; the second, ten words; and the third, twelve. Occasionally, it helps to take a profound, multifaceted theological truth and define it in simple, nontechnical terms.

First statement: *God does what He does by His grace.* Paul's first claim for being allowed to live, to say nothing of being used as a spokesman and leader, was "by the grace of God." Paul deserved the severest kind of judgment, but God gave the man His grace instead. Humanly speaking, Paul should have been made to endure incredible suffering for all the pain and heartache he had caused others. But he didn't, because God exhibited His grace.

That leads us to the second statement: *I am what I am by the grace of God.* It is as if he were admitting, "If there is any goodness now found in me, I deserve none of the glory; grace gets the credit."

In our day of high-powered self-achievement and an overemphasis on the importance of personal accomplishments and building one's own ego-centered kingdom, this idea of giving grace the credit is a much-needed message. How many people who reach the pinnacle of their career say to the *Wall Street Journal* reporter or in an interview in *Business Week*, "I am what I am by the grace of God"? How many athletes would say that kind of thing at a banquet in his or her honor? What a shocker it would be today if someone were to say, "Don't be impressed at all with me. My only claim to fame is the undeserved grace of God." Such candor is rare.

There's a third statement, which seems to be implied in Paul's closing statement: *I let you be what you are by the grace of God.* Grace is not something simply to be claimed; it is meant to be demonstrated. It is to be shared, used as a basis for friendships, and drawn upon for sustained relationships.

Jesus spoke of an abundant life that we enter into when we claim the freedom He provides by His grace. Wouldn't it be wonderful if people cooperated with His game plan? There is nothing to be compared to grace when it comes to freeing others from bondage.

REFLECTING ON GRACE

Describe one thing that God has done for you that reveals His awesome grace.

List four major accomplishments in your life. After each, write Paul's statement, "I am what I am by the grace of God." In what ways does this exercise change your view of these successes?

1.

2.

3.

4.

What relationship in your life will be most profoundly affected if you decide to let that person be what he or she is by the grace of God?

⬙ AWAKENING TO GRACE

1 Corinthians 15:9–11

For I am the least of the apostles, and not fit to be called an apostle, because I persecuted the church of God. But by the grace of God I am what I am, and His grace toward me did not prove vain; but I labored even more than all of them, yet not I, but the grace of God with me. Whether then it was I or they, so we preach and so you believed.

Paul's history did not disappear when he became a Christian. How does Paul use his past failures to promote deeper understanding of the grace of God?

In the passage, what did Paul mean when he says, "His grace toward me did not prove vain"?

Do you ever feel unfit for the tasks God has given you? How can God's grace help you?

⬙ WALKING IN GRACE

Using the statement, "I am what I am by the grace of God," write your own personalized statement regarding how God's grace affects your life.

To what person do you need to apply the words of the third statement, "I let you be what you are by the grace of God"? Explain.

Most New Testament writers mention the grace of God in both the greeting and closing of their letters. Using this model in your letters and e-mails, practice greeting people with a simple blessing of grace.

DAY 13

Who will free me from this life that is dominated by sin? Thank God! The answer is in Jesus Christ our Lord.

Romans 7:24–25 NLT

DEFINING LIBERTY

Without becoming needlessly academic, I want to define a term that I've been tossing around. What do I mean when I declare that the Christian has *liberty?* Essentially, liberty is freedom . . . freedom from something and freedom to do something.

Liberty is freedom from slavery or bondage. It is initially freedom from sin's power and guilt. Freedom from God's wrath. Freedom from satanic and demonic authority. And equally important, it is freedom from shame that could easily bind me, as well as freedom from the tyranny of others' opinions, obligations, and expectations.

There was a time in my life without Christ when I had no freedom from the urges and impulses within me. I was at the mercy of my master Satan and sin was my lifestyle. When the urges grew within me, I had nothing to hold me in check, nothing to restrain me. It was an awful bondage.

For example, in my personal life I was driven by jealousy for many miserable years. It was consuming. I served it not unlike a slave serves a master. Then there came a day when I was spiritually awakened to the charming grace of God and allowed it to take full control, and almost before I knew it the jealousy died. And I sensed for the first time, perhaps in my whole life, true love; the joy, the romance, the spontaneity, the free-flowing creativity brought about by the grace of a faithful wife, who would love me no matter what, who was committed to me in faithfulness for all her life. That love and that commitment motivated me to love in return more freely than ever. I no longer loved out of fear that I would lose her, but I loved out of the joy and the blessing connected with being loved unconditionally and without restraint.

331

Now that Christ has come into my life and I have been awakened to His grace, He has provided a freedom from that kind of slavery to sin. And along with that comes a freedom that brings a fearlessness, almost a sense of invincibility in the presence of the adversity. This power, keep in mind, is because of Christ, who lives within me.

In addition, He has also brought a glorious freedom from the curse of the Law. By that I mean freedom from the constancy of its demands to perform in order to please God and/or others. It is a freedom from the fear of condemnation before God as well as from an accusing conscience. It is freedom from the demands of other people, from all the *shoulds* and *oughts* of the general public.

Such freedom is *motivated*—motivated by unconditional love. When the grace of Christ is fully awake in your life, you find you're no longer doing something due to fear or out of shame or because of guilt, but you're doing it through love. The dreadful tyranny of performing in order to please someone is over . . . forever.

Grace also brings a freedom *to do* something else—a freedom to enjoy the rights and the privileges of being out from under slavery *and* allowing others such freedom. It's freedom to experience and enjoy a new kind of power that only Christ could bring. It is a freedom to become all that He meant me to be, *regardless of how He leads others.* I can be me—fully and freely. It is a freedom to know Him in an independent and personal way. And that freedom is then released to others so they can be who they are meant to be—different from me!

You see, God isn't stamping out little cookie-cutter Christians across the world so that we all think alike and look alike and sound alike and act alike. The body has variety. We were never meant to have the same temperaments and use the same vocabulary and wear the same syrupy smile and dress the same way and carry on the same ministry. I repeat: God is pleased with variety. This freedom to be who we are is nothing short of magnificent. It is freedom to make choices, freedom to know His will, freedom to walk in it, freedom to obey His leading me in my life and you in your life. Once you've tasted such freedom, nothing else satisfies.

Perhaps I should reemphasize that it is a liberty you will have to fight for. Why? Because the ranks of Christianity are full of those who compare and would love to control and manipulate you so you will become as miserable as they are. After all, if they are determined to be "cramped, somber, dull, and listless," then they expect you to be that way, too. "Misery loves company" is the legalists' unspoken motto, though they never admit it.

REFLECTING ON GRACE

What are some of the most obvious differences between a person in legalistic bondage and a person who has freedom in Christ?

What difference does it make in your life to know that you are free from demands to perform—for God or for others?

God directs His liberty toward us and *through* us to others. How does God's liberty allow you to graciously offer freedom to other people?

AWAKENING TO GRACE

Romans 8:1–14

Therefore there is now no condemnation for those who are in Christ Jesus. For the law of the Spirit of life in Christ Jesus has set you free from the law of sin and of death. For what the Law could not do, weak as it was through the flesh, God did: sending His own Son in the likeness of sinful flesh and as an offering for sin, He condemned sin in the flesh, in order that the requirement of the Law might be fulfilled in us, who do not walk according to the flesh, but according to the Spirit. For those who are according to the flesh set their minds on the things of the flesh, but those who are according to the Spirit, the things of the Spirit. For the mind set on the flesh is death, but the mind set on the Spirit is life and peace, because the mind set on the flesh is hostile toward God; for it does not subject itself to the law of God, for it is not even able to do so; and those who are in the flesh cannot please God.

However, you are not in the flesh but in the Spirit, if indeed the Spirit of God dwells in you. But if anyone does not have the Spirit of Christ, he does not belong to Him. If Christ is in you, though the body is dead because of sin, yet the spirit is alive because of righteousness. But if the Spirit of Him who raised Jesus from the dead dwells in you, He who raised Christ Jesus from the dead will also give life to your mortal bodies through His Spirit who dwells in you.

So then, brethren, we are under obligation, not to the flesh, to live according to the flesh — for if you are living according to the flesh, you must die; but if by the Spirit you are putting to death the deeds of the body, you will live. For all who are being led by the Spirit of God, these are sons of God.

What does it mean that you face "no condemnation" and are "set free from the law of sin and death"?

Contrast Paul's descriptions of a life led by the Holy Spirit and one controlled by the sinful nature. What are the results of each?

How can you be sure that you are walking according to the Spirit?

🐦 WALKING IN GRACE

Consider how Christianity would fare across the globe if all Christians were "cookie-cutter Christians." How does diversity among believers help to reach many different types, ages, races, and backgrounds of people?

How does diversity in your own congregation help to spread the gospel message? (Or, how would more diversity help your church be more effective?)

What specifically will you do this week to allow others the freedom to be who God has called them to be?

DAY 14

For when I tried to keep the law, I realized I could never earn God's approval. So I died to the law so that I might live for God. I have been crucified with Christ.

Galatians 2:19 NLT

DEFINING LEGALISM

*I*n contrast to yesterday's thoughts on liberty, what does it mean to say that *legalism* puts people under bondage? Legalism is an attitude, a mentality based on pride. It is an obsessive conformity to an artificial standard for the purpose of exalting oneself. A legalist assumes the place of authority and pushes it to unwarranted extremes.

In so many words, legalism says, "I do this or I don't do that, and therefore I am pleasing God." Or, "If only I could do this or not do that, I would be pleasing to God." Or perhaps, "These things that I'm doing or not doing are the things I perform to win God's favor." They aren't spelled out in Scripture, you understand. They've been passed down or they have been dictated to the legalist and have become an obsession to him or her. Legalism is rigid, grim, exacting, and lawlike in nature. Pride, which is at the heart of legalism, works in sync with other motivating factors. Like guilt. And fear. And shame. It leads to an emphasis on what one should *not* be, and what one should *not* do. It flourishes in a drab context of negativism.

Let's get specific. The one place on earth where we would most expect to be set free is, in fact, the very place we are most likely to be placed into slavery: the church. What happened in the first century can surely happen in the twentieth. Paul writes the Galatians of his surprise: "You were running well; who hindered you from obeying the truth?"

Allow me to amplify his thought—"When I was with you, some of you were into the 100-meter dash, others were doing the 440 with ease. Still others were into much longer distances . . . you were marathoners. The truth freed you and I distinctly recall how well you were running as well as how much joy you demonstrated. Who cut in on your stride? Who took away your track shoes? Who told you that you shouldn't be running or enjoying the race? Some of you have stopped running altogether" (Swindoll paraphrase).

How many Christians do you know who exercise the joy and freedom to be a person full of life, living on tiptoe, enjoying spontaneous living— as opposed to the numberless hundreds of thousands who take their cues from the legalists and live life accordingly? Isn't it surprising to anyone who has been set free that anybody would ever want to return to bondage? Surely, that must grieve our God.

REFLECTING ON GRACE

Describe the daily life of a Christian. In your answer, however, you cannot use negative expressions ("A Christian doesn't . . ." or "A Christian shouldn't . . .") and you can't use positive expressions that describe only rituals ("A Christian goes to church" or "A Christian reads the Bible"). See if you can describe a life that captures the joyous freedom mentioned in the quotation above.

How do you think you personally please God? What does the Bible say is the only way to please God?

Why do you think some believers return to bondage after being set free in Christ?

AWAKENING TO GRACE

Philippians 3:1–11

Finally, my brethren, rejoice in the Lord. To write the same things again is no trouble to me, and it is a safeguard for you.

Beware of the dogs, beware of the evil workers, beware of the false circumcision; for we are the true circumcision, who worship in the Spirit of God and glory in Christ Jesus and put no confidence in the flesh, although I myself might have confidence even in the flesh. If anyone else has a mind to put confidence in the flesh, I far more: circumcised the eighth day, of the nation of Israel, of the tribe of Benjamin, a Hebrew of Hebrews; as to the Law, a Pharisee; as to zeal, a persecutor of the church; as to the righteousness which is in the Law, found blameless.

But whatever things were gain to me, those things I have counted as loss for the sake of Christ. More than that, I count all things to be loss in view of the surpassing value of knowing Christ Jesus my Lord, for whom I have suffered the loss of all things, and count them but rubbish so that I may gain Christ, and may be found in Him, not having a righteousness of my own derived from the Law, but that which is through faith in Christ, the righteousness which comes from God on the basis of faith, that I may know Him and the power of His resurrection and the fellowship of His sufferings, being conformed to His death; in order that I may attain to the resurrection from the dead.

How does Paul view his former "perfect" life compared with his life in Christ?

Paraphrase Paul's words to describe what might be your own "confidence in the flesh."

WALKING IN GRACE

Considering the author's athletic metaphor, how well do you see yourself running the race? In what ways has legalism slowed your pace?

How much of your Christian walk is spent struggling through feelings of guilt, fear, and shame? What effect do these emotions have on your relationship with Jesus?

When you evaluate your life, to whom do you accredit your achievements, godliness, and success?

DAY 15

> So Christ has really set us free. Now make sure that
> you stay free, and don't get tied up again in slavery to
> the law.
>
> Galatians 5:1 NLT

FOUR ANTILEGALISTIC STRATEGIES

Grace killers cannot be mildly ignored or kindly tolerated. You can no more allow legalism to continue than you could permit a rattlesnake to slip into your house and hide. Before long, somebody is going to get hurt. So then, since liberty is worth fighting for, how do we do it? Where can our personal grace awakening begin? I can think of four strong strategies:

Keep standing firm in your freedom. I'm reminded of what Paul wrote in Galatians 5:1: "It was for freedom that Christ set us free; therefore keep standing firm and do not be subject again to a yoke of slavery." Stand your ground. Ask the Lord to give you courage.

Stop seeking the favor of everyone. This may be a stubborn habit to break, but it is really worth all the effort you can muster. If you're in a group where you feel you are being coerced to do certain things that are against your conscience or you're being pressured to stop doing things that you see no problem with, get out of the group! You're unwise to stay in situations where your conscience tells you it is not right. That is nothing more than serving men, not God. I don't care how spiritual sounding it may be, stop seeking the favor of everybody.

Start refusing to submit to bondage. Call it what it is: slavery. It's trying to be "spiritual" by performance. Think of how delightful it would be to get rid of all the anxiety that comes with the bondage to which you have submitted yourself; think how clean you could feel by being real again, or perhaps real for the first time in your adult life.

Continue being straightforward about the truth. That means live honestly. If you don't agree, say so kindly but firmly. If you are the only one, be true to yourself and stand alone. When you blow it, say, "I blew it." If you don't know, admit the truth. It's okay not to know. And the next time your kids spot hypocrisy, even though you may feel embarrassed, agree with them, "You know what, kids? You're right. I was a first-class hypocrite. What you saw and pointed out is exactly right." Tell them that. It may sound embarrassing to you now, but they will admire and respect your admission. And they won't grow up damaged. Best of all, they will learn to model the same kind of vulnerability and honesty, even if you are in vocational Christian work . . . *especially if you're in vocational Christian work.* Nobody expects perfection, but they do and they should expect honesty.

We need affirmation and encouragement to be all we're meant to be, and because so many people are rather delicate within, they need those who are strong to assist them in their fight for liberty. If for no other reason, liberty is worth fighting for so others can breathe freely.

If fighting for liberty sounds too aggressive to you, perhaps too selfish, then think of it as fighting so others can be set free—so others can be awakened to the joys and privileges of personal freedom. Those who do that on real battlefields are called patriots or heroes. With all my heart, I believe those who square off against legalism should be considered the same.

REFLECTING ON GRACE

Have you ever had to stand firm in your Christian freedom against legalists? Explain.

Of the four strategies mentioned above, which is the most difficult for you? Why?

In what areas of your life are you not living honestly?

Matthew 23:23–28

Woe to you, scribes and Pharisees, hypocrites! For you tithe mint and dill and cummin, and have neglected the weightier provisions of the law: justice and mercy and faithfulness; but these are the things you should have done without neglecting the others. You blind guides, who strain out a gnat and swallow a camel!

Woe to you, scribes and Pharisees, hypocrites! For you clean the outside of the cup and of the dish, but inside they are full of robbery and self-indulgence. You blind Pharisee, first clean the inside of the cup and of the dish, so that the outside of it may become clean also.

Woe to you, scribes and Pharisees, hypocrites! For you are like whitewashed tombs which on the outside appear beautiful, but inside they are full of dead men's bones and all uncleanness So you, too, outwardly appear righteous to men, but inwardly you are full of hypocrisy and lawlessness.

Jesus boldly compared the Pharisees with several objects to make a point. In your own words, write a brief explanation for each of Jesus' following metaphors.

The Pharisees as filthy cups:

The Pharisees as whitewashed tombs:

What guidelines did Jesus give the Pharisees to live more gracious lives?

✏ WALKING IN GRACE

Personally, what does it mean to you to live an honest life?

Whom do you know who has successfully stood firm in his or her freedom? Ask that person to support you in your battle against legalism.

Lift someone up in prayer this week who struggles with legalism and accepting God's grace. What are some simple ways you can exemplify God's freedom for that person?

DAY 16

So you should consider yourselves dead to sin and able to live for the glory of God through Christ Jesus.

Romans 6:11 NLT

CLAIMING OUR FREEDOM FROM SIN'S CONTROL

*I*n the wonderful sixth chapter of Romans, Paul presents three techniques for living by grace, above sin's domination. I find each one linked to a particular term he uses:

Know—"Or do you not know that all of us who have been baptized into Christ Jesus have been baptized into His death? . . . knowing this, that our old self was crucified with Him, in order that our body of sin might be done away with, so that we should no longer be slaves to sin; . . . knowing that Christ, having been raised from the dead, is never to die again; death no longer is master over Him" (vv. 3, 6, 9).

Consider—"Even so consider yourselves to be dead to sin, but alive to God in Christ Jesus" (v. 11).

Present—"And do not go on presenting the members of your body to sin as instruments of unrighteousness; but present yourselves to God as those alive from the dead, and your members as instruments of righteousness to God" (v. 13).

In order for us to live free from sin's control, free from the old master, with the power to walk a new kind of life, we have to *know* something, we have to *consider* something, and we have to *present* something.

Christ died for us on the cross. He was raised from the dead for us at the tomb. When we believed in the Savior's death and resurrection, we were "dipped" into the same scene. Our identity was changed. We didn't feel it, we didn't see it, we didn't hear it, but it occurred, nevertheless. When we came to Christ, we were placed into Him as His death became ours, His victorious resurrection became ours, His "awakening" to new life became our "awakening," His powerful walk became our powerful walk. Before we can experience the benefits of all that, we have to *know* it. The Christian life is not stumbling along, hoping to keep up with the Savior. He lives in me and I live in Him. And in this identification with Him, His power becomes mine. His very life becomes my life, guaranteeing that His victory over sin is mine to claim. I no longer need to live as a slave to sin.

"Now if we have died with Christ, we believe that we shall also live with Him, knowing that Christ, having been raised from the dead, is never to die again; death no longer is master over Him. For the death that He died, He died to sin once for all; but the life that He lives, He lives to God" (vv. 8–10).

You will meet well-meaning Christians who teach about crucifying one-self. But I have good news for you: That has already been done. You are in Christ. He was crucified once for all. He died for you so you never need to die again. Because we have our identification with Him, we have all the power needed to live the rest of our lives above the drag and dregs of slavery. Death to sin is an accomplished act, a finished fact. Theoretically, it has all been taken care of. A victorious walk begins with our *knowing* this fact. Christ's "Emancipation Proclamation" has put to death the whole idea of slavery to sin. Having died to sin's power, we are now free to serve our new Master.

REFLECTING ON GRACE

Explain briefly what you *know* about Jesus and what He has done for you.

Consider how it can be true that you are "dead to sin, but alive to God."

How can you *present* yourself to God as an "instrument of righteousness"?

AWAKENING TO GRACE

Romans 11:33–12:2

Oh, the depth of the riches both of the wisdom and knowledge of God! How unsearchable are His judgments and unfathomable

His ways! FOR WHO HAS KNOWN THE MIND OF THE LORD, OR WHO BECAME HIS COUNSELOR? Or WHO HAS FIRST GIVEN TO HIM THAT IT MIGHT BE PAID BACK TO HIM AGAIN? For from Him and through Him and to Him are all things. To Him be the glory forever. Amen.

Therefore I urge you, brethren, by the mercies of God, to present your bodies a living and holy sacrifice, acceptable to God, which is your spiritual service of worship. And do not be conformed to this world, but be transformed by the renewing of your mind, so that you may prove what the will of God is, that which is good and acceptable and perfect.

In what ways are you conformed to this world—either to the unredeemed world of sin or to the rule-filled world of legalists?

How does your mind need to be transformed?

What is the result of a transformed mind?

❧ WALKING IN GRACE

Christ's victory over sin is yours to claim! If you are waiting to claim it, for what are you waiting?

What does it mean for you personally to be "in Christ"?

How has your own life's journey reflected both the process of dying with Christ and living with Him?

DAY 17

 And you will know the truth, and the truth will make you free.

John 8:32

GRACE AND FREEDOM

With all this talk about grace and liberty, perhaps it's time for me to clarify something. Some may be asking: Doesn't liberty have its limits? Shouldn't folks restrain their freedom and occasionally hold themselves in check? Yes, without question. Grace can be and sometimes is— abused. By that I mean exercising one's liberty without wisdom, having no concern over whether it offends or wounds a young and impressionable fellow believer. But I must hasten to add that I believe such restraint is an individual matter. It is not to be legislated, not something to be forced on someone else. Limitations are appropriate and necessary, but I fail to find in Scripture any place where one is to require such restraint from another. To do so is legalism. It plugs up breathing holes. It kills grace. The best restraint is self-restraint that comes from the inner prompting of the Holy Spirit through the person and presence of Jesus Christ in each individual life. It's been my observation over the last thirty years that the vast majority of believers need to be freed, not restrained. Our job is to free people; God's job is to restrain them. God is doing His job much better than we are doing ours.

I like to think of certain verses in Scripture as those that help us breathe. By that I mean they encourage true freedom. They liberate! I suggest that all who wish to be free—truly free from bondage traps and legalistic prisons—read these verses again and again and again. I would suggest you type them on three-by-five cards and tape them to your bathroom mirror. Read them aloud each morning. They will help awaken grace within you on a daily basis. Here are a few that I often quote and claim:

It was for freedom that Christ set us free.
(Galatians 5:1)

For he who has died is freed from sin. (Romans 6:7)

For the law of the Spirit of life in Christ Jesus has set you free. (Romans 8:2)

What then shall we say to these things? If God is for us, who is against us? He who did not spare His own Son, but delivered Him over for us all, how will He not also with Him freely give us all things? (Romans 8:31–32)
So if the Son shall make you free, you will be free indeed. (John 8:36)

🕮 REFLECTING ON GRACE

In what ways do you relate to the author's statement: "Our job is to free people; God's job is to restrain them"?

In the past, which of these jobs have you taken as your main responsibility? What were the results?

Which of the previous verses would be your first choice as a theme verse for your own desire to practice Christian freedom? Why?

🕮 AWAKENING TO GRACE

Galatians 5:13–16

For you were called to freedom, brethren; only do not turn your freedom into an opportunity for the flesh, but through love serve one another. For the whole Law is fulfilled in one word, in the statement, "YOU SHALL LOVE YOUR NEIGHBOR AS YOURSELF." But if you bite and devour one another, take care that you are not consumed by one another.

But I say, walk by the Spirit, and you will not carry out the desire of the flesh.

How can freedom become an "opportunity for the flesh"? What would keep that from happening?

Describe two or three "footsteps" that illustrate what it means to "walk by the Spirit."

✆ WALKING IN GRACE

How could you use your freedom in Christ today to serve someone else in love?

What other ways can you think of for keeping those key "freedom verses" in view besides typing them on cards and taping them to a mirror?

What situations could you face today that will test your desire to walk by the Spirit as you live out your freedom in Christ?

But fortunately God doesn't grade us on our diet.

1 Corinthians 8:8 MSG

FREE TO EAT, OR NOT

A funny thing happened to me recently. One of the sound-and-light people at the church where I pastor (a real character!) heard me teach on the subject of freedom. A couple of weeks later he pulled a gag on me. With an impish grin he said, "You had a birthday recently, didn't you?" I nodded yes. He said, "You're originally from Texas, right?" By now I knew I was in for something! "Yep," I answered. He said, "Well, I have something for you." He put a small can in my hand about the size of a can of snuff. It was a can of armadillo meat. I groaned. The label read, "Pure Texas Armadillo—sun-dried and road-tenderized." The ingredients were printed on the other side: "Pure sun-dried armadillo, run over by a log truck three miles south of Pollok, Texas. Not over 20 percent hair and gravel. May contain foreign matter."

He told me that since I was such a believer in grace, I was free to eat it. I thought, *Whoa! This will gag a maggot!* My point? Because of grace, my friend can eat armadillo and I can eat armadillo. It's okay. It's fine if he wishes to, but it so happens that God has led me *not* to eat armadillo. (It's that "foreign matter" that concerns me.) But if you want to eat armadillo, that's great! Personally, I have my own personal list of dietary don'ts (which includes armadillo). You may not have that on your list, so in good Texas fashion, "git at it." I promise, I will not slander you or judge you as you munch on all that hair and gravel.

What in the world is all this about? Let me give it to you straight. Don't give me your personal list of dos and don'ts to live by! And you can count on this: I will never give you my personal list of dos and don'ts to follow! Being free means you have no reason whatsoever to agree with my personal list, nor should you slander me because it isn't exactly like yours.

That is one of the ways Christians can live in harmony. It is called living by grace, and it is the only way to fly.

⟨⟨ REFLECTING ON GRACE

What eating habits or favorite foods set you a little apart in your family or among your friends?

How does good-natured kidding over eating habits feel different from unbending rules that are imposed by a group or person about any area of life?

How does it set you free not to have to live by someone else's dos and don'ts and not to have to expect them to live by yours?

⟨⟨ AWAKENING TO GRACE

1 Corinthians 8:8–13

But food will not commend us to God; we are neither the worse if we do not eat, nor the better if we do eat. But take care that this liberty of yours does not somehow become a stumbling block to the weak. For if someone sees you, who have knowledge, dining in an idol's temple, will not his conscience, if he is weak, be strengthened to eat things sacrificed to idols? For through your knowledge he who is weak is ruined, the brother for whose sake Christ died. And so, by sinning against the brethren and wounding their conscience when it is weak, you sin against Christ. Therefore, if food causes my brother to stumble, I will never eat meat again, so that I will not cause my brother to stumble.

Why doesn't food "commend us to God" (or as Eugene Peterson put it, "God doesn't grade us on our diet")?

In the context of this passage, how would eating meat have caused a fellow believer difficulty? What might be a modern parallel?

How is Paul exercising freedom by choosing not to eat something he has the right to eat?

WALKING IN GRACE

Almost any behavior or choice can be described as something that "might cause a brother or sister to stumble." How will you balance personal freedom in Christ with the importance of considering the weaknesses or needs of others?

What personal spiritual benefits have you experienced from giving up or limiting certain habits out of a desire to express consideration for others?

In what situations have you learned the personal value of having to preserve a right in spite of the "demands or weaknesses" of others?

DAY 19

You shall walk in all the way which the LORD your
God has commanded you.

Deuteronomy 5:33

WHEN GOD SAYS DO OR DON'T

Now you say, "Well, what if we find a list of dos and don'ts in Scripture?" That is a very different issue! Any specified list in Scripture is to be obeyed without hesitation or question. That's an inspired list for all of us to follow, not someone's personal list. Let me encourage you to guide your life by any and all Scripture with all of your heart, regardless of how anyone else may respond. But when questionable things aren't specified in Scripture, it then becomes a matter of one's personal preference or convictions.

God has given His children a wonderful freedom in Christ, which means not only freedom from sin and shame but also a freedom in lifestyle, so that we can become models of His grace. Being free, enjoying your liberty, and allowing others the same enjoyment are hard to do if you're insecure. It is especially hard to do if you were raised by legalistic parents and led by legalistic pastors with an oversensitive conscience about pleasing everyone. Those kinds of parents and pastors can be ultracontrolling, manipulative, and judgmental. Frequently, they use the Bible as a hammer to pound folks into submission rather than as a guide to lead others into grace. Sometimes it takes years for people who have been under a legalistic cloud to finally have the courage to walk freely in the grace of God. Unfortunately, some who finally grasp this freedom go so far in it they abuse the grace of God by flaunting their liberty.

That can be just as tragic as those who don't go far enough. To return to one of my favorite words, we need the *balance*.

REFLECTING ON GRACE

Growing up, to what extent did legalism influence your walk with Christ? What was your response to this environment then and now?

Who can support you in maintaining balance as you emerge from a "legalistic cloud"?

Describe a time when others have used the Bible to guide you into grace. What happened? When have you used the Bible in this way?

AWAKENING TO GRACE

Romans 14:1–10

Now accept the one who is weak in faith, but not for the purpose of passing judgment on his opinions. One person has faith that he may eat all things, but he who is weak eats vegetables only. The one who eats is not to regard with contempt the one who does not eat, and the one who does not eat is not to judge the one who eats, for God has accepted him. Who are you to judge the servant of another? To his own master he stands or falls; and he will stand, for the Lord is able to make him stand.

One person regards one day above another, another regards every day alike. Each person must be fully convinced in his own mind. He who observes the day, observes it for the Lord, and he who eats, does so for the Lord, for he gives thanks to God; and he who eats not, for the Lord he does not eat, and gives thanks to God. For not one of us lives for himself, and not one dies for himself; for if we live, we live for the Lord, or if we die, we die for the Lord; therefore whether we live or die, we are the Lord's. For to this end Christ died and lived again, that He might be Lord both of the dead and of the living.

But you, why do you judge your brother? Or you again, why do you regard your brother with contempt? For we will all stand before the judgment seat of God.

According to Paul, what is the purpose of holding personal beliefs? How can you distinguish personal convictions from fundamental beliefs?

What is to be your attitude toward others regarding personal convictions?

In what ways does this attitude promote grace?

� WALKING IN GRACE

Consider the last disagreement you had with another Christian. If it centered on a personal conviction, are there ways you could have responded more graciously?

How can you find "balance" in your Christian life?

If you were raised in a legalistic setting, what can you do to break this pattern so that it is not repeated with the next generation?

DAY 20

*Choose to love the LORD your God and to obey him
and commit yourself to him, for he is your life.*

Deuteronomy 30:20 NLT

FREE TO CHOOSE FREEDOM

I wish I could guarantee all of us full freedom from sin 365 days a year,
but that is not possible—not so long as we are earthbound. Perpetual
sinlessness (theologians call it "sinless perfection") will not be ours to enjoy
until we are given glorified bodies and we are at home in heaven. The good
news is that we don't have to sin on a constant, day-after-day basis. Grace
has freed us to obey Christ.

> But thanks be to God that though you were slaves of sin, you
> became obedient from the heart to that form of teaching to which
> you were committed, and having been freed from sin, you became
> slaves of righteousness. (Romans 6:17–18)

Wonderful, wonderful truth! Choosing righteousness, we enjoy a
lifestyle marked by God's blessings, stability, and strength. Grace frees us
to choose. We can decide to walk with God and draw strength from Him
to face whatever life throws at us. Or we can decide to walk away from
God and face the inescapable consequences. The next time you are
tempted to yield to your old master, remember this: Grace invites you to
return and find forgiveness, but it doesn't automatically erase the scars
that accompany sin; some could stay with you for life.

In spite of the terrible consequences sins may bring, grace also means
we allow others the freedom to choose, regardless. To do otherwise abuses as much as those who use their freedom as a license to sin. I am a firm
believer in mutual accountability, but grace means I will not force or
manipulate or judge or attempt to control you, nor should you do those
things to me. It means we will keep on helping others to freedom by pro-

viding breathing holes. It means we deliberately let go so each of us can grow and learn on our own; otherwise, we shall never enjoy the liberty of an open sea. For most of us, letting others go is neither natural nor easy. Because we care, it is more our tendency to give people hints or advice. The thought of letting them fail or fall is extremely painful to us, but God treats us like that virtually every day of our lives. We tend to clutch, not release . . . to put people in our frame and not allow them any breathing holes unless and until they accept the shape of our molds.

𝒢 REFLECTING ON GRACE

How can God's grace of giving us freedom to choose be both wonderful and dangerous at the same time?

List three ways you can deliberately let go of someone you've been attempting to control:

1.

2.

3.

Define the difference between mutual accountability and manipulation. In which of your relationships have you experienced each one?

𝒢 AWAKENING TO GRACE

John 15:5–14
I am the vine, you are the branches; he who abides in Me and I in

him, he bears much fruit, for apart from Me you can do nothing. If anyone does not abide in Me, he is thrown away as a branch and dries up; and they gather them, and cast them into the fire and they are burned. If you abide in Me, and My words abide in you, ask whatever you wish, and it will be done for you. My Father is glorified by this, that you bear much fruit, and so prove to be My disciples. Just as the Father has loved Me, I have also loved you; abide in My love. If you keep My commandments, you will abide in My love; just as I have kept My Father's commandments and abide in His love. These things I have spoken to you so that My joy may be in you, and that your joy may be made full.

This is My commandment, that you love one another, just as I have loved you. Greater love has no one than this, that one lay down his life for his friends. You are My friends if you do what I command you.

According to the passage, how can you abide in Christ's love?

What are the benefits of choosing to obey Christ?

How does Jesus link your personal obedience with an expression of grace toward others?

✍ WALKING IN GRACE

Watching a loved one make mistakes can be devastating. How can you display a caring spirit while still allowing them freedom to choose?

What specific "breathing holes" do you desire in your life? What "breathing holes" have others asked you to give them?

Do you have a specific person you've been afraid to release? Today, pray for strength to relinquish that person to Christ's authority.

DAY 21

Don't you realize that whatever you choose to obey becomes your master?

Romans 6:16 NLT

CAREFUL WARNING TO ALL WHO ARE FREE

*E*ven those who live in a free country need warnings. So we shouldn't be surprised that God gives His own a few warnings lest we abuse our privileges as people under grace. These warnings are set forth in verses 16 through 23 of Romans 6. None of them is complicated, but to grasp each one we'll need to concentrate. For some reason, this information is not commonly heard in many churches today, so we must be taught to handle grace rather carefully. An overall principle is woven into the words of verse 16:

> Do you not know that when you present yourselves to someone as slaves for obedience, you are slaves of the one whom you obey, either of sin resulting in death, or of obedience resulting in righteousness?

If you were to ask me to give you in one sentence what the balance of chapter 6 is teaching, it would be this: *How we live depends on the master we choose.* "Do you not know that when you present yourselves to someone as slaves for obedience, you are slaves of the one whom you obey?" Why, of course! Submission to a master is tantamount to slavery to the same master. And what are the alternatives?

There are only two: "either of sin resulting in death, or of obedience resulting in righteousness." Every day we live, we have a choice to do what is right or what is wrong. When we send our young children off to school, we tell them, "Now, sweetheart, you need to know that Mom and Dad won't be there to make your decisions. You will find some kids at school who will encourage you to do what is right, and you'll find others who will lead you to disobey and do what is wrong. Make the right choice. Select your friends carefully. Be smart."

REFLECTING ON GRACE

Recall the last choice you faced that forced you to choose between right and wrong. What process did you go through to make your decision?

What tools does God's grace give you to make right choices in your life?

What does the phrase "slaves to obedience" bring to mind? How do you relate to this term?

AWAKENING TO GRACE

Galatians 5:16–23

But I say, walk by the Spirit, and you will not carry out the desire of the flesh. For the flesh sets its desire against the Spirit, and the Spirit against the flesh; for these are in opposition to one another, so that you may not do the things that you please. But if you are led by the Spirit, you are not under the Law. Now the deeds of the flesh are evident, which are: immorality, impurity, sensuality, idolatry, sorcery, enmities, strife, jealousy, outbursts of anger, disputes, dissensions, factions, envying, drunkenness, carousing, and things like these, of which I forewarn you just as I have forewarned you, that those who practice such things will not inherit the kingdom of God. But the fruit of the Spirit is love, joy, peace, patience, kindness, goodness, faithfulness, gentleness, self-control; against such things there is no law.

What does this passage regard as the conflict inherent in every choice you make?

Give specific examples of when your life clearly produced either the fruit of the Holy Spirit or the fruit of your sinful nature.

With which fruit of the Spirit do you struggle the most?

WALKING IN GRACE

Consider the people you've chosen to surround you. What kinds of choices do they make and encourage you to make?

How does your presence influence the choices of others?

If someone were to look at your life yesterday, last month, or last year, who would your actions reveal your master to be?

DAY 22

You have forgiven the guilt of your people—yes, you have covered all their sins.

Psalm 85:2 NLT

Two-Dimensional Grace

Grace comes to us in two dimensions, vertical and horizontal. Vertical grace centers on our relationship with God. It is amazing. It frees us from the demands and condemnation of the Mosaic Law. It announces hope to the sinner—the gift of eternal life, along with all its benefits.

Horizontal grace centers on our human relationships. It is charming. It frees us from the tyranny of pleasing people and adjusting our lives to the demands and expectations of human opinion. It gives relief—the enjoyment of freedom along with all its benefits. It silences needless guilt and removes self-imposed shame.

Few people realize better than non-Christians how guilt-ridden many Christians are. A lady in our congregation tells of a conversation she had with a fellow student while the two of them were students at the Berkeley campus of the University of California. He knew she was a Christian, and he made it painfully clear that he had no interest whatsoever in her faith. When she asked why, his answer bore the sting of reality: "Because the most guilt-ridden people I know are Christians. No thanks."

This is a good time for me to ask you two probing questions. Only you can answer them:

Do you add to others' guilt, or do you lessen it?

Are you the type who promotes another's liberty or restrains it?

Both questions have to do with attitude, don't they? We do what we do with others because of the way we think. Our attitude, therefore, is crucial. It is also at our mercy. We have full control of which attitude we shall have: charming and gracious, or restrictive and rigid. Liberty or legalism will be the result. Depending on our attitude, we are grace givers or grace killers.

� REFLECTING ON GRACE

If you admitted that you have added to others' guilt or attempted to restrain their liberty, what have been the key motives behind your actions?

To what extent do you allow your attitudes or feelings to direct your actions? What can you do to make sure your attitude stays at your mercy?

As you read these devotionals, which type of grace—vertical or horizontal—do you find yourself spending the most time focusing on? Pray that your relationship with God and others may *both* be flooded with grace.

� AWAKENING TO GRACE

Luke 6:37–42 NIV

"Do not judge, and you will not be judged. Do not condemn, and you will not be condemned. Forgive, and you will be forgiven. Give, and it will be given to you. A good measure, pressed down, shaken together and running over, will be poured into your lap. For with the measure you use, it will be measured to you."

He also told them this parable: "Can a blind man lead a blind man? Will they not both fall into a pit? A student is not above his teacher, but everyone who is fully trained will be like his teacher. Why do you look at the speck of sawdust in your brother's eye and pay no attention to the plank in your own eye? How can you say to your brother, 'Brother, let me take the speck out of your eye,' when you yourself fail to see the plank in your own eye? You hypocrite, first take the plank out of your eye, and then you will see clearly to remove the speck from your brother's eye."

While speaking to the crowd, what did Jesus reveal as the key to demonstrating a spirit of grace?

According to this passage, what consequences follow maintaining an attitude that adds to someone else's guilt?

How does Jesus' illustration regarding the blind leading the blind relate to someone who judges another?

WALKING IN GRACE

What kind of picture do your words and actions paint about Christianity to nonbelievers? How do you know?

Have you been a grace giver or a grace killer? What is one step you can take to become a grace giver?

DAY 23

And whatever you do or say, let it be as a representative of the Lord Jesus, all the while giving thanks through him to God the Father.

Colossians 3:17 NLT

GUIDING GRACE

*I*n his letter to the Romans, Paul goes into great detail regarding the issue of personal freedom—greater detail than almost anywhere else in his writings. In the fourteenth chapter, for example, he sets forth four very practical guidelines that can be followed by all who are serious about releasing others in grace. My hope is that we not only learn what they are but, equally important, that we spend our days following them.

Guideline 1: *Accepting others is basic to letting them be.* The problem was not a meat problem, it was a love problem, an acceptance problem. It still is. How often we restrict our love by making it conditional: "If you will (or won't), then I will accept you." Paul starts there: "Accept one another!" In other words, "Let's allow each other the freedom to hold to convictions that are unlike our own . . . and accept them in spite of that difference." Those who didn't eat (called here "weak in faith") were exhorted to accept and not judge those who ate. And those who ate were exhorted to accept and not regard with contempt those who did not eat. The secret lies in accepting one another. All of this is fairly easy to read as long as I stay on the issue of eating meat. That one is safe because it isn't a current taboo. It's easy to accept those folks today because they don't exist!

Guideline 2: *Refusing to dictate to others allows the Lord freedom to direct their lives.* I especially appreciate the statement at the end of verse 5: "Let each man be fully convinced in his own mind." Give people room to make up their minds. Do you have a few new converts who are a part of your life and ministry? Do you want to help them grow toward maturity? Here is how: Let them grow up differently. Let them learn at their own pace, just like you had to learn, including failures and mistakes. If you really want grace to awaken, be easier on them than others were on you. Don't make up their minds—let them! Don't step in and push your weight around—give them plenty of space. Whatever you do, don't control and manipulate them to get what you want.

Be an accepting model of grace. Refuse all temptations to be a brother basher or sister smasher. We already have too many of them roaming around the religious landscape. And nothing catches the attention of the unsaved world quicker than those times when we Christians beat up on one another. Don't think the unsaved world doesn't notice our cannibalism.

Guideline 3: *Freeing others means we never assume a position we're not qualified to fill.* This, in one sentence, is enough to stop any person from judging another. We're not qualified. We lack full knowledge. How often we have jumped to wrong conclusions, made judgmental statements, only to find out later how off-base we were—then wished we could cut out our tongue.

Guideline 4: *Loving others requires us to express our liberty wisely.* In other words, love must rule. I'm not my own, I'm bought with a price. My goal is not to please me; it is to please my Lord Jesus, my God. It is not to please you; it is to please my Lord. The same is true for you. So the bottom line is this: I don't adapt my life according to what you may say; I adapt my life according to the basis of my love for you because I answer to Christ. And so do you.

Reflecting on Grace

What godly sounding conditions have you tried to put on others before accepting them as brothers and sisters in Christ?

Which of the author's four guidelines, if followed, would change your relationships with others the most? Why?

Why is it so important to allow new Christians to grow up differently in Christ than you did?

🐝 Awakening to Grace

1 Corinthians 10:25–33

Eat anything that is sold in the meat market without asking questions for conscience' sake; FOR THE EARTH IS THE LORD'S, AND ALL IT CONTAINS. If one of the unbelievers invites you and you want to go, eat anything that is set before you without asking questions for conscience' sake. But if anyone says to you, "This is meat sacrificed to idols," do not eat it, for the sake of the one who informed you, and for conscience' sake; I mean not your own conscience, but the other man's; for why is my freedom judged by another's conscience? If I partake with thankfulness, why am I slandered concerning that for which I give thanks?

Whether, then, you eat or drink or whatever you do, do all to the glory of God. Give no offense either to Jews or to Greeks or to the church of God; just as I also please all men in all things, not seeking my own profit but the profit of the many, so that they may be saved.

What practical guidelines for grace did Paul set up in this passage?

According to Paul, how should your conscience play a part in deciding your actions?

In what ways can you—a believer set free in Christ—exemplify grace to nonbelievers?

WALKING IN GRACE

All Christians are weak in some areas and stronger in others. Honestly identify several weaknesses and strengths in your own life.

Name some close friends who hold different convictions than you do about various *spiritual* matters. How have you maintained a relationship of grace with them in the midst of your differences?

Today, how will you turn your focus away from pleasing others to pleasing the Lord?

DAY 24

*When I am with those who follow the Jewish laws, I
do the same, even though I am not subject to the law,
so that I can bring them to Christ.*

1 Corinthians 9:20 NLT

A Few Actions That Signify Grace

I want to focus our attention today on the concluding verses in Romans
14. Read verse 19 slowly and thoughtfully. "So then let us pursue
the things which make for peace and the building up of one another."
On the basis of that great statement, consider the first of four action
steps.

1. *Concentrate on things that encourage peace and assist others'
growth.* An idea that works for me is to filter whatever I do through a
twofold "grid"—two questions that keep me focused: (a) Is this going to
make a lot of waves, or will it encourage peace? (b) Is this going to hurt
and offend, or will it help and strengthen my brother or sister? Let's commit ourselves anew to encouragement and affirmation.

2. *Remember that sabotaging saints hurts the work of God.* "Don't
tear down the work of God for the sake of food." (v. 20). You sabotage the
saints when you flaunt your liberty, knowing that they have convictions
against it. That is not fair. Frankly, that is fighting dirty. Scripture calls it
"regarding with contempt," and counsels us against it. Enjoy your liberty
with discretion.

3. *Exercise your liberty only with those who can enjoy it with you.* I
repeat, that means to keep it private and personal. What others don't know
can't hurt them. That's not deception; it's wise and necessary restraint. It
isn't prompted by hypocrisy but by love.

4. *Determine where you stand and refuse to play God in anyone else's
life.* That may sound simple and easy, but it is tougher than it may seem.
Be absolutely sure you are right, then press on, regardless. By letting others be, you free yourself to give full attention to what God is trying to make

of you. You have neither the time nor the energy to keep holding on. Love demands that you let go.

Reflecting on Grace

In your closest relationships, you're probably well versed on the other person's hot buttons. How might you "concentrate on peace" in these friendships?

When confronting legalism, anything you do has the propensity to cause waves. How can you remain spiritually free while exercising self-restraint with certain people?

What other actions would you add to this list as good advice (not strict rules) for balanced, gracious living?

Awakening to Grace

1 Corinthians 9:19–23 NLT

This means I am not bound to obey people just because they pay me, yet I have become a servant of everyone so that I can bring them to Christ. When I am with the Jews, I become one of them so that I can bring them to Christ. When I am with those who follow the Jewish laws, I do the same, even though I am not subject to the law, so that I can bring them to Christ. When I am with the Gentiles who do not have the Jewish law, I fit in with them as much as I can. In this way, I gain their confidence and bring them to Christ. But I do not discard the law of God;

I obey the law of Christ. When I am with those who are oppressed, I share their oppression so that I might bring them to Christ. Yes, I try to find common ground with everyone so that I might bring them to Christ. I do all this to spread the Good News, and in doing so I enjoy its blessings.

In these verses, how does Paul illustrate a clear understanding of both his freedom in Christ and the dedication to grace?

What is Paul's ultimate motive in becoming like a Jew or a Gentile?

Where do Paul's personal beliefs intersect with the convictions held by people from different backgrounds?

WALKING IN GRACE

Regarding the fourth action step, how can you "determine where you stand" in your beliefs?

Sensitivity begins with awareness. Identify people in your life with whom you will be able to exercise more freedom and those with whom you need to be more sensitive.

Choosing never to exercise your freedom, even in private, as some ultra-cautious gesture toward others, wastes God's beautiful gift of grace! In what particular area do you need to be less self-conscious about exercising your freedom?

Day 25

 The human body has many parts, but the many parts make up only one body. So it is with the body of Christ.

1 Corinthians 12:12 NLT

Agreeing about Disagreements

*A*s much as we may pursue peace, and as positive and tactful as we may be, there will still be occasions when disagreements arise. As one wag put it, "Life ain't no exact science," which brings me to the first of four facts with which everyone (well, most of us) would agree.

1. *Disagreements are inevitable.* Throughout this book, I have emphasized the value of variety and the importance of individuality. The downside of that is it leaves the door open for differing opinions. I say downside only because those inevitable differences can lead to strong disagreements. There will be opposing viewpoints and a variety of perspectives on most subjects. Tastes differ as well as preferences. That is why they make vanilla and chocolate and strawberry ice cream, why they build Fords and Chevys, Chryslers and Cadillacs, Hondas and Toyotas. That is why our nation has room for Democrats and Republicans, conservatives and liberals—and moderates. The tension is built into our system. It is what freedom is all about, including religious freedom. I am fairly firm in my theological convictions, but that doesn't mean you (or anyone) must agree with me. All this explains why I place so much importance on leaving "wobble room" in our relationships. One's theological persuasion may not bend, but one's involvements with others must. Leaders are especially in need of leaving "wobble room" if they hope to relieve steam from inevitable tensions.

2. *Even the godly will sometimes disagree.* When I was younger I had difficulty with this one. I couldn't understand how two people who loved the Lord with equal passion and who believed the Bible with equal zeal could come to different conclusions. In my two-by-four mind I was con-

vinced that all godly minds held to identical conclusions. Not so! To my amazement, I soon discovered that there were not only various opinions on the same subject but that God had the audacity to bless those who disagreed with me. I believe it was Dr. Bob Cook, while he was president of The King's College, who wisely said, "God reserves the right to use people who disagree with me." I'll go one step further, for I am now convinced that God is not nearly so narrow as many of His people are. I find that God is much easier to live with than most of His followers . . . far more tolerant, certainly full of more grace and forgiveness than all of us are.

Unlike us, when He forgives, He forgets the transgression and removes it as far as east is from west. Perhaps you have heard of the man who loved the Lord, but he couldn't seem to conquer a particular sin. Time and again through the week he would come before the Lord and confess the same transgression. In all sincerity, he would tell God how much he hated what he had done and how grateful he was for God's grace in forgiving him. Wouldn't you know it, by Saturday of that same struggling week he was back on his knees: "Here I come again, Lord, with the same sin . . . asking Your forgiveness and claiming Your cleansing." To his surprise, he heard God's audible answer: "What sin?"

There will be no denominations in heaven, no categories of Christians—only the vast company of the saints, and only then will there be perfect harmony of heart and complete unanimity of agreement. Until then, count on it, even the godly will disagree.

3. *In every disagreement there are the same two ingredients:* (a) an issue and (b) various viewpoints. The issue is usually objective and involves principles. The viewpoints are subjective and involve personalities. And therein lies the sum and substance of a clash, which could be defined as a disagreement over an issue because of opposing points of view. I will be candid with you: Every time I have remembered those two basic ingredients in the midst of a disagreement, I have been able to keep calm and think clearly. When I have forgotten them, almost without exception I have failed to negotiate my way through the clash with wis-

dom. Furthermore, I have regretted something I said in the heat of verbal exchange. Those two simple ingredients have never failed to help me keep cool. Why? The next fact will explain.

4. *In many disagreements each side is valid.* As "liberal" as you may think that sounds, chew on it before you toss it aside. On numerous occasions when I have encountered a brother or sister who felt as strongly as I about the other side of the argument, I came to realize it was not so much an I-am-right-and-you-are-wrong matter as it was an I-see-it-from-his-perspective-and-you-from-that-perspective matter. Both sides of most disagreements have strengths and weaknesses, which means neither side is an airtight slam dunk. Nevertheless, any disagreement can lead to a serious, permanent rift in a relationship . . . and sometimes (this may surprise you) that is God's will. There are times God chooses to spread the good news of His Son rapidly in different directions by having two capable servants of His have a major disagreement. As they separate and minister effectively in two different locations, He accomplishes a greater objective than their being in agreement.

REFLECTING ON GRACE

Consider a time when you experienced a disagreement with a fellow brother or sister in Christ. How did you choose to look at the situation? What were the consequences of that choice?

Whom do you know that God has chosen to use despite (or because of) a disagreement with you?

How can you stand firm in your theological persuasion while maintaining a flexible involvement with others?

◇ AWAKENING TO GRACE

Acts 15:36–41

And after some days Paul said to Barnabas, "Let us return and visit the brethren in every city in which we proclaimed the word of the Lord, and see how they are." Barnabas wanted to take John, called Mark, along with them also. But Paul kept insisting that they should not take him along who had deserted them in Pamphylia and had not gone with them to the work. And there occurred such a sharp disagreement that they separated from one another, and Barnabas took Mark with him and sailed away to Cyprus. But Paul chose Silas and left, being committed by the brethren to the grace of the Lord. And he was traveling through Syria and Cilicia, strengthening the churches.

What disagreement is presented in these verses? Who are the major characters involved and what were their positions?

What positive effects on the ministry came from the separation of Paul and Barnabas?

What do you learn from this situation about God's ability to use such disagreements to His glory?

◇ WALKING IN GRACE

Give examples of how you could demonstrate "wobble room" in one of your troubling relationships.

In your next disagreement (and there will be a next one), concentrate on separating the issue from the two or more viewpoints being presented. How might this exercise change your perspective in the disagreement?

What are several benefits of having diverse opinions within the body of Christ? What are some of the challenges? Where does grace fit in?

DAY 26

See that no one pays back evil for evil, but always try
to do good to each other and to everyone else.

1 Thessalonians 5:15 NLT

MODELING GRACE THROUGH DISAGREEABLE TIMES

*L*et me offer several comments that may help you handle future disagreeable times in a gracious manner.

First, *always leave room for an opposing viewpoint.* If you don't have
room for an opposing viewpoint, you're not going to do well when you
have teenagers. Teens can be among our best teachers. I know ours have
been. They haven't always been right, nor have I. However, I have learned
in rearing teenagers that they are great at pointing out another point of
view, if nothing else than just to make me think, just to challenge me, just
to remind me that there is another way of viewing things. I can assure you,
it has helped me in my ministry. It has certainly helped me in my relationship with those to whom I am personally accountable. Opposition is
good for our humility.

Second, *if an argument must occur, don't assassinate.* An argument—
even a strong clash—is one thing, but killing folks is another. I have seen
individuals in an argument verbally hit below the belt and assault another's character. I've seen a lot of mudslinging happen in arguments related
to the work of the church. I've seen brutal character assassinations occur
in the name of religion—in public speaking as well as in writing—and
they are all ugly memories. No need for that. If we must fight, let's fight
fair.

Third, *if you don't get your way, get over it; get on with life.* If you don't
get your way in a vote at a church, get over it. The vote was taken (if the
church has integrity, the vote was handled with fairness), now get on with
it. Just press on. And don't rehearse the fight or the vote year after year.
The work of God slows down when we are not big enough to take it on the
chin and say, "We lost!" Having been raised in the South, I didn't know

the South lost the Civil War until I was in junior high school . . . and even then it was debatable among my teachers. Be big enough to say, "We lost." Grace will help.

Fourth, *sometimes the best solution is a separation.* There is good biblical support for this, remember. Paul and Barnabas simply couldn't go on together, so they separated. If I can't go on with the way things are in a particular ministry, I need to resign! But in doing so I should not drag people through my unresolved conflicts because I didn't get my way. If separation is the best solution, doing it graciously is essential. If your disagreements are starting to outweigh your agreements, you ought to give strong consideration to pulling out. Who knows? This may be God's way of moving you on to another dimension of ministry.

✑ Reflecting on Grace

What is your response when mudslinging takes place in your presence? How can you respond graciously yet firmly?

Sadly, many times separation in ministry is often the *first* solution instead of the last. What can you do to encourage unity and grace in your ministry?

Name the last time you allowed an opposing viewpoint to teach you humility.

✑ Awakening to Grace

1 Corinthians 6:1–8
Does any one of you, when he has a case against his neighbor, dare to go to law before the unrighteous and not before the

saints? Or do you not know that the saints will judge the world? If the world is judged by you, are you not competent to constitute the smallest law courts? Do you not know that we will judge angels? How much more matters of this life? So if you have law courts dealing with matters of this life, do you appoint them as judges who are of no account in the church? I say this to your shame. Is it so, that there is not among you one wise man who will be able to decide between his brethren, but brother goes to law with brother, and that before unbelievers? Actually, then, it is already a defeat for you, that you have lawsuits with one another. Why not rather be wronged? Why not rather be defrauded? On the contrary, you yourselves wrong and defraud. You do this even to your brethren.

What was Paul's advice to believers for handling disagreements in the early church?

According to Paul, what would be the result if believers resolved their disagreements as unbelievers do?

Paul's closing advice to let yourself be wronged sounds unfair and out of place in today's world. What spiritual and mental benefits could be gained from following this suggestion?

WALKING IN GRACE

Today, do your best to listen to an opposing viewpoint. What would it mean to let someone win an argument or disagreement in order to save the friendship?

Modeling Grace through Disagreeable Times

Gracious separation in ministry is not the same as separation in marriage. If you've experienced more disagreements than agreements with your spouse, what can you do to work toward graceful resolution while keeping your marriage strong?

What argument have you been holding on to because you didn't get your way? Will you let it go today in prayer?

DAY 27

For I am confident of this very thing, that He who began a good work in you will perfect it until the day of Christ Jesus.

Philippians 1:6

AWAKENING GRACE

Want a boost of encouragement? Our God is working toward that end in all of His children. It is His constant pursuit, His daily agenda, as He points us toward our final destination, "the Celestial City," as Bunyan calls it. Having cleansed our hearts of the debris of inward corruptions and the dust of sin's domination, God is now daily at work awakening grace within us, perfecting our character and bringing it to completion.

As I think about our becoming people of awakening grace, I believe at least three things are involved in the process:

First, it *takes time.* Learning anything takes time. Becoming good models of grace, it seems, takes years! Like wisdom, it comes slowly. But God is in no hurry as He purges graceless characteristics from us. But we can count on this, for sure: He is persistent.

Second, it *requires pain.* The "dust" in our room doesn't settle easily. I know of no one who has adopted a "grace state of mind" painlessly. Hurt is part of the curriculum in God's schoolroom.

Third, it *means change.* Being "graceless" by nature, we find it difficult to be anything different. We lack it, we resist it, we fail to show it, but God never stops His relentless working. He is committed to our becoming more like His Son. Remember? "He who began a good work . . . *will* carry it on to completion" (NIV).

REFLECTING ON GRACE

What recurring trial in your life might actually be part of God's curriculum as He teaches you grace over time?

What pain have you seen or experienced as a result of a specific gracious act that you did? How might you relate that pain to Christ's pain on the cross?

Compare your life now with how you were five years ago. In what ways has God continued His work of grace in you?

AWAKENING TO GRACE

Romans 8:28–29

And we know that God causes all things to work together for good to those who love God, to those who are called according to His purpose. For those whom He foreknew, He also predestined to become conformed to the image of His Son, so that He might be the firstborn among many brethren.

How does this passage confirm that grace awakening is a process that involves time, pain, and change?

According to the passage, how can you reconcile your painful struggles in life to God's grace?

What does it mean to you that you have been "predestined to become conformed to the image" of Christ?

WALKING IN GRACE

Reflect upon the three areas involved in becoming a person of awakening grace. After each, record personal experiences that God has used to teach you about each one.

Grace takes time:

Grace requires pain:

Grace means change:

Describe a specific time this past week when you saw God at work in your daily life to promote gracious living.

Imagine that God's good work in you has been fully completed. What things have changed in your life? Choose one insight to pray about today.

DAY 28

He has removed our rebellious acts as far away from us as the east is from the west.

Psalm 103:12 NLT

GRACE THAT RELEASES

One characteristic of a grace awakening ministry deserves special attention: *release from past failures*. A ministry of grace doesn't keep bringing up the past for the purpose of holding it over people. There is an absence of shame. Paul addresses this in 1 Timothy 1:12–14:

> I thank Christ Jesus our Lord, who has strengthened me, because He considered me faithful, putting me into service, even though I was formerly a blasphemer and a persecutor and a violent aggressor. Yet I was shown mercy because I acted ignorantly in unbelief; and the grace of our Lord was more than abundant, with the faith and love which are found in Christ Jesus.

You may be surprised to know that the apostle Paul had every reason to feel ashamed. He was one whose past was dreadful: "formerly a blasphemer . . . persecutor . . . violent aggressor." Then how could the same man write, "I am not ashamed" (2 Timothy 1:12)? He gives us the answer here in 1 Timothy 1:14: Grace was more than abundant. Blasphemy had abounded in his past, but grace superabounded. Violence and brutality had abounded, but grace superabounded.

What if it read "divorcee"? What if it read "homosexual"? What if it read "addict"? I realize it reads "blasphemer, persecutor, aggressor." But what if it read "prostitute" or "ex-con" or "financial failure" or "murderer"? In a grace-awakened ministry, none of those things in the past are allowed to hold those people in bondage. They are released, forgiven, and the believer is allowed to go on to a new life in Christ.

Grace releases people, not only from sin but from shame. Do you do that in your ministry? Or do you make a note of those things and keep reminding yourself when that particular name comes up: "Well, you know, you'd better watch her" or, "You've gotta watch him." Do you give people reasons to feel greater shame? Who knows what battles of shame most folks struggle with? It is enormous.

✺ REFLECTING ON GRACE

Paul acknowledged his past failings without allowing them to bring him back under the control of guilt. How well have you been able to do that? Why?

How close do you come to Paul's example of separating humility and shame?

What sins abound today that are commonly regarded as difficult for God to erase? In what ways has your ministry combated this assumption?

✺ AWAKENING TO GRACE

Hebrews 4:13–16

And there is no creature hidden from His sight, but all things are open and laid bare to the eyes of Him with whom we have to do.

Therefore since then we have a great high priest who has passed through the heavens, Jesus the Son of God, let us hold fast our confession. For we do not have a high priest who cannot sympathize with our weaknesses, but One who has been tempted in all things as we are, yet without sin. Therefore let us draw near with confidence to the throne of grace, so that we may receive mercy and find grace to help in time of need.

Grace That Releases

How do these verses display a balance between God's sovereignty regarding your sin and God's grace in His relationship with you?

Through whom does God enact His grace toward humanity?

How does Jesus model a spirit of total acceptance and understanding of personal weakness?

WALKING IN GRACE

Describe a time in your ministry when grace abounded. What specifically led to such gracious gestures?

Have you ever warned others about a specific individual's past sins? How can you be an example of someone who truly wipes the slate clean?

Be someone who people can depend on for unconditional love and grace! Start building this reputation today by releasing someone in his or her walk with Christ. Who will be the first beneficiary of your desire to practice grace?

Day 29

 So again I say, each man must love his wife as he loves himself, and the wife must respect her husband.

Ephesians 5:33 NLT

MARITAL GRACE

*T*he more the grace of God is awakened in a marriage, the less husbands will attempt to control and restrict and the less wives will feel the need to "please no matter what." It makes marriage easier to manage.

• Grace releases and affirms. It doesn't smother.

• Grace values the dignity of individuals. It doesn't destroy.

• Grace supports and encourages. It isn't jealous or suspicious.

I know whereof I speak. For more years than I care to remember, I was consumed with jealousy. I was so insecure and fearful it wasn't uncommon for me to drill Cynthia with questions — petty, probing questions that were little more than veiled accusations. It is amazing she endured it. Finally, we had one of those famous showdown confrontations every married couple has had. No need to repeat it, but she made it painfully clear that I was smothering her; I was imagining things she never even thought of doing . . . and it had to stop. Her words hurt, but she did the right thing. I took her seriously.

I went to work on this ugly side of my life. I confessed my jealousy to Cynthia. I assured her I would never again treat her with such a lack of trust. I asked God for grace to help, for relief from the destructive habit I had formed, for the ability to love and give myself to this woman without all the choking conditions. I distinctly recall how much an understanding of grace helped. It was as if grace were finally "awake" in my life, and I could appropriate its power for the first time. It seemed to free me, first in small ways, and finally in major areas. I can honestly say today that I do not entertain a single jealous thought. Grace *literally* wiped the slate clean.

Marital Grace

❧ REFLECTING ON GRACE

How does the awakening of grace assist in balancing a marriage?

Consider what each of the following promises means for your marriage.

Grace releases and affirms my spouse.

Grace values the dignity of my spouse.

Grace supports and encourages my spouse.

Which of the above concepts is most difficult for you right now? Explain.

❧ AWAKENING TO GRACE

Ruth 3:1–11

Then Naomi her mother-in-law said to her, "My daughter, shall I not seek security for you, that it may be well with you? Now is not Boaz our kinsman, with whose maids you were? Behold, he winnows barley at the threshing floor tonight. Wash yourself therefore, and anoint yourself and put on your best clothes, and go down to the threshing floor; but do not make yourself known to the man until he has finished eating and drinking. It shall be when he lies down, that you shall notice the place where he lies, and you shall go and uncover his feet and lie down; then he will tell you what you shall do." She said to her, "All that you say I will do."

So she went down to the threshing floor and did according to all that her mother-in-law had commanded her. When Boaz had eaten and drunk and his heart was merry, he went to lie

> *down at the end of the heap of grain; and she came secretly, and uncovered his feet and lay down. It happened in the middle of the night that the man was startled and bent forward; and behold, a woman was lying at his feet. He said, "Who are you?" And she answered, "I am Ruth your maid. So spread your covering over your maid, for you are a close relative." Then he said, "May you be blessed of the* LORD, *my daughter. You have shown your last kindness to be better than the first by not going after young men, whether poor or rich. Now, my daughter, do not fear. I will do for you whatever you ask, for all my people in the city know that you are a woman of excellence."*

How did Ruth display an attitude of trust in her relationship with her mother-in-law?

In what ways did Boaz show Ruth grace in her vulnerable state?

What resulted from Boaz's grace toward Ruth?

WALKING IN GRACE

Recall a confrontation in your marriage that caused you to reassess your feelings toward your spouse. Was that conflict resolved in a deeper understanding of grace? Why or why not?

What areas of your marriage could benefit most from an attitude of grace on your part?

How far are you willing to go in order to secure grace in your marriage? What steps can you take to start this process?

DAY 30

God loves the person who gives cheerfully.

2 Corinthians 9:7 NLT

The Attraction of Gracious Giving

When I consider the magnetic effects of gracious giving, four qualities immediately emerge. First, grace is so attractive: *Grace individualizes the gift.* When you give by grace, you give individually. You give proportionately to your own income. You have needs, and you have an income to meet those needs. That combination is unlike anyone else's on earth. You are an individual. When you give on that basis, your gift is an individual kind of *gift*. We are not all shoved into a tank, blended together, then "required" to give exactly 50 percent. (Though if everyone gave 50 percent, we would have such an enormous surplus in God's work we would not know what to do with the extra . . . but I'm sure we'd quickly find out.) It is much more individualized than that. Grace, remember, brings variety and spontaneity.

Here's the second reason grace is so attractive: *Grace makes the action joyfully spontaneous.* "Not grudgingly or under compulsion, for God loves a cheerful giver" (2 Corinthians 9:7). I never have been able to understand why everyone in the church looks so serious during the offering. Wouldn't it be great if when the offering plates are passed in church next Sunday that instead of grim looks, stoic silence, and soft organ music you heard laughter? I can just imagine: "Can you believe we're doing this?" "Put it in the plate, honey. Isn't this great? Put it in!" . . . followed by little ripples of laughter and applause across the place of worship. Wonderful! Why not? Deep within the heart there is an absence of any compulsion, only spontaneous laughter. The word *cheerful* is literally a Greek term from which we get the word "hilarious." "God loves a *hilarious* giver."

Now for a third reason grace is so attractive: *Grace enables us to link up with God's supply line.* Look at verse 8 of 2 Corinthians 9: "And God is able to make all grace abound to you, that always having all sufficiency in everything, you may have an abundance for every good deed." When we possess an attitude of grace, we give. We give ourselves. We give from what we earn. And He, in turn, gives back in various ways, not matching gift for gift, but in an abundance of ways, He goes beyond.

Fourth: *Grace leads to incomparable results.* "Because of the proof given by this ministry, they will glorify God for your obedience to your confession of the gospel of Christ and for the liberality of your contribution to them and to all, while they also, by prayer on your behalf, yearn for you because of the surpassing grace of God in you" (2 Corinthians 9:13–14).

REFLECTING ON GRACE

Describe a specific time when an act of giving to others produced an abundance of well-being in your own life.

Besides money, with what has God gifted you that you can use to bless others?

How might the idea of being a "hilarious giver" change the way you give?

AWAKENING TO GRACE

2 Corinthians 8:12–15 NIV

For if the willingness is there, the gift is acceptable according to what one has, not according to what he does not have. Our desire is not that others might be relieved while you are hard pressed, but that there might be equality. At the present time your plenty will supply what they need, so that in turn their plenty will supply what you need. Then there will be equality, as it is written: "He who gathered much did not have too much, and he who gathered little did not have too little."

According to the passage, where should you begin when you want to give?

How did God set up a system of balance in giving?

What did Paul point out as one of the most important aspects to remember in giving?

WALKING IN GRACE

Take a moment to consider the manner and amount you give to the Lord. Are there certain aspects of your life that you've refused to share?

In what other ways is your giving individualized and unique in the family of God?

What places in your church or community need a gift that you are able to supply? If you can't think of one, start asking people about their needs and what you can do to help meet them.

*Sin is no longer your master, for you are no longer
subject to the law, which enslaves you to sin. Instead,
you are free by God's grace.*

Romans 6:14 NLT

FREE INDEED

My hope has been to create an appetite for grace that is so strong
nothing will restrain us from pursuing the freedom and spontaneity
it can bring—a longing so deep that a new spiritual dawn, a "grace awakening," if you will, cannot help but burst through the wall of legalism. Since I
am a Christian minister, much of my involvement and exposure is in the
realm of the church and Christian organizations. It has been my observation that even here most folks are not free; they have not learned to accept
and enjoy the grace that has come to us in Jesus Christ. Though He came
to set us free, it saddens me to say that many still live behind the wall of
bondage. Regrettably, the stones of constraint are everywhere to be found.
Instead of being places of enthusiastic, spontaneous worship, many churches and Christian ministries have become institutions that maintain a system
of religion with hired officials to guard the gates and to enforce the rules.

In vain I have searched the Bible, looking for examples of early
Christians whose lives were marked by rigidity, predictability, inhibition,
dullness, and caution. Fortunately, grim, frowning, joyless saints in
Scripture are conspicuous by their absence. Instead, the examples I find
are of adventurous, risk-taking, enthusiastic, and authentic believers
whose joy was contagious even in times of painful trial. Their vision was
broad even when death drew near. Rules were few, and changes were
welcome. The contrast between then and now is staggering.

The difference, I am convinced, is grace. Grace scales the wall and
refuses to be restricted. It lives above the demands of human opinion and
breaks free from legalistic regulations. Grace dares us to take hold of the
sledgehammer of courage and break through longstanding stones. Grace

invites us to chart new courses and explore ever-expanding regions, all the while delighting in the unexpected. While others care more about maintaining the wall and fearing those who guard it, grace is constantly looking for ways to freedom. Grace wants faith to fly, regardless of what grim-faced officials may say or think or do.

There is a "grace awakening" loose in the land. Will you become a part of it? While you take your turn with the sledgehammer and pound away, a host of us are standing near, and some of us may be half a world away, cheering you on. Don't think of it as a lonesome, isolated task. You are breaking through to freedom, and no one is more delighted than the Lord Jesus Christ, who has promised you His grace. Never forget His words: "If therefore the Son shall make you free, you shall be free indeed." Stay at it. By the grace of Almighty God, the new movement will someday sweep across every continent, and the longstanding wall that has kept people in bondage for centuries will come tumbling down. And we shall all, at last, be free indeed.

✎ REFLECTING ON GRACE

How will you continue to fuel your appetite for grace after you put this book down?

What longstanding stones still need to be broken in your life and ministry?

When legalism creeps in, what will be your strategy for retaining Christ's promise of true and lasting freedom?

✎ AWAKENING TO GRACE

Colossians 2:13–23 NLT

You were dead because of your sins and because your sinful nature was not yet cut away. Then God made you alive with

*Christ. He forgave all our sins. He canceled the record that con-
tained the charges against us. He took it and destroyed it by
nailing it to Christ's cross. In this way, God disarmed the evil
rulers and authorities. He shamed them publicly by his victory
over them on the cross of Christ.*

*So don't let anyone condemn you for what you eat or drink,
or for not celebrating certain holy days or new-moon ceremonies
or Sabbaths. For these rules were only shadows of the real thing,
Christ himself. Don't let anyone condemn you by insisting on
self-denial. And don't let anyone say you must worship angels,
even though they say they have had visions about this. These
people claim to be so humble, but their sinful minds have made
them proud. But they are not connected to Christ, the head of
the body. For we are joined together in his body by his strong
sinews, and we grow only as we get our nourishment and
strength from God.*

*You have died with Christ, and he has set you free from the
evil powers of this world. So why do you keep on following rules
of the world, such as, "Don't handle, don't eat, don't touch."
Such rules are mere human teaching about things that are gone
as soon as we use them. These rules may seem wise because they
require strong devotion, humility, and severe bodily discipline.
But they have no effect when it comes to conquering a person's
evil thoughts and desires.*

According to the passage, what are several things you are no longer condemned for now that you are alive with Christ?

What does Paul say is the relationship between rules and Christ?

In these verses, what real power does obeying rules have in becoming godly?

WALKING IN GRACE

Which believers in the Bible do you most identify as "adventurous, risk-taking, enthusiastic, and authentic"? How could you use their lives as a model for your own grace awakening?

Name one thing you can do to make your church a more welcoming atmosphere of grace.

Take time to pray for a real grace awakening in your family, your church, and yourself. In all your relationships, be an instrument of grace today!